The Space
Between Us

The Space Between Us

EXPLORING THE DIMENSIONS
OF HUMAN RELATIONSHIPS

Ruthellen Josselson

SAGE Publications
International Educational and Professional Publisher
Thousand Oaks London New Delhi

For information address:

 SAGE Publications, Inc.
2455 Teller Road
Newbury Park, California 91320
E-mail: order@sagepub.com

SAGE Publications Ltd.
6 Bonhill Street
London EC2A 4PU
United Kingdom

SAGE Publications India Pvt. Ltd.
M-32 Market
Greater Kailash I
New Delhi 110 048 India

Printed in the United States of America

Library of Congress Cataloging-in-Publication Data

Josselson, Ruthellen.
    The space between us: exploring the dimensions of human relations
/ Ruthellen Josselson.
        p.   cm.
    Originally published: San Francisco: Jossey-Bass Publishers, 1992.
    Includes bibliographical references and index.
    ISBN 0-7619-0126-4 (pbk.: alk. paper)
    1. Interpersonal relations.   I. Title.
HM132.J675   1996
158'.2—dc20   95-32812

01 10 9 8 7 6 5

Sage Managing Editor: Claudia A. Hoffman

To my parents,
Anne and Martin Lefkowitz,
to my daughter,
Jaimie,
to Hanoch,
and to all the other people
I have loved

Contents

Preface

In our highly individualistic age, people have become ashamed of needing others. The therapeutic message that has formed the spiritual core for our age has been to do it alone, attending to the self. Psychology understands the self better than it understands connections between people.

Patients so frequently ask me, "But what *can* I expect from my husband? from my friends? Am I being greedy, expecting too much? Is what I want what everyone else has? Or is my disappointment 'just life' and I have to accept it?" As therapists, we have learned to dodge these questions. We don't answer because we don't know. If we do answer, we tend to do so out of our own experience of life rather than out of any science that might instruct us. Yet as theorists and experts on relatedness, we ought to be able to do better than that.

Increasingly, however, our patients come to us not with symptoms but with "living pain" (Yalom, 1989), and much of this anguish is traceable to dissatisfaction with their connections to others. While we have a viable theory of internal life, relations between people can be depicted only by encasing them in the language of psychopathology. Needing support from another gets defined as "dependence"; worrying about another's well-being is seen as a symptom of "codependence." As a culture, we talk easily now about sex, and we can even discuss money straightforwardly. What causes us embarrassment is to talk about love.

How we think about love is central to our identity and to our quest for meaning in our lives. Yet each person (and each culture) thinks about love differently, emphasizing different aspects of this phenomenon with many faces. So even if we could overcome our shame and talk about love, we would find that our meanings are different. And in endeavoring to sort out those differences, we would quickly run out of words to say what we mean. In our haste to understand symptom formation, we have been inattentive to conceptualizing what gives meaning and vitality to life. Where is the language of adult relatedness? How do we need each other as and when we grow up?

This book is an effort to develop a consensual vocabulary of the ways people link themselves to each other. I describe what people actually do and how they feel in their relationships and how their needs in relationships might develop over time.

In talking to a great many people about their relationships over the course of their lives, I have learned that people relate to each other in an astonishing variety of ways, some leaning more heavily on certain kinds of relating, other people emphasizing other relational experiences. My task here is to draw a tentative map of the roads that connect people so we can think more sharply about them and understand better what we need from others and what others need from us.

Origins of the Work

While studying identity in women, I became increasingly impressed by the centrality of relatedness in human development, and I was aware of how few theoretical tools I had with which to make sense of the relational phenomena before me. I set out, then, both to read what our best thinkers have said about relationships and to talk to people about what has mattered most to them in their own relationships. This book is an effort to integrate phenomenology and theory, using the one to illuminate the other. If height, width, and depth are the three dimensions of a figure, what are the dimensions of a relationship as they appear from the inside? What do people mean to others? How do we make use of others in our own development?

The theory I have relied on derives mainly from psychoanalytic object relations and self psychology approaches. I also include some work from developmental psychologists and from other writers whose work I think furthers the model I develop. Because of the constraints of space, I leave it to others to think about how my model of relatedness might intersect with the social psychology literature on interpersonal attraction and with the family therapy literature. I do not present either of these bodies of work here.

For the phenomenological side of this project, I used intensive interviews to help me think more clearly about "lived experience." My approach was less that of a formal study and more a way of trying to hear better how people experience themselves in relationships. My first step in interviewing people about their relationships was to ask them to draw a "relational space," mapping with circles the most important people in their lives. They were asked to begin with how their relational space would have looked to them at age five, then at five-year intervals up to their present age. These drawings formed the basis for an in-depth interview about how each person on each diagram had been important to the person being interviewed. What was the relational atmosphere? What were the important moments? How did each person's importance change as the interviewee got older? (For more detail about these interviews or to see what a relational space map looks like, see Resource A in the back of the book.)

Most interviews took between three and five hours. The interview itself took place in the context of a relationship, and my aim was to offer myself as a nonjudgmental and interested Other. Because these were research subjects and not patients, I was freer to listen diffusely. And I did not listen as an expert. I was a student, trying to learn how people make others important to them.

Most people found the experience of the interview interesting, valuable, and even moving. Many cried during the interview— tears from being profoundly touched by gratitude or remembered love, tears of not-yet-healed wounds of loss or disappointment. By the end of the time together, I felt intensely close to the person I had interviewed, but also exhausted and overwhelmed. Many of those I spoke with got in touch with me at least once afterward—usually to say how meaningful the experience had been to them, and perhaps to discover whether it also had meaning to me.

I interviewed people who I thought might have something

to teach me, but I did not make an effort to stratify or compose my sample formally. I interviewed fifty-five people, and I have data from twelve more interviews conducted by my students. Subjects ranged in age from eleven to ninety-three and represented a variety of ethnic and cultural backgrounds. Most of the subjects were between thirty and fifty. (I "specialized" here, because I found that these people had the widest range of connections and could tell me the most about this variability.) I tried to find highly articulate people to interview. Talking about the "hows" of relatedness is very difficult: I wanted to maximize the possibilities of people being able to get their experiences into words.

I have jumbled and disguised stories to preserve confidentiality, but all the case histories remain emotionally (if not factually) true.

Overview of the Contents

An exploration of eight dimensions of relatedness, introduced in Chapter One, forms the core of this book. In Chapter Two, I consider in detail how the phenomena of relatedness have been treated in psychology and in society, and I critique the dominance of the self in psychological theory. This chapter proposes that a model of "Yearning (Wo)Man," in contrast to Freud's "Guilty Man," serve as the prototype for a theory of development founded in an appreciation of the centrality of relatedness. Having grounded my model of relatedness in this way, I present each dimension in successive chapters. Each one integrates some relevant research and theory, as well as an exploration of how the dimension is expressed phenomenologically in people's lives. At the end of the book, I explore the ways in which women and men differ in their approaches to relatedness, and I finish with an integrating chapter on love.

For each dimension, I present a detailed relational biography of a person whose life focuses on that form of interpersonal exchange. I have chosen to present one "whole life" for each chapter— in other words, to present a person's story in its entirety—in order to show the *pattern* of relatedness, the tapestry that is central to understanding a person's developmental course.

I have avoided "pathologizing" people or commenting on

ways in which their needs could be construed as neurotic. Remember: we have a theory of development in which all needs for others (except for sexual fulfillment) can be viewed as neurotic, or worse. As much as possible, I have avoided the use of the word *dependent*, because that is what we have always been taught all relationships are. When people have been in therapy, I say so and explore why and how it affected them. I freely draw vignettes from my own clinical experience when I need them to illustrate a point. When I have found no telling example from either my subjects or my patients, I have turned to literature—or, as a last resort, to my own experience. My approach assumes that it is healthy and necessary to need each other; the problem before us is to be able to say how.

Audience

I have written this book for people who would like to better understand the genesis and experience of human relationships—that is, for students of psychology, social work, counseling, and interpersonal communication. I have also written for the practitioners of psychotherapy, social work, counseling, and developmental psychology who inevitably encounter these issues all through their work. I write in hopes that they, too, can better understand people's struggles with and gratifications from relationships. I hope that this schema might be useful both in research and in therapy. I think that the therapeutic situation, both in its undertaking and in its process, is fundamentally relational. This book presents a new framework for listening to and thinking about our patients/clients in relationship to us and to others.

Overall, this book is for all who might like to join the dialogue about what we need from others. We must be able to discuss these matters without getting sentimental or embarrassed, without romanticizing or disparaging. This is where I believe an adequate human psychology must begin.

Acknowledgments

A book such as this is a vehicle for the thinking and input of a great many people and a product of my relationships with them. There are the people who have shared with me, orally and in their writing, what sense they have made out of the phenomena that intrigue me. To these, I owe a great intellectual debt. In this book, I rely heavily on the British object relations theorists as well as the influence of Harry Stack Sullivan and Erik Erikson. I am especially indebted to Josephine Klein, whom I never met but whose wonderful book gave me the inspiration I needed to do this. David Scharff, in a lecture I attended, made the distinction between the "arms-around" and "eye-to-eye" experiences of the infant, and it came to me that these kinds of relational distinctions were exactly what our theory needs.

I first presented these ideas at the fiftieth reunion of the Psychological Clinic at the University of Michigan. I am grateful to my colleagues there for affording me that opportunity to speak and to those whose enthusiastic response fueled this effort. I wrote this book while on a Fulbright scholarship at the Hebrew University in Jerusalem, and I wish to thank the Fulbright Commission for its support. I am especially grateful to Amia Lieblich, my companion and colleague during that time, who always made time to read my newest paragraphs and consider seriously my latest formulations. Her insight and support are woven through this book.

Then there are the many people who nourished my work by listening to me, sharing their ideas, encouraging me, or critiquing various drafts of the manuscript. Here I would like to thank Gracia Alkema, Orli Bach, Leslie Brown, Eileen Higham, James Marcia, Ofra Mayseless, Beverly Palmer, Diane Pomerantz, Pamela Sheff, Hadas Wiseman, and Irvin Yalom. Special thanks to Judy Armstrong and Hanoch Flum, who did all of the above reliably and with great thoughtfulness. I also thank my students April Sewell and Cindy Spence and my former student and colleague Sharon Weiss for doing some of the interviews and offering their perspectives on the material.

I am deeply grateful to all the people, whom I cannot name, who shared their lives with me in the relational interviews. Their stories moved me, made me feel that I was close to what is really important to understand, and gave me the determination to tell others.

Baltimore, Maryland   Ruthellen Josselson
January 1992

The Author

Ruthellen Josselson is both a practicing psychotherapist and Professor of Psychology at Towson State University, where she directs the Clinical Concentration Program. She received her Ph.D. in clinical psychology from the University of Michigan. The 1994 recipient of the Henry A. Murray Award from the American Psychological Association, she has also been a Visiting Professor at the Harvard Graduate School of Education and Fulbright Professor of Psychology at the Hebrew University in Jerusalem.

Her previous book, *Finding Herself: Pathways to Identity Development in Women* (1987), focuses on female development. Dr. Josselson is also the coeditor of the annual *The Narrative Study of Lives* and author of many articles on adolescence, women, and narrative.

But what is it all about? People loose and at the same time caught. Caught and loose. All these people and you don't know what joins them up. There's bound to be some sort of reason and connection. Yet somehow I can't seem to name it.

—Carson McCullers,
The Member of the Wedding

Chapter I

The Discourse of Relatedness

But still the heart doth need a language.

—Samuel Taylor Coleridge, translator of *The Piccolomini*,
by Friedrich von Schiller

People create their lives within a web of connection to others. The cast of characters in a life and the nuances of interconnection provide the richness, the intricacy, the abrasion, and much of the interest in living. Life unfolds as a kaleidoscope of relationships, with varying pieces in shifting arrangements.

Psychology has only recently begun to consider seriously the developmental course of human connection in its subtlety and variety. Until now, psychological theory of development has occupied itself instead with explication of the self. Self-esteem, self-control, self-awareness, and individual achievement have dominated psychological theory. Other people have been recognized only as "objects" for the gratification of instinctual needs and of the needs of the growing and differentiating self. Relationship as a goal, interconnection as an aim—these had no place in our theories. Where the phenomena of interpersonal connection in human life were acknowledged at all, they served merely as backdrop for the more apparent dramas of self.

People who study and treat women (Miller, 1976, 1984; Gilligan, 1982, 1990; Josselson, 1987), people who study and treat adolescents (Grotevant and Cooper, 1985; Apter, 1990), people who work with families—all have called for and begun to develop a theory that takes account of human interconnection and recognizes

1

relatedness as the central plot of development. Converging voices proclaim that we cannot have a viable theory of human development unless we can schematize development that takes place within, through, and for relatedness.

Relationship and Language

Yet writers and theorists who have taken up this challenge have been stymied by the lack of language to describe these phenomena. (See especially Gilligan, 1982; Miller, 1976; and Heilbrun, 1988.) We become inarticulate when it comes to addressing how people intermingle with others, how we need others and need them to need us. *Love* is perhaps the least definable word in our lexicon, and vague, all-inclusive terms such as *affiliation, communion,* and *intimacy* take us only part of the way. The nature of relationship has remained enshrouded partly because we have so few words and agreed-upon concepts to indicate the ways in which people connect themselves to others. Language shapes our view of reality (Palmer, 1969). Because our speech in this realm is so restricted, we end up with a cultural mythology of human intercourse that overemphasizes the easily described phenomena of individuality and ignores or distorts interpersonal bonding. When we wish to know people, we are therefore more likely to ask about what they do than about how they love. But in fact we would know them better if we knew how they are with others and what they want from them.

Relationship itself has become a hackneyed word, made to carry so many meanings that it ceases to have much connotative force. Eve, for example, has a "relationship" with her mother, her husband, her daughter, her friend, and her car mechanic, and each connection has its own special form. If, however, one were to ask her how her "relationship" is, she would undoubtedly understand the question to refer to a heterosexual pair bond and to be inquiring as to the relative "goodness" of that bond. The manner in which this very generic word is commonly used says a great deal about our cultural assumptions. Unmodified, the word *relationship* means actual or potential sexual partner; relationships are to be characterized along a continuum of good or bad; relationships are to be "had" rather than created in the flow of intention, action, and response between people. Using these cultural assumptions as a starting point in this hypothetical interview of Eve, we might learn that she feels that she "has a good relationship." But this is only a very small bit of the richness of Eve's connection to others.

Self and Other

From many directions, the portents echo one another: relatedness is central—to physical health, to longevity, to meaningful social life, and to the growth and development of the self.[1] It has been rare in our science that so many avenues have led us in the same direction.

Psychodynamic theory began at an individualistic extreme. Freud bequeathed a legacy of concern with intrapsychic conflict, where the focus is squarely within the individual: other people are of interest only as objects of drive expression. The drama of human life in this model takes place in the counterpoints among impulse, reality, and morality. We conjure other people when we need them, but it is our fantasies of them and our own role in creating them that is of interest to the psychoanalyst. Later writers, such as Fairbairn, Guntrip, Winnicott, and Sullivan, who broke with Freud and made relatedness prominent in their developmental schemas, were kept out of the mainstream and seldom taught. The resurgence of interest in the British object relations theorists has followed the need to expand the monadic focus of classical psychoanalysis. This work, however, exists either in piecemeal form or with the relational concepts themselves bent and reshaped to fit a model of separation and individualism. (For a full discussion and critique of relational concepts in psychoanalysis, see Mitchell, 1988; Klein, 1987; Jordan, 1986.)

Although the work of object relations theorists has introduced and legitimized the study of how people connect to one another, it has focused largely on infantile relationships. The effort of these theorists has been to understand how early experience is recorded in the development of the self. Infantile experience, despite being preverbal, is concrete and basic. We can know, for example, absolutely and concretely, what it feels like to be held or to fall, to feel hungry or to feel filled up, to feel cold or to feel pain. These aspects of sensation and perception of life are primary, incontrovertible, and universal.

While these early experiences form the basis for later development, cognitive development soon introduces the possibility of interpretation of experience. As we come to experience ourselves as discrete selves and become able to think about ourselves and others, our direct experience with others is mediated. Perception become apperception; we experience on the basis of our previous experience and within the cognitive categories that order our experience. As a result, relatedness becomes richer, broader, more complex, and more differentiated as development proceeds. Capacities for relatedness emerge over time; they build on but are not reducible to infantile roots. And the need for relatedness continues. Bowlby (1988) points out that the idea that the adult need for others is a sign of regressive dependency needs is one of the most dangerous ideas promulgated by modern psychiatry.

The last taboo in our psychological reflections on the human experience is not sex or money but love. How can we talk about love without sounding hopelessly sentimental and muddle-headed? Can we think about the dimensions and developmental history of love and connection and maintain ourselves as analytical and psychological rather than literary? It seems to me that the work that lies ahead is to parse the domain of relational needs, to map the dimensions of what we need from others, and to learn about how this progresses developmentally. In this book, the themes of development will unfold in eight aspects of relational connection; separateness is relegated to accompaniment.

Eight Dimensions of Relatedness and the Metaphor of Space

At birth, the cord that tied us prenatally to our mother is cut, and we are alone. We are thrust into separateness, physically bound within the confines of our body. If we are women, we can contain another, in pregnancy, within our physical body space. But we can never again be physically joined to another. Relationship becomes the only means of overcoming the space between us.

Psychologically, we are also doomed to separateness. No one else can ever think exactly my thoughts as I think them or know precisely how I feel. We cannot even know, for example, that what I see and call blue is not what you see when you say red. But we reach out and try to overcome that separateness. With speech, we try to describe our inner experiences to one another. Or we share our lives and needs in various ways. Or we get as close as we can physically. When we do these things, we feel as if there is something "between" us. And we speak in those terms: "Is there something between you and him?" Interpersonal life, then, is an effort to connect and, in connecting, to overcome this psychological and physical space. Different ways of interrelating are different methods of transcending the chasm that parts us. The "between"—the way the space is filled or reverberates—becomes all-important.

There are many ways in which we reach through the space that separates us to make connections—ways that vary throughout life—and many motives that impel us to do so. Relatedness involves other people as objects of desire (as when we need someone to satisfy a particular need), but relatedness also serves as a context for the experience of the self. Theorists who have taken on the task of explicating relational experience have tended to do so emphasizing a particular aspect of connection. D. W. Winnicott, for example, taught us much about holding, and John Bowlby called our attention to attachment. Sigmund Freud, of course, viewed all relational connection as an aspect of sexual (libidinal) drive. More recent writers, such as Jean Baker Miller and her colleagues at the Stone Center, have highlighted the importance of responsiveness and mutuality, and Carol Gilligan has gotten us thinking about the dilemmas of care and connection, fundamental to selfhood, that are organizers of identity as well as moral thinking. Each theorist, however, ends up with a unidimensional model. By putting these models together, we can construct a figure with many sides.

The psychological and the physical are always metaphorically (and often linguistically) linked. Thus, when we feel deeply the experience of another, we say that we feel "touched."

Conversely, we might hold the hand of another to feel emotionally close to him or her. We can have sex with a stranger and feel psychologically "untouched," and we can have profound intimate contact by looking in someone else's eyes.

Throughout this book, then, I will use the physical and the

psychological as metaphorically interchangeable. Our limited language of relatedness requires that we rely on metaphor to grasp its various phenomena. By focusing on dimensions, I am shifting the usual perspective to try to add clarity to what has become vague and impenetrable. Inevitably, some of what seemed sharp before, such as the distinction between the physical and the psychological, will dissolve into soft focus.

There are eight primary ways in which we overcome the space between us. They involve, actually or metaphorically, a way of transcending space, of reaching through space (or being reached) and being in contact with each other. As each dimension emerges in the developmental history of the individual, each is concrete and basic. As development proceeds, each way of connecting becomes more symbolic, less physical and spatial, but no less crucial. Each dimension of relatedness has its own channel, its own origin and course. Understanding each dimension uniquely allows us to understand the confluence of the streams that create the character of relatedness in adult life.

Holding is the first interpersonal experience and represents security and a basic trust that what is essential will be provided. In holding, we experience ourselves as contained by another; powerful arms keep us from falling. Throughout life, we need to feel held in developmentally more mature idioms, but we continue to need to be contained, bounded, and grounded in order to grow.

A bit later in earliest development, babies learn to discriminate their mothers from the other people around, making possible *attachment* to this one very particular other person. The innate propensity to attach to others structures some of the most fundamental processes throughout life, including the painful vulnerability to loss that is part of our human core. When we are attached, it is as though we were clinging to someone, holding on with our limbs, keeping close. Throughout life, we continue to form attachments (if we are fortunate), and these are often at the center of our existence.

From the beginning of life, basic biological drives seek gratification. In infancy, the need to suck—the earliest form of libidinal life—forms a third configuration of interpersonal experience. Here, in the realm of *passionate experience,* others are objects of drive gratification. This pleasure-seeking orientation will organize experience in different ways and at different levels of intensity throughout the life course. Contacting others through our drives is the mode of passionate relating: overcoming separateness through sexual union or its symbolic expression. The pleasures of touch and the possibilities of uniting in boundaryless bliss are powerful means of transcending space.

In eye-to-eye relating, we overcome space through the communication of eye contact, finding ourselves in the other's eyes, having a place in the other. In *eye-to-eye validation*, we connect by existing in and for someone else. As early in development as we become able to know an other as an Other, we begin to use the other as a mirror to learn about ourselves. What the infant first sees in the mother's eyes forms a core of the infant's sense of self—the beginning of a process that continues in more refined and complex ways throughout life.

After existing for a time in this world of Others, we begin to notice that some are bigger, stronger, and more able to do things than we are ourselves. When we idealize and identify with others, we reach up for them, try to climb through the distance that separates us; we try to be where they are as a way of expanding ourselves. *Idealization and identification* are ways of linking to powerful others and striving to become like them (or to control them).

As the person grows through childhood and the self matures and becomes more aware of others, the child eventually discovers the possibilities of engaging the self with others and becomes able to experience companionship, which is a form of *mutuality*. In mutuality, we stand side by side with someone, moving in harmony, creating a bond that is the product of both people—an emergent *we* in the space between.

When we are embedded with others, we "fit in" like a piece of a jigsaw puzzle; we are comfortable in our role, our "place." It is not usually until adolescence that the concern with having a place in society becomes paramount. Yet younger children also make important their sense of belonging to one group rather than another, differentiating themselves and at the same time experiencing communality. The experience is one of being part of, belonging—the dimension of *embeddedness* with others.

Finally, but all along, the developing person has been learning about taking care of others, offering the self to others' needs, bridging the space through *tending and care*. In tending, we hold others, cradling them (actually or symbolically) in our arms.

All of these modalities, then, are forms of reaching through the space that separates us, both physically and psychologically. Any given relationship may involve more than one of these dimensions, simultaneously or sequentially. The metaphor of spatial orientation is useful in cutting through confusing verbalizations to clarify how people are oriented toward each other and what they need to feel connected.

These dimensions of relatedness unfold simultaneously and often independently, although they may interpenetrate and incorporate each other. They are not, however, reducible one to another. Because human life is of a piece, the dimensions shade into one another; they do not stay separate and distinct (as well they should not). But each has its own coherent center, its own fundamental phenomenology; each has its own metaphor and form of expression. Thinking in these terms allows us to move beyond thinking of all human connection as rooted in and metaphorically experienced as "good feeding."

How and toward whom love is expressed varies by culture. Yet there are certain fundamental human propensities for connection that find expression in some form universally. Social mores and traditions regulate the rituals and forms through which people are held or recognized or idealized, but the processes of these eight dimensions remain identifiable.

No doubt there are other ways to describe a multidimensional relational space; perhaps there are even more than eight dimensions. The dimensions chosen here are drawn from the modalities that theorists have already brought into focus, juxtaposed with one another so that relatedness emerges as a multifaceted process.

The first four dimensions are primary: holding, attachment, passionate experience, and eye-to-eye validation. They are present either from the beginning of life (the need to be held and the need for drive gratification) or shortly thereafter (as in attachment and awareness of eye-to-eye response). The second four dimensions require cognitive maturation and may not develop until late child-hood. Idealization and embeddedness require a concept and expe-rience of the self, as well as the capacity to think about how one is positioned in regard to others. Mutuality and tending, also very much concerned with responsiveness to others, require development out of egocentrism and into a world of others.

When we look at the phenomenology of personal experience, however, we find that the dimensions that a particular theorist has made central may be only tangential in a given life. Although each of the dimensions is probably present to at least some extent in everyone's life, people often develop along particular relational pathways that highlight one or two relational themes in favor of others. Thus some people tell life stories marked by needs for pre-serving attachment and caring for others, while other people's sto-ries focus on an attempt to be seen by others as a certain kind of person—perhaps successful or desirable or intelligent. Still others stress that their life project is to be like someone they admire; they consecrate their life to realization of idealization. There are many ways to interconnect with others: I have chosen to explicate the eight that, based on reading and hundreds of hours of interviewing, seem most salient and useful to me.

In making the choice to look at the dimensionality of related-ness from inside the person, I recognize that I cannot also see re-latedness from the outside. Such traditional issues as power and aggression, most visible to an observer, are now more hidden from view. No one says, for example, "Ray mattered a lot to me because I could have power over him and control him." People are, how-ever, apt to say, "I was so afraid that Ray would leave me that I did everything I could to keep him close to home." Rage, too, is cer-tainly present in the interviews, but it is reactive to disappointment or betrayal.[2] The focus in the chapters that follow is, by design, on what people want and need of others.

People remember selectively, of course, and I rely on retro-spection for the phenomenological part of my explication of re-latedness. Undoubtedly, the memory of those I interviewed made their relationships more consistent than they may have been in reality (although many people enjoyed relating the drama of *chang-ing* relationships). Reminiscences themselves serve a psychological function: memory of relatedness serves in balancing the self. And sometimes it is not until a distance of years allows perspective on a relationship that we can see what another person has really meant.[3] The focus in the interview was on what the relationship meant to the person over the years, and there is room for understanding that a given relationship might mean different things at different times.

Before proceeding with an explication of these dimensions, however, we must explore more carefully how this model of relatedness may fit within psychological theory.

Chapter 2

Yearning (Wo)Man

Only I discern—
Infinite passion, and the pain
Of finite hearts that yearn.

—Robert Browning, "Two in the Campagna"

Freud's model of human development depicts Guilty Man, Man (and Woman) battling impulses in order to form a society. In Kohut's model of Tragic Man, people are fated never to realize the ambitions of the nuclear self. When we focus on the dimensions of relatedness in human development and human life, we create a picture of Yearning (Wo)Man, in which people are destined always to want more connection with others than is possible, aching to overcome inescapable aloneness. In Freud's model, anxiety calls up the need for defenses. In Kohut's theory, narcissistic overexcitation is warded off. In this model, it is painful longing that we must keep out of consciousness lest it disrupt or undo us.

Fairbairn wrote that "the experience of rejection in the presence of excitement due to the stirring of urgent need constitutes a traumatic situation of the highest order for the child" (1954, p. 115). Rejection of our urgent needs for each other continues to be traumatic, and people go to great lengths to avoid such longing when the risks of rebuff are great.

As a culture, we have similarly tended to ward off concern with experiences of relatedness. They make us too vulnerable. American culture prefers what seems controllable, what is achievable through will and striving. Interpersonal responsiveness is too capricious, it seems—too unaffected by our efforts. To need others

11

seems like a weakness. After all, it was his need for Delilah that cost
Samson his strength.

Balancing Individualism and Relatedness

The problem of the balance in life between self-interest and concern
for others is ancient and unresolvable. In each era, humankind has
tended to stress one at the expense of the other. Certain epochs have
emphasized duty and responsibility, social or moral expectation, as
the center of human motivation. In the post-Freudian era, on the
other hand, we have tended to eschew a guilt-dominated orientation
to life in favor of self-expression and individual freedom. In this
framework, relatedness to others becomes a matter of what leads to
self-fulfillment. Therefore, the modern solution to an unfulfilling
relationship is to leave it in search of a better one. Responsibilities
to children and to friends are secondary to the necessities of career.
Participation in the social and civic good is often ignored in favor
of activities that bring financial rewards. It is difficult in this age
even to talk about these things without sounding hopelessly reac-
tionary or preachy.

Sociologists and social critics are increasingly alarmed by the
radical individualism of American culture and the concomitant
overvaluation of the self (Lasch, 1978; Bellah and others, 1985). The
centrality of the self in modern psychology is both cause and con-
sequence of this cultural tilt. By glorifying selfhood and individual
enterprise, psychology has both absorbed American values and encouraged a social philosophy that puts the interests of the self at the
helm. As a result, the current dominant psychological narrative of
human development is a tale of human beings set adrift from each
other, pursuing their course of "autonomy" and "independence."
Thus psychology joins the culture of narcissism in shared idolatry
of the self, bestowing praise on self-reliance, self-expression, self-
awareness, and self-fulfillment. And in paying such homage, both
our culture and our psychology deny our essential dependence on
each other.

As society becomes more individualistic and places less value
on human interconnection except as a means of productivity, psychological (as well as physical) space for meeting becomes scarcer.

There are few places in which we find each other now, little time for being with. In our mobile society, the community, the extended family, the temple, and the neighborhood have all weakened as bulwarks of human exchange. And those few relational institutions that *do* remain (such as marriage and the family) begin to crack under the strain of carrying all the relational needs that we have but are too ashamed to acknowledge openly.

We have, as a culture, overloaded the institution of marriage with so many expectations that it crumbles beneath the psychological burden. The family is increasingly a beleaguered phenomenon, shunted to the sidelines of cultural interest. Similarly, friendship is becoming an activity that people wish they had time for. Yet we grow only with and through others. Devaluation of relatedness is another form of destroying our environment: we trample on that which constitutes our world.

All the while, those of us who are psychotherapists see more and more people who come to therapy in distress about relationships. Beneath the individualism, the focus on self, the careerism and greed of modern life is an intense yearning for each other, a yearning for connection, a yearning for the responsiveness and contact that warms and enriches life. Complaining of the vulnerability inherent in needing something important from someone else, people ask us what—or who—can be changed. Others bring us their efforts to defend against this vulnerability: the schizoid brings withdrawal; the narcissist brings self-focus; the anorectic brings preoccupation with body weight as a substitute for the people she wishes she could control. All are engaged in desperate attempts to need other people less fervently. All will improve when they become able to recognize, to bear, and to channel their needs for others.

Ethel Person (1988) points out that the subject of love has been ignored in twentieth-century scientific discourse. The elevation of reason and the dismissal of feeling have led us away from the truth of our own experience. "We blink away the actualities of our condition—the feelings, drives, dreams, and desires that express, with painful accuracy, the depths at which we really *live*. Not where we think or imagine we should live, or where society advises us to live, but where our lives are fueled and our deepest satisfactions experienced—this is what we disregard. We allow ourselves too

often to live lives that are secondhand and largely theoretical, devoted to goods we do not truly desire, to gods in whom we do not
truly believe" (p. 19). In this rational century, we may not yearn.

Martha Nussbaum (1986) develops a similar position in her
philosophical treatise on Greek tragedy. She points to a fundamental duality of human existence: the human being is an agent but
also a plant. As plants, we are vulnerable to happenings in the
world. Our destinies are influenced by how people treat us. As people who love, we expose ourselves to the caprice of events outside
our control. No wonder, then, that Western culture prefers an ethic
and a Weltanschauung of agency and strength.

Our needs for relatedness make us vulnerable to rejection and
to the possible shameful exposure of our neediness, especially in a
culture that so values self-reliance and independence. A veritable
industry has developed to try to wean people away from such needs,
to persuade them that they can really do it all on their own. Self-
help books are consumed by people hoping for a formula that will
enable them to need less from others. This focus on the self at least
distracts people from their needs for affection and response. Yet the
multitude of books and articles that we read about relationships—
how to conduct them, how to solve problems in them, how much
space to allow them in our lives—satisfy our craving to articulate
the deep stirrings in us about our connections to other people. They
speak to our most tender spot. We are fragile in this regard: what
we need most we cannot control.

Approaches to the Psychological Study of Relatedness

One major hindrance to the study of relatedness has been the pe-
culiarly American polarization of autonomy and connection. In this
view, one can *either* be invested in the energies and activities of the
self (as valued in American culture) *or* one can be preoccupied with
and occupied by others in relationships (perceived as weak, inferior
forms of endeavor). But this polarization has made it impossible to
understand many important phenomena. A psychology dominated
by centrality of the self, for example, has proved quite ineffective in
making sense of the development of women.

In contrast to men, whose development emphasizes separation and boundaries, women grow through increasingly complex and differentiated forms of communion with others. Women, to whom relatedness tends to be central, anchor themselves in a web of interrelationship with others—relationships that exist at varying levels, with differing degrees of importance and distinct nuances and shadings of liaison. And as we look more clearly at how women do these things, we notice that men do similar things, only more furtively, not attending to or talking about them as much.

Relatedness and individuality are not dichotomous. Action takes place only within a relational matrix; the self is realized through others; development concerns both maintaining our ties to others *and* differentiating from them. As Gilligan put it, "We know ourselves as separate only insofar as we live in connection with others, and . . . we experience relationship only insofar as we differentiate other from self" (1982, p. 63).

Our study of women has taught us that valuing the interpersonal does not have to exclude competence and creativity, that cooperation and group effort can effect progress, that knowledge can be connected, passionate, and contextual as well as hypothetico-deductive and authority-based (Belenky and others, 1986). If relatedness does not have to obviate competence and autonomy, we can be less frightened of it; so we, as psychologists, have become more willing to shine our lamp on it and see what takes place. But even though we are now more sympathetic to the serious study of the interpersonal, we lack both navigational instruments and road maps. This is a different sort of place, this interpersonal sphere. It exists in the realm of the subjective and affective, the symbolic and the transcendent. Much of what really matters here is beyond words.

Many writers have commented on the basic dualities of human life beyond Freud's division into work and love: doing and being (Erlich and Blatt, 1985; Guntrip, 1971), self-definition and interpersonal relatedness (Blatt, 1990), the instrumental and the expressive (Parsons, 1964), clinging and thrill-seeking (Balint, 1959)—all are different names for the two axes of human life. David Bakan (1966), working with these same dualities, denotes them as polarities of agency (which involves self-assertion, mastery, distinction, and separateness) and communion (which encompasses contact, union, and cooperation).

Bakan goes further than naming and exploring the duality, however. He also points out that it is in the nature of the agentic side of human nature to separate itself, often forcefully, from its communion aspect. Thus the agentic view of human development stresses the attainment of agentic forms (self-expression, individuality, and control) while disowning and repressing the communion side (which, by its nature, endeavors to overcome separateness, to connect, to be at one with, to participate). A theory told from the agentic viewpoint in agentic language stresses developmental movement toward action, competence, individuation, and comfort with aloneness. Such a stance, by its nature, disavows communion. A theory written in the language of agency cannot illuminate compassion or care or the capacity to love—the states of being-with that are beyond time or sequence. Is it possible, then, to have a theory told from the communion side, or is theory-making itself an agentic form? Can we have a relational theory of development that details more differentiated forms of making contact with each other while not disavowing movement toward self-realization? Such a theory would trace the growth of self-in-relation (Miller, 1976, Gilligan, 1977) postulate individuation toward greater belonging and sharing, and see development as moving not toward separation but toward increasingly complex relatedness.

Part of what is wondrous about human beings is that we are capable of many complex and varied forms of being with each other. The ebb and flow of our efforts to have our needs met by each other and in spite of each other is the wellspring of literature and theater. Religion and ethics take on the task of teaching us how we *ought* to be with each other. And the fascination with human interaction promotes itself in the analysis that people do of each other in a form of conversation designated as gossip.

Within developmental psychology, however, this liveliness of human interchange is nowhere apparent. The effort in developmental psychology has been to view human growth as proceeding from dependence to autonomy and to account for the processes by which more and greater aspects of experience are taken over by the self. In our current state of knowledge, individual developmental history is depicted as a movement from merger to separateness. The metaphorical picture of the "lone self" is one we can draw well: the

Lone Ranger forms the developmental ideal of autonomy, self-sufficiency, and mastery. But how are we to describe the ways in which human beings are inexorably embedded in and with others, even in defining their selfhood? The Lone Ranger, after all, would not have been the same without Tonto.

Relationships are the Brownian motion of psychology. They are hard to study because they do not stay still. Relationships are recursive: people in relationships modify each other. Our theories have tended to behave as though either the self or the other were static. We have, for example, only recently been able to contain theoretically the fact that "mother" is not a fixed entity—in other words, that the mother is in part shaped by her child's responses. Winnicott (1965d), for example, begins his theory by stating provocatively that there is no such thing as a baby; there is only the mother-child unit.

People in mature relationships modify themselves in order to accommodate to others. So the fact of a relationship being gratifying or meaningful to the participants reflects subtle and complex processes of mutual adaptation. It makes no sense, then, to ask about the self who is in the relationship. Rather, we must inquire about the self-in-relationship and about the relationship as it exists in the self. People bring aspects of themselves to a relationship based on their perception of the other and the other's needs. Similarly, the existence of a certain kind of relationship might indelibly alter one's own characteristics.

Self Versus Other: Separation or Connection

Like the conundrum of the chicken and the egg, a theory of psychological development has to begin its story with either self or other, separateness or merger. Either the tale begins with the self merged and growing toward separateness or with the self as separate and growing toward connection. And which starting point is chosen colors the way the developmental story unfolds.

One way to begin the story is to make the assumption of otherness and to envision the infant as part of a symbiotic mass, physically separated but still psychologically merged. If we begin this way, development becomes a narrative of separation, of firming boundaries, of detaching, of learning to do for oneself, of developing a self out of the primordial fusion with otherness. (In contemporary developmental theory, this position is best represented by Margaret Mahler [Mahler, Pine, and Bergman, 1975].) Developmental progress becomes synonymous with greater and deeper self-awareness.

Another way to begin the story is to assume the self as preexisting and to envision the infant as born separate and alone, disconnected and helpless. Development then becomes a story of learning to attach, to connect, to find ways of meeting one's complex needs for contact with the human environment. Daniel Stern (1985), who has written about the interpersonal world of the infant from this perspective, believes that development is a process of learning about "being with others." In his view, there is no symbiotic phase. Experiences of union occur only to the extent that a sense of core self and core other exist. In this narrative orientation, developmental progress occurs along the track of greater and more differentiated connection to others. As we grow, we become able to relate to others in more complex ways, which means that the nature of our interaction with others becomes that much more multifaceted.

And this is not simply an academic debate. A sense of human development as originating in fusion and moving toward separateness supports a psychology that views normality and health in essentially separatistic terms. These metapsychological disputes affect the lives of people who go to psychotherapists with their conflicts and symptoms. If we are "separatists," we are likely to locate the problems in faulty separation-individuation and counsel people to more firmly reinforce their boundaries and to better tolerate aloneness. If we are "connectionists," we think in terms of helping people to improve and enlarge their bonds with others.[1]

Increasingly, we understand psychological conflict as resulting from distortions in relatedness, from being haunted by inner representations of past painful interactions with others, and from failures of the effort to have one's needs met. Inner conflict may also result when a person is overwhelmed by another's insatiable or inappropriate needs or is inadequately responded to by important others.

As humans, we need much from others in order to exist, and

yet we are imperfect providers of the emotional supplies necessary to others. Frequently, discord and conflict within relationships exist because of unevenness of emotional supplies. A person gets a part of what he or she needs from another only by leaving some other important need unfulfilled. Such compromises of life are also the compromises of psychopathology.

But to tell the story of development solely from the point of view of relatedness would repeat the same error that telling the story of development from the point of view of separation has always done. Relatedness and separation are recursive processes.[2] Separation from others firms the self, makes boundaries palpable, and allows for greater differentiation of self from others. And these factors produce greater responsiveness in relationships. In this vein, many theorists (such as Balint, 1952b, Erikson, 1968, and Kernberg, 1980) have pointed out that true intimacy is possible only between separate people. The clearer we are about who we ourselves are, the more we are able to risk ourselves with another. The more certain we are about our own boundaries, the freer we become to experience a range of affect and interconnection with others.

Greater responsiveness and availability in and to relationships in turn remold the self. Our experiences with others teach us something about ourselves as well. We must always revise our inner model of ourselves in light of our interpersonal experience. We know and realize ourselves only in, through, and with others.

Separation and connection, then, are interpenetrating processes. To make matters even more complicated, both always involve both an internal and an external aspect. The internal aspect always includes a representation of the self, a representation of the other, and an affect to join them. The external aspect always affects others' experience and representations of us and their likelihood of future responsiveness. Said in other words, when we are together, we are both separate and connected. Whatever happens between us will create some emotional response in me as well as a change in my image of you and my image of myself. The changes in my image of you and of myself (including my image of myself-in-relation [to you]), will also influence how I will treat you in the future. What happens between us will likewise affect you in your thinking about me and will influence how you treat me in the future. When people talk about their lives, they talk this recursive language naturally and simply. Developmental theory, on the other hand, stammers and sputters, divides up relational experience between the proponents of the inner and the champions of the outer, highlights the self and allows others to be relegated to chiaroscuro, or becomes so vague about what interpersonal experience is that we are each free to project our own meanings into the theory and think that we are communicating with each other.

Relatedness and Psychotherapy

As psychology and psychoanalysis begin moving the candle to illuminate this relatively unexplored area, they do so with the same kinds of candles that have shed light on other problems. For the clinical psychologist and the psychoanalyst, the frame of reference for the understanding of relatedness is the understanding of the relationship that is best known: that between therapist and patient. In the transference, the patient's customary modes of relating to and fantasizing about others are dramatically visible. The patient does not need to tell: the therapist need only experience what the patient brings. No relationship has ever been understood in more detail, in all its conscious and unconscious, loving and hating, conflictual and whole aspects.

Yet limiting our understanding of relationships to these phenomena blinds us in three ways. First, the therapeutic relationship is a nonmutual one. One person, willing to accept the role of "patient," comes to another, cast in the caregiving role of "therapist," for help. The "patient" is in need; the therapist is to respond to or to help to understand the needs. By design, the therapeutic setting replicates parent-child positions. No wonder, then, that our psychological theory is so exclusively focused on parent-child dynamics. Within the therapeutic consultation, we rarely have an opportunity to view anything else.

Second, patients are people who come to us with difficulties in life—symptoms or conflicts. All such problems bespeak difficulties of some sort in relationships. While it may be true that patients are very often just as "normal" as nonpatients, and sometimes even more so, we are nevertheless hearing about experiences that are dominated by emotional distress rather than experiences of people whose lives are smoothly functioning.

Limiting our understanding to the transactions in the therapeutic relationship blinds us in yet a third way. The clinician hears mostly about what is relationally disturbed and is often unaware of other, more mature relational levels of functioning in a patient's life. We might know, for example, that a patient tends to become hostile and punitive when he feels aroused to closeness and intimacy with a woman, and this might be the focus of therapy; but what we may miss is his generosity and warmth as a mentor to younger men in his firm. We may never hear about the importance of his tennis partner as a confidant or the joy he knew collecting stamps with his grandfather. These relationships are part of our patient's health (after all, not all of him is diseased) and therefore may be overlooked in our task of helping him to better integrate his ambivalence toward women.

Although over time we will, as therapists, witness many aspects of the patient's inner relational patterning in the transference, there is much more that we will not see. While this may not hinder our therapeutic efforts, it seriously cripples our theory. In turn, our crippled theory leads us not to attend clinically to those very aspects of a patient's life that may be the source of his or her trouble (or a potential wellspring of strength).

Marjorie, for example, consulted me for depression and an inability to choose a career or find a love relationship. We worked in individual therapy for a year. During that time, she formed a highly positive transference to me that allowed her to gain some inner emotional distance from her mother, who was controlling and demanding. Marjorie had the sense that nothing she could ever do would please her. At the same time, her mother seemed to have "promised" her that one day she would meet a man who would take care of her and solve all of her problems. Marjorie, at the age of thirty-three, was beginning to fear that this would not happen. To choose a career of her own meant to disengage from the Prince Charming fantasy of her life that she shared with her mother.

Marjorie was bright, insightful, and self-observant. Yet in spite of our best efforts, we could not see what it was that kept her from having a relationship with a man. Certainly, she was too extreme in her idealistic expectations; but after being in therapy for a while, she could see this and was trying to temper it. She said that she had many friends, and indeed she seemed to be personable and appropriate. She worked hard in therapy, yet I often had difficulty listening to her. I found it hard to make emotional contact with her self-pity and entitlement. I decided to put her in a therapy group.

In the group, the picture changed dramatically. It became clear almost immediately that she simply dismissed other people, almost did not see them. She was seriously unable to be emotionally responsive to others. Lacking any empathic capacity, she simply reacted to other members of the group by making moral judgments. None of this had been apparent in the individual therapy; it was neither in the transference nor in any other aspect of the relationship between her and me. Nor did it *ever* appear in our relationship, even in the group. With people she "looked up to," a whole different pattern of relational orientation appeared.

One could, of course, say that if I had been a better therapist, I would have been able to pick up on all of this in the individual therapy. Perhaps so. But I have come to believe that what we see so clearly focused in transference are those aspects of the early relationship with parents that center on issues of dependency, control, competition, approval, and so on. Because the therapeutic relationship is necessarily nonmutual and unequal, we learn most about how a person experiences nonmutual and unequal relationships. In helping people resolve their conflicts in these areas, we help them remove troubled infantile, no-longer-relevant pieces from their ongoing adult relationships. So far, so good. But we then assume that if we take away neurotic, repetitive, infantile wishes from adult relationships, the person will be able to have "enduring, satisfying, mutually gratifying" relationships. As though such relationships were fundamental givens, only hidden beneath transferentially based distortions!

The paradigm of transference does not illuminate mutual relationships, and it is with "peers" that people must articulate their lives. And it is this process of interpersonal integration that we are just beginning to investigate.

To be sure, in psychoanalysis and psychotherapy we learn more deeply about what people want of others than in any other method. We need, however, some theoretical breadth to add to the depth.

It may be humbling for us as therapists to discover that we do not have central importance in our patients' schemas of relatedness. I was surprised to see how often people I interviewed for this study who had been in psychotherapy or in a lengthy psychoanalysis placed their therapists and analysts in far reaches of their life space (or left them out altogether). We have meaning to our patients, certainly, but in a different way than "real" people in their lives have meaning.

Relatedness and Developmental Psychology

Another major effort to understand relatedness has come from developmental psychology, which uses its research tools to investigate the normal. In this tradition, we find an attempt at breadth but a lack of depth. The problem here is that the instruments of developmental research are far from the depth psychology that the clinician knows. Developmentalists most often utilize questionnaires and attempt to understand phenomena such as love by asking a large sample of undergraduates to answer questions such as, "On a scale from 1 to 7, how often do you feel that people want to get closer to you than you want them to?" To the ear of the clinician, accustomed as he or she is to ambivalence and contradiction and to the complexity that gives texture to all relationships, this is a limited form of investigation. The definition of relational phenomena by a measurable laboratory procedure is likewise limited. Attachment, for example, has come to be synonymous with how a twelve-month-old responds to his mother after a brief separation arranged by an experimenter. The focus in such developmental studies moves quickly to problems of operationalization or problems of measurement, relegating concerns about the meaning of such experiences to the sidelines.

In the search for replicable methods that can be widely (and usually quickly) utilized, developmental psychology gets caught in a process of devising a measure, relating it to many variables, finding discrepancies in results, arguing over what the measure really measures after all, and then losing interest in it and moving on to another measure, repeating the cycle. It would be very difficult to tell a coherent "story" of the development of relatedness from developmental research, although there have been some promising and thoughtful studies of such phenomena as loneliness, friendship, and empathy. Too often, once developmental psychology gets one of these "variables" clearly in view, the person disappears. Therefore, there are studies of loneliness that tell us nothing about people who are lonely or why they are lonely—or even how they are lonely. We just learn such things as that "we are faced with the task of interpreting the interrelationship of self-perceived trait competence and skills, coactor-perceived skills and observer-perceived skills with the experience of loneliness over time" (Spitzberg and Hurt, 1987).

Or else we learn about how people experience themselves in terms of the researcher's definitions of love. (People doing research on love have been known to tell undergraduate subjects who have never been in love to fill out the questionnaire as they imagine they would respond if they *had* been in love!) Or we learn that female adolescents are more likely to disclose personal things about themselves to their friends than are male adolescents. But why, and what does it feel like?

In order to study relatedness adequately, we must, in Husserl's phrase, return to the "things themselves." In the phenomenology of people's experience of relatedness, we can best view the interweaving and patterning, the differentiation and complexity of the threads that tie people to each other.

My effort in the present study has been to try to marry the best tools of both clinical and developmental psychology and the framework of object-relational thinking to suggest a phenomenologically based schema of dimensions of relatedness.[3] I aim to try to find out what people mean when they talk about love. What do we need of each other?

The Multidimensionality of Adult Relatedness

Our tendency to "reduce" adult relatedness to its infantile origins keeps us from knowing explicitly about the importance of relational connections in adult life. Clearly, adults have many, many experiences—important experiences—that are not possible in infancy. And relationships change over time as the person matures. Cognitive growth and change lead us to reinterpret our earlier experiences to be consistent with later ones. We rethink painful events that have happened to us in ways that neutralize their sting. Cognitive development also radically alters the growing person's capacity for experience itself. Theorists have essentially ignored these experiences, however, or have attempted to reduce them to whatever infantile threads can be found. Thus we overcome the problem of adult complexity by simply blinding ourselves to it.

Where theorists have written of relationships, they have tended to take one dimension and explore it, leaving us, as readers, to fill in the rest. Freud, for example, taught that the aims of healthy development were *lieben und arbeiten*. That is a wonderful phrase. When I read it, I think that Freud meant what *I* mean by "love," and you think that he meant what *you* mean. But what did *Freud* mean by *lieben*—"to love"? He seems, based on the rest of his writings, to have meant "to have mutual genital orgasms" (which is also what Erikson thought he meant). Freud, after all, was focused on the development and vicissitudes of the libido. Therefore, the endpoint of healthy development was the channeling of libido into nonperverse sexual activity within social bounds. We assume that Freud really meant more than this, but in fact he did not comment on how housework should be distributed within a couple or on needing others for empathic resonance or on why men feel so good after a night of poker with "the guys." Similarly, Bowlby (1969), who has done so much to direct our attention to the importance of real relationships, writes that "attachment gives meaning to life," here seeming to include all else that is good in relationships that is not specifically attachment.

Theorists have offered us intensive and sensitive portrayals of aspects of connection. Now we are perhaps ready to assemble these threads and see how they knit themselves together in the fabric of a life. Few relationships are unidimensional, nor are many relationships omnidimensional. We can feel valued by and attached to someone without a sexual/libidinal component, for example. We can idealize someone and be sexually involved without experiencing any resonance or mutuality. And so on. Each relationship has its own "recipe." This is a study of the ingredients and what we know about them so far.

Relational Moments Versus Relational Environments

Relationships are built of millions of interactions across a spectrum of affect and responsiveness. Which ones, then, shall we study? Shall we look at the "big moments" or at the ongoing milieu that results from but is not defined by any particular episode? We may know, for example, that Arlene's father was an alcoholic and abandoned her and her mother when she was seven years old. She recalls two occasions on which he was drunk and hit her. This information would seem to characterize Arlene's image of her father, until we further learn that her father used to delight in her, call her his little princess, and spend hours playing dominoes with her.

Relationships, then, must be characterized by their thematic background as well as their more visible dramatic moments. Connections between people have rhythms beyond their content. These ways of being together are the hardest to verbalize, because they involve emotional tone and mutual interpersonal adaptation. It is not so much the "what" of the interaction as the process that forms its core.

Every relational environment is unique, even though many different moments may occur within each environment. Within a Beethoven symphony are many varied passages that together comprise the symphony. Similarly, if it were possible to close my eyes and ears to the content of my interactions with someone who matters to me and just listen to the relational music, carried on affect and responsiveness, reverberating in closeness and distance, resonance and discord—if I could rely solely on these nonverbal and noncognitive sensations, I would still know exactly whom I was with. Only the greatest of writers have ever been able to evoke the feel of two people being together, so difficult is it to articulate the "atmosphere" of an ongoing relationship.

We are perhaps most conscious of this relational music when we encounter an old friend after many years. Most people have had the experience of "picking up" just where they left off with such a friend. I think, though, that what is "picked up" is not at all the content, although that is easily enough filled in. What is picked up is the old music, which both people remember, although neither could have remembered it alone. The old friends, with their beings, find that they each respond in the same old ways, laugh at the same old things, and have similar tensions and symmetries to those that used to be there. Immediately and inevitably, the old patterns reappear. Unconsciously, we preserve the choreography that, regardless of the new dialogue, is the essence of the connection.

The Patterning of Relatedness

Where we have tried to understand the interpersonal world, it has been through observation of specific and particular relationships. There is much written on marriage, for example, and on mother-child relationships. Only recently have investigators begun to consider friendship and the interconnections among siblings. But these approaches, in trying to get a highly complex relationship under the microscope, necessarily overlook the context in which each relationship occurs. Who there is in our life influences who else we need and how we need them.

Eve, for example, had a troubled and distant relationship with her critical, unloving mother. Eve's grandmother, however, was devoted to her and responsive to her needs; she supplied the support and warmth that her mother did not offer. These relationships were delicately juxtaposed, and Eve's psychological situation would have been entirely different had her grandmother not been available in the way she was.

Relationships always occur in existing systems, enhancing, counterpointing, or clashing with others already there. An adolescent boy and an adolescent girl fall in love. What could be more natural, more ordinary? But if one is embedded in a family named Montague and the other in a family named Capulet, we have an enduring tragic tale.

Studying individual relationships abstracted from their larger relational contexts, then, gives us very narrow information. A study exploring mother-daughter relationships, using Eve as a subject, would discover her distance from and disappointment in her mother. Her sense of rejection and anger would be primary.

What would be missed, however, would be Eve's substitution of her grandmother for her mother and the fact that Eve was adequately held and validated early in life—but by her grandmother.

The pattern of relatedness has far-reaching effects on development, forming the "cocoon" out of which the human continues to emerge. Ignoring this patterning, focusing only on specific dyadic relationships, researchers fail to find direct psychological or behavioral linkages between generations (Ricks, 1985). Despite years of highly funded research, there are few developmental rules linking parental behavior or personality characteristics to the fate of the child. Yet we know that early development has profound consequences for later life. The answer to this dilemma must lie in the patterning of relatedness. It is not how things go with a particular person but the whole interpersonal network that ultimately shapes development. We must extend our view to observe the healing effects of later nutrients on early deprivation. Although people harm each other, they also offer solace and sustenance to assuage prior hurt. And as individuals grow, more people become available to meet their developmental needs. The ability to find and attract necessary others decreases the individual's dependence on people who may be inadequate or disappointing (Wolf, 1980). We must take this longer view.

As a field, psychology has conceptualized only a limited stratum of relational life. We assume that most of what is developmentally central takes place in the complex ties between parent and child. Nods are given to siblings, generally in terms of rivalry. Then, with a brief glance toward generic "peers," the focus again shifts to a single heterosexual relationship, which we assume will produce offspring; and *again* we can be interested in parent-child dynamics, again from the viewpoint of the child. Life as lived is far more various; relationships take place between and among many Others. The family saga and sexual partnering are only small pieces of the relational network that shapes a life, as we shall see.

Chapter 3

Holding

She looked from one to the other, and she saw them established to her safety, and she was free. . . . Her father and her mother now met to the span of the heavens, and she, the child, was free to play in the space beneath, between.

—D. H. Lawrence, *The Rainbow*

Of all the ways in which people need each other, holding is the most primary, the least evident, and the hardest to describe. Holding contains the invisible threads that tie us to our existence. From the first moments of our life to the last, we need to be held—or we fall.

The earliest sensations the infant experiences are those of being grounded or held. After the secure and compact enclosure of the womb comes the vastness of space in which falling is a terrifying danger. The experience of being held is the experience of feeling "arms around." The warmth of body contact and the possibilities for molding to the other are aspects of being held, but the most fundamental sensation is one of strong arms grounding, keeping one from falling.

Winnicott (1965c) makes holding central to his idea of the necessary conditions of "good-enough" mothering. What babies need most is an adequate "holding environment"—an environment that makes possible the emergence of their own innate potential. This is the most fundamental of the relational contexts in which psychological growth unfolds. As a result of holding, the infant is gradually able to take over some of the functions of his or her caretaker and become a separate person who "lives with." But Winnicott's "good-enough" mother does a great deal more than feed, which was the central aspect of Freudian and post-Freudian mothers. The "holding" mother intuitively manages the environment to allow her infant a full range of experience without allowing need, affect, or stimulation to be too overwhelming too often (Winnicott, 1975b). The result of holding is an infant who is not only sufficiently fed but who feels real, who, in Winnicott's phrase, is able to "reach the difficulties of life" (1975c). The infant must be adequately held to exist as a self.

Bion, similarly, in his concept of the "container," speaks to arms-around sensations that are both literal and metaphorical. The infant needs from the mother the security of a container that will stay intact regardless of his or her impulses or destructiveness. Bion adds to Winnicott's formulation the idea that the container will also be able to transform unpleasant and overwhelming sensations that the baby experiences. By absorbing and managing what threatens to strain the coping capacity of the baby, the "container" helps to manage and to mitigate overwhelming emotional experience (cited in Grinberg, Sor, and de Bianchedi, 1977). Thus the container encloses and protects and makes safe what is inside.

In order to be able to move away from the mother, the baby has to internalize a sense of being adequately held. As mobility increases, the adequately held baby begins to explore the environment. Mahler's (Mahler, Pine, and Bergman, 1975) concept of "rapprochement" describes the phenomenon of the adventurous baby returning at intervals to her mother for "refueling" or "touching base." While these phenomena can be understood in attachment terms (see Chapter Four), they also relate to holding; the "fuel" here is the holding itself, and the "base" is the arms-around experience. Often, in fact, babies in the rapprochement stage return to their mothers just for a hug—a literal expression of arms around. Mahler also describes the toddler who runs off, only to be swept up in the arms of a parent. The child comes to see that the world is bounded rather than infinite: the strong arms make safe limits in space. (Throughout life, people are bounded and limited by others.)

Babies sometimes fall, of course. It is important that arms are available to pick the baby up again, quickly, restoring the sense of groundedness and security. Babies calm when they feel held again, when they feel the enclosure of the arms around.

The experience of this boundedness draws a circle of safety in which one may live. Although with time and development the circle widens, distressed adults may still need to be physically held. Adult needs for holding are rarely discussed, however. We can read long discourses on the development and phenomenology of sexuality, but there is little written on hugging, which provides the arms-around experience throughout life. Instinctively, we hug or hold someone who is suffering or frightened (with my arms I will try to keep you from falling into despair). But adults learn to be ashamed of yearnings to be held. It is often easier to obtain sex than holding; there are many clinical reports of people who seek sexual contact as a way of obtaining the holding that they really need.

As the baby grows, focus shifts from the container in which mobility takes place toward action and purpose. The arms-around experience is the background to the more conspicuous experiences of initiative and adventure. Holding functions, when they are optimal, now become transparent. As development proceeds, experiences of being held move from the physical to the emotional realm and become more symbolic. We are held by people who rarely touch us physically; we can be held by institutions and ideas. But we always retain our need for the feeling of boundedness (Fromm, 1941). The "holding" of infancy becomes the "support" of later years.

Thereness

Throughout the interviews I conducted, the word my interviewees most frequently used in describing their most important relationships was *there*.[1] How is your husband, your mother, your friend important in your life? I would ask. He or she is "there," would be the reply. Consistently—and somewhat surprisingly—this is what was *most* important. And people could rarely say more about what "thereness" is. Most, when asked for a definition, would look at me searchingly, intently, and say something like, "She was there. Just always *there*. I just knew she was there." *There* seems to be a word that describes a fundamental psychological experience that cannot be further broken down. As best I can understand it, the "thereness" of someone speaks to holding. It is an expression of what can be taken for granted; it is all-important background.

Cal, for example, spoke of the "thereness" of his grandfather. He never felt close to him: his grandfather was a distant, forbidding patriarch who never took a particular interest in him. But when his grandfather died (when Cal was twenty-five), Cal felt less safe in the world. His grandfather had been a keystone of the family. When he died, Cal felt the family break apart; he no longer felt confident that there was a strong family caretaker who could somehow put things right. Without being fully conscious of it, Cal had always thought of his grandfather as strength, as the place he could go if he were really in trouble. This is what Cal meant by his experience of his grandfather's "thereness."

In earliest experience, one can be held only by someone who is physically "there." But holding offers the feeling of support as well. Later in life, we still need that support from people—a sense of people's "thereness" that seems to prevent us from falling.

While going through a divorce that she initiated from a husband who was unresponsive and demeaning to her, Emily, a patient of mine, began developing massive anxiety attacks. During such an attack, she could not breathe normally: she would find herself alternately holding her breath and hyperventilating. She had a recurring sense of falling, and she would grab at the arms of the chair in an attempt to anchor herself. Despite repeated medical examinations, no physical basis for these symptoms could be found.

In a dramatic moment during one of her therapy sessions, Emily remembered a repressed childhood incident. At four years old, she was in a lake with her father. He was playfully dropping her in the water, then lifting her up again, making affectionate and exciting sounds. Then he lost both his balance and his hold on her. In remembering this, Emily reexperienced the sensation of falling through the water, of flailing about unsupported for what seemed like an interminable time. She realized that this was the same feeling of falling that she had been reexperiencing for so many weeks. The memory of falling in the water was the connection, of course, to her difficulties in breathing.

Having remembered the incident, Emily then could link her terrifying anxiety attacks to her sense that, although she was relieved to have ended her relationship with her husband, she felt in danger of falling; she was no longer able to rely on her husband's support or on the structure of the life they had built together. Unconsciously, Emily was experiencing the divorce as falling helplessly through the water.

Falling is one of the most terrifying of sensations. It is an experience of utter loss of control, of losing one's moorings, of complete helplessness and powerlessness. We cannot fly: we are creatures who have to have something beneath us. The exercise of our selfhood and our autonomy is absolutely dependent on our being adequately grounded.

In an existential sense, to be aware of the essential groundlessness of the human condition is to be overwhelmed by the sensation of falling. Ultimately, there is nothing that holds us, yet we can live only by denying this fact and resting ourselves against what we can experience to be firm and solid.

After we have moved beyond our mother's arms, the experience of being held or having more symbolic arms around us resides in the family unit. This is the first of the "holding environments" that are necessary to growth across the life cycle. Children who have been held well feel safe enough and protected enough to begin discovering aspects of themselves in the world (still returning to the family as a holder or ground). Such children have internalized what Erikson (1968) calls a sense of "basic trust"; they have an expectation of support from the world. Based on early good-enough holding, children reach out for experience with the expectation that the world will not let them fall.

Part of what initiates the adolescent identity crisis is the cognitive capacity to experience the absence of holding. With a shock of betrayal, adolescents (at least some adolescents) see human groundlessness for the first time. They discover both that parents cannot really protect them and that they themselves are not likely to achieve omnipotence or immortality. Rage against fundamental human helplessness, which had been hidden in the happy illusions of childhood, often underlies adolescent troublesome behavior. "What is the meaning of life?" the adolescent asks, as he or she comes to understand the inescapable fact of death, the abyss into which *all* will fall.

This reaction is not limited to adolescence, of course. Eve had always felt held and protected by her grandmother, and she preserved this sense after her grandmother's death (when Eve was nine) by adopting a prayer her grandmother had taught her as a ritual.[2] She recited the prayer every night of her life until her son became seriously ill. Then her experience of existential groundlessness and fear destroyed the power inherent in the prayer. She had to realize that the magic words could not keep her or her son safe.

The holding experience is a complicated one to understand, because it is neither cognitively realistic nor emotionally intelligible. The sense of holding exists between fantasy and reality: we feel held even though we know that we are not. We rely on people even though we know that they cannot promise us safety. It is the juxtaposition of knowing and not knowing that gives our need to be held its distinctive cast. Yet as soon as we know surely that we are not held, we seek other ground.

After Eve had her experience of existential terror and gave thanks for the survival of her son, she regrounded herself in an ideal of family happiness. Although she had to learn to live closer to the edge of the precipice, she found a way to feel held by family harmony—a harmony so much in contrast to the chaos and disruption of her childhood.

People who serve as "holding others" in adulthood are like the transitional objects of childhood: one cannot ask too precisely if this person was found or created. We experience ourselves to be held by a net we weave out of our imagination and out of our contacts with people as they are. At the very least, we need others who will allow us to "find" them and rely on them. Some people can feel held only by not putting others to the test, while other people must test others again and again, obsessively worried that they will let them down. (We frequently see both kinds of people in our consulting rooms.)

The holding other is not so much a person in his or her own right but exists as a ground, or what Winnicott calls an "environment." In an individual's later development, groups can become holding environments—places or people who contain or ground us while we exercise some aspect of our autonomy or skill. Universities, when they function well, hold their students while they learn. Students come to rely on faculty or university resources for the refueling that they need as they explore ideas, dispute and debate theories, and try to find their own intellectual path. Good professors do not only teach; they learn how to hold their students well. They learn to bear their students' doubts and anxieties as well as their idealism and their excesses. And they know not to let their students know too dramatically or too soon that they, too, lack answers.

We have come to understand that one of the most serious pathognomonic features of development is insufficient holding—an insufficiency that occurs not as a traumatic moment but as an ongoing absence. In the absence of adequate holding, which is the frame for psychological development, emotional growth cannot occur. Inadequately held people become overwhelmed by persecutory fears, trying to live as though there were no ground beneath them, unable to trust. In such instances, substances such as drugs or alcohol can become symbolic holders, reliable sources of solace; addiction at least structures life.

Emotional Holding and the Stimulation Barrier

The arms-around experience not only keeps us from falling but also encloses and protects us. Enfolded in arms, we have a barrier between ourselves and whatever might be hurtful or overwhelming in the world. In arms, we have an extra layer of protection from the world. We sense that buffer even though we may be unclear what part of it comes from ourselves and what from outside.

A good-enough mother, in her holding function, manages things so that her baby is not overstimulated. She senses how much stimulation is welcomed and can be tolerated. An adequate holding environment leaves the baby free to develop in a state of being; the infant does not always have to react. In the state of optimal holding, the self can come into existence free of external intrusion.

When holding is not adequate, there is danger of what Winnicott (1975a) calls "impingement." If stimulation is more intense that the ego functions of the infant can bear, traumatic injury may result, leading to the use of dissociative defenses. Not only is self-development interrupted, but the growing person becomes fearful of what may come from the outer world. The infant's energy must be directed toward keeping the world from intruding (much as we react when loud noises distract us from work).

Good holding environments in later life similarly provide a container in which people can explore their own capacities free of the demands and clamor of the outer world. A good teacher, for example, affords pupils the right to explore, to err, and not to know. Similarly, the therapist learns to welcome the quiet spaces in psychotherapy as moments for the patient to exist as a self.

People often come to psychotherapy because they need to be held while they do the work of emotionally growing. They need a structure within which they can experience frightening or warded-off aspects of themselves. They need to know that this structure will not "let them down." They also need to trust that they will not be impinged upon by unwanted advice or by a therapist's conflicts or difficulties. Psychotherapy, because of clinicians' efforts to analyze what takes place, is one of the best understood of holding environments. Therapists "hold" patients as patients confront aspects of their memory and affective life that would be too frightening or overwhelming to face alone. (One of my patients once described her experience of therapy as my sitting with her while she confronted the monsters inside.) Therapists continue to hold patients even as patients rage at them in disappointment, compete with them, envy them, or yearn for them. Adequate holding continues despite the pain of relatedness.

Good friends also contain and hold stimulation for each other. We often "unload" on each other feelings that are too intense to bear, wanting only for the other person to bear them with us, not to be destroyed by them. Emotional support is often simply this kind of containment, which absorbs what is overstimulating, thereby rendering it less noxious. I am told that Spanish has a slang phrase for this process: in literal translation, I can ask someone to "be a bank for me"—that is, ask someone to keep and safeguard my feelings for me, allowing me to be free of them (Marcos Lichtmajer, letter to the author, Feb. 1990).

Emotional Support

In support, people do what they can to keep another from falling. Being supported is the experience of being tended, of having a stronger figure act on one's behalf to provide what one needs. In earliest life, the helpless infant's basic needs for food, comfort, and warmth are provided by caregiving others. Later, the child needs someone's fingers to hold on to while learning to walk. Still later, the growing child needs to be advised and guided while learning to navigate through the increasing complexity of the world. The experience of being adequately held in this way—protected and steered—is distinct from the experience of affection or approval.

Natalie spent many years trying to understand the contradictions in the way she was parented. "My mother was very warm and loving. With both my parents, there was a lot of physical affection. Lots of hugging and kissing, and my mother always told me how wonderful I was and how much she loved me. But I knew that neither of my parents could solve any problems. I felt like an orphan." Natalie drew three aunts on her relational chart and described them as "a regiment who provided for us. They brought us what we needed, sometimes took me out for ice cream, later offered help with our homework. I got a lot of love from my mother, but it was her life project to change my father, to make him be responsible. She never did, but most of her energy went to try to make something out of him; then she got too tired and worn out to do anything else. I got this sense that if your parents don't try to change things for you, you're not really important to them. I feel like I've had to learn everything on my own." Natalie felt affection and approval from her mother, but not the holding that she needed.

The support component of holding, then, has its prototype not only in the child's physical needs being met but also in the child's having someone to hold on to and be guided by while learning to walk. Having such supports to clutch while making transitions is necessary throughout life. My research subjects tended to talk about their need for "support" most when they were describing instances of venture and risk or when life structures were changing. A wish to be fully oneself or to follow a path in life that differs markedly from family expectations necessitates a great deal of support from others.

Mark, for example, whose parents wished him to go to college, relied on the support of a sympathetic uncle to bear his parents' disapproval while he became a dancer. Mark recalls the derision not only of his parents but also of his contemporaries, who viewed dancing as effeminate and foolish. He painfully recalls being laughed at and teased. At these times, he would think of his uncle's supportive message: the important thing in life is to become what you are, and to hell with what others think. Mark spoke of having "held on" to these words of his uncle when he felt doubtful and uncertain about his choice.

We feel supported when we have someone who believes in us—who is *behind* us. This sense of the word *support* is very much within the holding metaphor. Memories of supportive moments and relationships evoked profound gratitude from the people in my study. Sometimes support became the basis of a long attachment or friendship; in other instances, the supportive relationship lasted only long enough for the person to traverse whatever chasm was threatening, only as long as the support was required.

We can look at how people respond to those who are grieving. They bring over casseroles, offer practical help, do whatever they can—as if to say, "I am here and available for what you may need, although I know that I cannot provide what you *really* need" (that is, the dead person). Those who try to comfort the bereaved person try to dramatize symbolically that the world continues as a container. In support groups, people make themselves available to each other to fill in whatever resources the person might be missing. In AA groups, for example, the "buddy" is the support who is there to help a person refrain from drinking. He is a person to "fall back on" when one's impulse control wanes.

This form of support is an intricate, paradoxical process, because it provides externally the possibility of doing what the person wants to do anyway. Warren calls Ed so that Ed can tell him not to take a drink, which is just what Warren knows Ed will do. There is something about Ed's "thereness," however—the fact that he is willing to "contain" Warren's impulse and not be overwhelmed by it— that makes it possible for Warren to master the impulse as well. Thus our patients bring to us what they cannot contain. When it does not destroy us, they, too, can continue functioning.

Meaning Systems as "Holders"

In adult life, holding forms the basis for adult experience; it is the rock on which life is built. It is rarely a dominant relational theme, except for those who feel unable to function independently. For most people, holding becomes abstracted into a meaning system and as such becomes the container that orders and makes sense out of all other relationships. Thus belief in the institution of marriage moors a marital relationship through turbulent, ungratifying times. Religious beliefs make it possible to endure affliction. We are held by larger systems of meaning (often depersonified) that anchor our lives and comfort us by providing something "to hold on to."

For some people, meaning-making holding functions are located in specific people rather than in institutions or abstract ideals. Marris (1982), in trying to understand severe grief, suggests that for some people loss of a loved one can be equivalent to loss of all meaning and sense in the world. In such cases, the loved person serves not just as an attachment figure but also as a carrier of that which contains and structures life. Loss of a holding person is thus experienced as falling through space, without purpose or place in the universe. (There is no evidence, however, that it is more or less valuable, healthy, or mature to be held by institutions or ideas rather than people. Ideals and people are equally fragile.)

This meaning-making holding function of others generally becomes clear only when there is a crisis or severe disruption in the predictable ordering of an individual life. In the Holocaust, for example, people had to look for ways to be held when all rationality and predictability in their world had ceased.

Rachel

Born in a small village in Hungary early in the 1940s, Rachel witnessed the murder of both of her parents when she was three years old. She had no understanding then that they were Jewish resistance fighters, but she remembered people talking about how dangerous it was for anyone to take her in.

Nevertheless, a former maid of her mother's arrived to take her home. A year later, the maid and her family were also killed.

> Nanny [the maid], her husband, and I were all outside
> having a picnic. We heard the sounds of the Gestapo,
> and they told me to hide under the blanket. I re-

member great fear. The Gestapo stepped on the
blanket, took them into the house. I remember
hearing loud noises, but I stayed under the blanket.
After a very long time, I walked into the house. The
house had been ransacked. The walls were bare. I remember seeing them lying on their backs on the floor.
I felt fear. That was the strongest emotion I felt
throughout the war.

In the morning, her sister came and found me
in the shrubbery. She was a devout Catholic. She told
me that these people were not good people, were
against Christ. She said she'd raise me as one of her
children, gave me a cross to wear, and never let me out
of the yard.

Despite all the turmoil, I felt very much cared
for and cared about. I remember the sensation of being
held. People were going out of their way to take care
of me and to keep me alive. I knew that a lot of sacrifice was going on around me. I was told many times
that my mother had asked [Nanny] to take me and
raise me as her own. My mother suspected she would
not survive the war. I don't really remember my
mother, but I remember her hair, and I remember the
sense of being held. Through that time, I was always
feeling I was cared about while all the people
changed.

When she was five, Rachel was discovered and taken to a
concentration camp. She was permitted to survive only because she
was to be used in medical experiments. In the camp, a woman who
had lost her own child became attached to Rachel and tried as best
she could to be a comfort to her. This lasted for two years—until
she, too, was killed.

After the war, Rachel was adopted by British foster parents
whom she experienced as cold and unloving. Caught themselves in
a troubled, violent marriage, they had hoped that a lovable adopted
daughter could be a peacemaker between them. In retrospect, Rachel can now see that her foster father, anticipating an "orphan,"

was at some level expecting Shirley Temple. Instead, Rachel appeared—thin, diseased, shaven-headed, and so terrified of hunger
that she could not learn table manners. She sensed his profound
rejection of her from the very beginning. Her foster parents did,
however, provide for her financially and made it possible for her to
receive an excellent education.

In a short time, Rachel learned what was required to "make
it" in her new world. She learned that the most important thing was
to be liked, so she systematically set about making herself likable.
She became a top student and very popular, but she never spoke of
her previous life. Keeping this more "real" part of her experience
private prevented her from making deep emotional connections
with anyone. "Once I learned to play by the rules of living in upper-
middle-class London, I turned out to be the dream child. I never
talked about the Holocaust or about my inner life. I got some perverse pleasure out of how well I had fooled them, how well I had
played by their rules."

When she was seventeen, Rachel left her foster parents and
moved to Israel. There, in a land that understood the Holocaust
and was founded as a homeland for Jews, Rachel found the people
and the social values that felt like a bedrock on which she could
build a real life. With the Israeli man who was to become her husband, Rachel felt for the first time grounded enough to open herself
to authentic contact with other people. She felt "held" enough to
marry, have children and friends, have a career helping others, and
struggle in all the myriad ways that everyone else struggles to be in
emotional connection with others.

Rachel's poignant history is illuminating in many ways, but
it is particularly instructive about the experience of holding. It is
remarkable, for example, that Rachel profoundly remembers the
sensation of being held even while familiar and loved others were
unpredictably being murdered and taken from her. Because of that,
Rachel was able to build a structure of existence out of the sense that
someone would come forward to try to care for her, that sooner or
later someone would be "there." The people might change, but the
caring function would continue to exist in the world. This experience echoes, of course, Anne Frank's wrenching assertion that "in

spite of everything, I believe that people are really good at heart"
(1952, p. 233)—words uttered in the midst of that same world gone
mad with destruction.

But once safe, Rachel could not feel fundamentally held by
a society that could not, despite its material benefits and her success
on its terms, contain her experience. Only when she was able to
nestle within the container of a social and ethnic ideal was she able
to begin to allow the true unfolding of herself. Israel, for Rachel,
represented a way of "making sense." And, with this holding environment in place, she could begin to work through some of the
scars of her traumatic early life.

Loss and trauma, even at much less dramatic levels than
Rachel's, can severely damage people's expectations of "good-
enough" care. At such times, the holding functions of existence are
in doubt and the earth quakes as we stand on it. As we grow, we
internalize certain expectations of how the world operates in relation to us, and these become central to our psychological preservation. Other people, then, to the extent that we (inevitably) ground
our existence in them, have the capacity to contain or to traumatize
us.

Annette's early adult life was centered on her family, which
she described as "very average." She was occupied primarily with
taking care of two young daughters. She and her husband had a
compatible but emotionally distant relationship and were concen-
trating their energies on renovating a newly purchased house.
While waiting for the final touches on the house, they moved into
a rented apartment. One day Annette received a shocking document
from her husband's lawyer. It informed her that her husband had
left the country with another woman and did not plan to return. He
had sold their new house and taken all the couple's money with
him. Only that month's rent had been paid. Within two weeks,
then, Annette and her daughters went from relative affluence to
welfare and food stamps. Beyond the deprivation and humiliation,
beyond the disruption and necessity of finding employment and
reorganizing her life, beyond the rage and helplessness, Annette said
that the worst thing was the discovery that something like this could
happen. She had always thought that she was protected by laws as
well as shared human standards of fairness and honesty. (She had

also thought that she was protected by her husband.) Never had she dreamed that someone could so completely and irredeemably "pull the rug out from under me."

Again, then, in Annette is the imagery of falling as a way of describing the loss of meaning. What one counts on as the framework of one's life turns to dust. Annette fell into suicidal despair, from which she emerged holding on to the necessity of taking care of her children, to keep them from similarly falling in space.

The holding function of relatedness not only provides care and meaning; it also provides hope. When we feel held, we can orient ourselves toward the future. This is Jerome Frank's (1963) view of the essence of psychotherapy. We are able to be helpful to patients, to "hold" them, not only because of our direct ministrations but because we offer hope. It is our own belief in a system of meaning that (presumably) holds us that makes it possible for our patients to benefit. If that is so, it does not matter too much which ritual we prescribe—whether we ask people to keep a log of every time they feel angry or to lie on a couch for ten years and say whatever comes to mind—the real therapy is that we *hold,* and that makes it possible for our patients to hope. What is important from the patients' point of view is that our ritual of meaning-making be compatible enough with theirs to serve as a shared meaning system—a meaning system on which they, too, can rest.

Chapter 4

Attachment

These are ties which, though light as air, are as strong as links of iron.

—Edmund Burke,
Speech on Conciliation with America, March 22, 1775

Attachment is related to, but different from, holding.[1] In attachment we "hold on" and thereby feel less alone. We can be attached to people by whom we are not held, and we can be held by people to whom we are not attached. Infants feel held long before they feel attached, because attachment systems develop later. Although these two threads of connection are closely interwoven throughout early childhood, they often diverge in adult relatedness. But both are essential. While the opposite of holding is falling, the opposite of attachment is aloneness (or loss). Being alone, like falling, is a terrifying experience.

If holding is in the arms, attachment is in the touch, the glance, the voice—in short, in the sense of proximity. Attachment resides in an experience of emotional linkage—the sense that space can be overcome if necessary, that there is togetherness despite space. When we are attached to someone, we need know only that that person is within reach of our call and will likely respond.

Attachment grows over time: one cannot "fall in" attachment. Consistency of response leads to the expectation that someone will continue to be available. Repeated unavailability of particular attachment figures tells us that we cannot count on them anymore; they may offer us other things in the relationship, but not the security of predictable responsiveness, which is the foundation of attachment.

Whereas being held is passive, attachment is an active process of clinging to someone (either actually or symbolically) in order to reduce our anxiety. Attachment and the affection that accompanies it is one of the most profound of human experiences. Despite vagaries of passion and care, despite fortune and the vicissitudes of life, attachment is our sense of emotional belongingness.

The Essence of Attachment

Bowlby, the most important theorist of attachment, begins by taking issue with the psychoanalytic view that reduces the adult search for comfort and care to regressive dependency needs. In Bowlby's (1969, 1973, 1980, 1988) view, attachment is a fundamental innate need, as biologically rooted as needs for food or sex. Attachment serves an ethological and evolutionary need for protection and is expressed in behavior designed to maintain closeness and accessibility of the attachment figures. Rooted in this biological need for proximity, attachment is a primary need. Over the life course, the attachment system traverses a developmental pathway, and the expression of need for closeness, security, comfort, and care is an *adult* expression of attachment need rather than a regression to infantile modes of behavior.

Our clinical experience tends to support Bowlby's observation that many of the most intense emotions arise during the formation, maintenance, disruption, and renewal of attachment relationships. The unchallenged maintenance of a bond is experienced as a source of security and the renewal of a bond as a source of joy. In Bowlby's view, much of the psychopathology of emotion is a psychopathology of affectional bonds.

Attachment has to do with clinging rather than with sucking or satisfaction of oral needs, as classical psychoanalytic theory would have it. That such a basic need exists phylogenetically was demonstrated dramatically by Harry Harlow (1974). In Harlow's experiments, monkeys raised with either cloth or wire surrogate mothers preferred the cloth "mothers," regardless of which one supplied the milk. The need to be comforted through clinging was more insistent than the need to be fed. The necessity of finding an attachment figure is urgent as soon as the infant is able to discriminate those available in the environment.

From early infancy, the infant can discriminate the attachment figure—usually the mother—by smell and sound. By the second half of the first year of life, the infant will protest if given into the care of another person. At this point, the infant has the cognitive capacity to represent the attachment figure, to make comparisons, and to protest the unfamiliarity.

Bowlby sees attachment as organized by a control system that uses communication to regulate distance from attachment figures. The need for proximity to attachment figures is greatest during times of distress or emotional pain. Anxiety about attachment is greatest when there are threats to the continuation of a relationship.

Attachment in Young Children

Although Bowlby is careful to reiterate that attachment behavior continues throughout life and remains as important in adulthood and old age as it was in childhood, attachment has been easiest to study in young children.[2] For one thing, attachment behavior at an early age is more observable. Children physically seek out an attachment figure when anxious, and this can be observed experimentally in the laboratory.

Mary Ainsworth, a colleague of Bowlby's, devised the "strange situation" as a way of researching attachment behavior in young children (Ainsworth, Blehar, Walters, and Wall, 1978).[3] The child is temporarily removed from the mother and placed in a playroom. Then the child's response on being reunited with the mother is carefully observed (and identified as secure, anxious-ambivalent, or anxious-avoidant). Secure children protest the mother's absence but remain confident that she will return, and they greet her enthusiastically when she does. Anxious-ambivalent children are uncertain about the responsiveness and availability of the mother, and they treat her ambivalently when reunited with her. They approach her angrily and resist her efforts to reach out to them, setting in motion an endless struggle between inner wishes for closeness and angry resistance to it. Anxious-avoidant children do not have confidence in their mother's responsiveness and do not seek her out or greet her on her return. They seem to be trying not to need her. These patterns of attachment have been shown to be predictive of behavior to age six (Main and Cassidy, 1988), indicating the stability of the child's early experiences of attachment.

How the child has come to expect to be treated in terms of responsiveness and availability shapes his adjustment to school as well as his approach to other social relationships. Self-reliance, for example, occurs most frequently in a context of secure attachment. Bullying and other antisocial behaviors are characteristic of those children with anxious-avoidant attachment patterns. Secure children are most emotionally open: feelings of sadness, anger, and loneliness are available to them, perhaps because their basic security affords them the capacity to manage these feelings. Insecure six-year-olds, by contrast, avoid the expression of feeling, responding to a projective task with passivity or disorganization (Main, Kaplan, and Cassidy, 1985).

Attachment in Adolescents and Adults

Even into late adolescence, those with secure attachment styles show the best adjustment. Using an interview that produces the same classification of attachment patterns, Kobak and Sceery (1988) showed that college students who thought of their parents as loving and available during distressing events were most able to modulate their negative feelings when under stress. They both felt and were viewed by others as less anxious and more socially competent than their peers. By contrast, those college students who were "dismissing" (that is, avoidant) of attachment perceived relationships as distant and unsupportive and tended to respond to situations in a way that Bowlby has called "compulsively self-reliant." These are people who do not trust that others will be there for them and tend toward hostility and more distant relationships with others. The late-adolescent concomitant of the anxious-ambivalent children— the "preoccupied" group (primarily female in Kobak and Sceery's study)—were the most anxious about their attachments, felt least competent, and reported the most symptoms. Their peers also perceived them to be highly anxious.

Mounting research evidence has demonstrated the positive effects of secure attachment in early childhood and the negative effects of insecure attachment. Attachment history also shapes parenting and is likely to have profound effects into the next generation (Main, Kaplan, and Cassidy, 1985). Our "working models of attachment" (Bowlby, 1969) are rooted in our experiences with our earliest attachment figures and come to be a set of expectations of how others will treat us. If we had a responsive, available attachment figure early in life, we are more likely to expect others to be available, predictable, and responsive to us in adulthood. (We are also more likely to be available, predictable, and responsive to others who are attached to us, but that gets ahead of the story.) Conversely, if we were rejected or disappointed in our attachment needs, we are likely to try to avoid attachments, to screen out awareness of attachment issues, and to try to rely only on ourselves. If our attachment figure was unpredictable—sometimes responsive and sometimes distant—or if our attachment figure asked us to take care of him or her, we are likely to become anxious about attachment, perhaps even preoccupied with it, always fearful of abandonment, always searching for someone to be there for us.

Bowlby's "working models of attachment," very much like object relations theorists' concepts of internal objects, are ways of describing what the developing person has learned about what he or she might expect from people in the way of bonding or availability. But Bowlby believes that these working models, unlike internal objects, develop based on real experience rather than fantasy. Were people there and responsive in childhood? Did parents use threats of abandonment as a form of discipline?

Recognizing the need to be attached as fundamental and primary helps us to reinterpret much of our formerly misinformed theory of development. That attachment needs persist throughout life is a sign of healthy rather than pathological (dependent) development.

Our theory of adolescence has been misguided in this respect. With the focus on separation and autonomy in the theory of adolescent development, health has become associated with detachment from and disavowal of ties to the "primary object"—that is, the parents (Blos, 1962). The logic in this reasoning is that attachment would somehow obstruct the exploration of self that is the hallmark of adolescence. Quite to the contrary, however, it is the securely attached adolescent who is most likely to be competent and venture-some in the struggle for identity. With development, relationships to parents are revised, but attachment persists. Adolescents work to maintain their primary attachments despite developmental changes in their views of self and others (see Salzman, 1990; Grotevant and Cooper, 1985; Frank, Avery, and Laman, 1988). By adulthood, these attachments have generally endured. Nearly all of the people whom I interviewed reported continued attachment relationships with one or both parents throughout life. Many of those who had had breaks in attachment reported refinding their parents at a later time, often with even more intense feelings of attachment. We often value even more that which we have almost lost.

From adolescence onward, the individual is likely to become attached to new people as well as parents—most often people of the same age and of the opposite sex. Any one of these relationships may replicate in intensity the attachment of early childhood, al-though attachment may be diffused among a number of important others.

Theoretical insistence on the processes of adolescent "detach-ment" from parents has tended to obscure adolescents' preoccupa-tion with attachment. So much of what is lumped as "peer involvement" is in reality exploration into what one can expect from others outside the family in terms of loyalty, reliability, and affection. Adolescents try to discover which of their friends can be counted on, and in what way. Who will be "there" when needed for company or comfort? In many ways, adolescents use their friends as well as their families as secure bases from which to explore. Ado-lescents talk about "having" someone, which makes it possible to venture into relationships with others. "I 'have' Elaine," says Linda, "so I can go with the other girls and see if they like me. If not, I can always go see what Elaine is doing."

So much of the pain of adolescence is disappointment with the capriciousness and unreliability of attachments at this age. These rejections and betrayals color an adolescent's expectations of others for a long time afterward, and skepticism about trust and friendship reaped from adolescent injury may persist into adult life.

Paula told of her "best" friendship with Suzanne, which began in the sixth grade and lasted through high school. The girls were always together and often dressed alike. Suzanne was a little ahead of Paula in being interested in boys, but whenever she had a date, she would tell her date to bring someone along for Paula. They each had other friends, but their understanding was that they would make plans with other friends only when they could not do something together. They always spent Saturday afternoons together at the mall—hanging out, shopping, being where things were happening. One Saturday Suzanne said that she had to go visit an aunt with her mother, so Paula, unable to find other companionship, went to the library to get some books. Riding the bus home from the library, she passed the mall and saw Suzanne and another girl from their class walking together. Paula remembers intense pain and an inability to comprehend what she had seen. Only after much emotional wrenching could she come to understand that Suzanne had lied to her and had preferred to be with someone else. Paula never mentioned this episode to Suzanne, but she never again believed her when she said she had something else she had to do. And never again did Paula feel that she could *completely* trust anyone. It was not that she had no trust at all, but she always reminded herself that others could hurt and could betray.

The individual reaches adulthood, then, with many experiences of attachment, both in and out of the family. In this context, the adult must intertwine life with others in order not to feel alone. But adult attachment, because of its less clear behavioral manifestations, is harder to study (Ainsworth, 1982; Weiss, 1982). The field of psychology knows little about attachment past infancy or to people other than the mother (Ainsworth, 1989).

While Bowlby ties attachment to the reduction of anxiety, Robert Weiss (1982) tries to define it as the absence of loneliness. In adult life, attachments are often most apparent in their absence, when the sharp pains of loneliness signal that something vital is missing. When present, attachment is likely to pass by unnoticed, reflected in feelings of familiarity and continuity. Adult attachment seems more to be anchored in constancy and what can be taken for granted, in a sense of an accustomed haven from the strangeness and surprises of the world.

A sense of reliability, familiarity, continuity, and constancy of important others seems to underlie the "secure base" of adult attachment. And just as in childhood, the sense of a secure base seems to be necessary for exploration and self-development. We can venture away only to the extent that we trust that there is someone to whom we can return and be greeted, if not with affection, at least with response. Bowlby points out that attachment behavior and exploration are antithetical. When we feel secure in attachment, we are likely to explore, to be aware of the self and its adventures. Only when frightened, ill, or tired are we likely to try to regain attachment figures. Secure attachment in adulthood, then, is not likely to be demonstrated so much in behavior (although many adult relationships have clear attachment rituals, such as birthday celebrations or regular phone calls) as in an inner sense of a peopled world. The securely attached adult feels in proximity to an important other (or others), whether or not that person is geographically close.

Although we must be *held* by someone experienced as strong enough to keep us from falling, we may be *attached* to someone weak. As Fairbairn (1954) notes, it is the responsiveness of the other, rather than the kind of response, that matters most. Georgia spoke of calling her easily upset mother to tell her about having gotten fired from her job. "I know that if I tell her, she'll only worry, and that won't do me any good; but still, her worrying makes me feel better." Just knowing that someone is emotionally responsive helps.

If, as Bowlby insists, attachment is a biologically and ethologically rooted system, the experience of attachment is not necessarily cognitively explicable. We need to have attachment figures because that is how we are programmed. Not to have such people in our lives is to feel intolerable aloneness pain.

Separation and Loss: The Dark Side of Attachment

In contrast to feelings of being held, the attachment experience is specific. We attach to a particular person and will not accept substitutes. (We can, however, be held by many.) To attach, then, is to risk the pain of loss and the necessity of grief.

Separation distress is a signal that an attachment system is threatened. In the same way that signal anxiety in classical psycho-analysis is a warning to the ego that overwhelming panic may be approaching, separation distress warns that unbearable aloneness (abandonment) is imminent. In the face of separation distress, the person (of any age) protests, pleadingly or angrily. In the young child, all other functions and behavior cease as the missing person is sought. The child cries, protests, insists that the person to whom he is attached be restored. Under parallel conditions, the adult may cry and beg, get angry, and try through coercion or a whole repertoire of other relational skills to restore the attachment bond.

What we need from our attachment figure is responsiveness; the nature of the response seems to be less important than the simple existence of the response. *Any* response sustains an existing attachment—that is, any response except neglect. Expressions of attachment behavior are an effort to evoke a response. "Be in emotional contact" is the demand.

Because of the intense need for the attachment figure, children quickly learn which actions and appeals procure a response and which do not. This type of interpersonal learning continues through adolescence and into adulthood. Through intricate and subtle transactions of approach and response, the shape and style of attachment relationships are established. Angela reports, "All through high school, my best friend called me at exactly 6:10 every night. Even though we might have just seen each other a few hours earlier and there was nothing new to report, we spoke to each other right after dinner. And when the phone would ring and everyone in my family knew it was her, I just felt so good to know that I had this friend and I could count on her." Most attachment relationships develop such rituals.

Conversely, learning about attachment means learning about how much is too much. At what point are demands for response likely to overburden the attachment figure and cause him or her to withdraw? Eric, for example, a twenty-five-year-old patient, would become so anxious if his new girlfriend did not telephone when she said she would that he would work himself into an angry pout. When he finally reached her, he would be unable to relate to her except with sarcasm and rage. She would then accuse him of being too demanding and possessive and threaten to end their relationship. Eric's intense need for attachment thus threatened the possibility of his having it. Some people so much fear being like Eric—fear driving away the people they need—that they balk at establishing attachment relationships at all.

One of the worst experiences in life is to call a friend in a moment of need and have no one be there. To call without response is to know utter aloneness in the world, utter desolation. As a result, many people develop rigid defenses against attachment experiences. If we never attach, we are never vulnerable to loss or abandonment. "I always leave people before they can leave me," said one of my patients, terrified above all of the experience of loss and abandonment.

The Experience of Attachment in Contemporary Life

As lifetime commitments become exceptional and human bonds are revealed as increasingly fragile in late-twentieth-century life, more and more people struggle with the problem of making attachments. "I want to be with someone who will never leave me," say many of my patients. But they cannot keep from knowing that no one will ever *not* leave them. Just as the paradox of holding is that we are doomed to hold on to something that is itself ungrounded, the paradox of attachment is that we must be attached to people whom we will ultimately lose. The fears of loss and abandonment, then, always shadow attachment, however subconsciously or obscurely. When too great, such fears preclude attachment, claiming for the self the very aloneness that is feared.

Within the fluidity, mobility, and disjunction of modern life, our attachments form the continuity. And part of what we mourn in loss is the fragility of even this most intense form of human bond.

When attachment systems are functioning smoothly, they are subliminal. They are not unconscious, but neither are they the focus of our attention. They are part of what is necessary, like the air that we breathe. Securely attached adults have an awareness of the "thereness" of someone, which means that the other can be counted on to be responsive to them. But within secure attachment, as with adequate holding, the awareness of the tie to the other becomes part of the background. Because of our attachment figure, we feel not alone and therefore free to turn our attention to our pursuits and interests. Bowlby describes an attachment relationship as "a Hub around which a person's life revolves not only when he is an infant or a toddler or a schoolchild but throughout his adolescence and his years of maturity as well, and on into old age. From these intimate attachments a person draws his strength and enjoyment of life" (1969, p. 442). The attachment relationship, then, is a wellspring, a resource. It means that someone is "there" for us, not to satisfy a particular need or purpose, but to be with, so that we may feel not alone.

As I have noted, the fact of responsiveness is more important than its character. Even a negative response is preferable to no response at all. An angry parent, for example, is at least *present*. As a result, it is quite possible to remain intensely attached to people who are highly abusive toward us or who fail to fulfill other of our important needs. The power of the attachment system can supersede all other needs and can even supersede reason. Thus the battered woman returns to the husband who beat her. The husband of an alcoholic believes one more time his wife's promise to stop drinking and returns to her. Sometimes these are dependent people; more often they are intensely attached.

Many adults speak of their need to "belong" to someone, which seems to be an adult expression of attachment. They want to feel claimed, existing as another's possession. It is intensely important for some people to be called "my" by someone—"my wife" or "my son." That possessive is a sign of reliable connection: someone will be taking them along through life. The "belonging" aspect of attachment seems to represent its permanence. Orphaned child survivors of World War II concentration camps, even when well cared for afterward, often fervently fantasized a mother to "belong" to— to *irretrievably* belong to—and this need persisted despite whatever kindness or affection may have been offered by others (Moskowitz, 1983). By belonging, one is linked in the chain of existence.

Other people, on the other hand, experience "belonging" as imprisonment. Because they see it as infringing on their autonomy, they experience attachment at a greater distance and in a different idiom. They often fear attachment and the claims it may make on their selfhood.

There are large individual differences in how tightly one

must cling to *feel* attached. Some adults maintain a sense of attachment through infrequent phone calls; others must "touch base" each day to know that the attachment remains reliable.

Attachment, then, is part of what people mean when they describe someone important to them as "there," but the "thereness" of attachment is different from the "thereness" of holding. In attachment, a biologically and ethologically based need for bonding, grounded in but finally independent of the need to seek proximity to a protective adult, leads the person to connect the self firmly to another in a linkage and sense of togetherness that assuages a sense of aloneness. In attachment, unlike holding, the bond needs to serve no other purpose than responsiveness in a context of continuity. Attachment relationships may involve sexuality, mutuality, holding, embeddedness, or any of the other relational dimensions, but they do not have to. This is one of the reasons that it is so difficult to articulate the experience of attachment: a person is "there." There for what? There for me. There so I can feel not alone.

In his thoughtful reflections on adult loneliness, Weiss (1987) wonders just exactly what it is in adult attachment that keeps away loneliness. He notes that it does not seem to be that the attachment figure is a confidant or a sexual partner or even a source of security. Rather, it is a sense of lives intertwined, emotionally linked. This is hardly precise, but it is the best we can express.

Attachment behavior after childhood, then, is most likely to be visible when there is something amiss in the attachment system. When events threaten the continuation of attachment relationships, exploration ceases and attention is riveted on the restoration of the attachment bond. Nearly all researchers who have set out to study attachment end up studying loss. Our treasured others are in sharpest relief when we lose them or are in danger of losing them. Where loss is, attachment was. One of the great difficulties in studying attachment, then, is the fact that it is a faint penumbra when smoothly functioning; it glows bright only when disrupted.

Harriet's mother died when she was sixteen, and she was largely responsible for the care of her five younger siblings for the next year. When she went away to college, she met Wally, who seemed to offer her the affection and devotion that she had counted on from her mother. She appreciated Wally's steadiness and loyalty and came to count on his "being there" for her. They got married after college. During their first fifteen years together, Harriet kept herself from being aware of any disappointments in the relationship. They were a team; they worked hard together, had many interests and activities, and enjoyed lots of friends. They had always expected to start a family once they felt financially settled enough.

The eventual discovery of Wally's infertility led to a crisis in their marriage. Harriet's anger at him for letting her down on such an important issue opened the floodgates to other suppressed resentments. Harriet now became aware of Wally's workaholism, his passivity and inability to respond to her emotionally, and his lack of sexual interest in her. Years of effort, some with the aid of therapy, made it clear to Harriet that Wally would not change; he was an introverted man who shied away from emotional intimacy. This realization left her with a painful dilemma.

Harriet felt that if she had to accept a life without children, she needed more emotional sustenance in her primary relationship. She wanted more involvement and empathy from Wally, as well as more sex. Yet whenever she made the decision to separate from him, the full weight of her attachment to him, imperceptible in periods of her anger, would encumber and paralyze her. To view the longing she felt for him at such times as dependency would be a grievous error. She needed him because she was attached to him. What Harriet experienced of this deep need was an awareness that no one would be there to pick her up at the airport after a trip. No one would know when she got home after a late night of work. No one would go with her to family events or celebrations. Harriet was aware that she *could* do all of these things on her own, yet the pain of giving the shared component up felt overwhelming.

Someone who knows where you are, who meets your plane, who goes with you to family events and to movies—these are the adult expressions of a "secure base." What is often confusing to patients and to therapists is that the particular action is in itself immaterial. For example, a patient may be genuinely puzzled about why it is so important that his wife set his next-day clothes out for him each night. After all, he is capable of doing that himself. But he neither wants to nor really feels able to; something in him would be disrupted and out of balance if he were to. In some cases, this might indeed be dependency, but it is more likely a sign of attachment.

When an attachment figure is available and responsive, we feel secure—but relatively unaware of the complex emotional and psychological operations taking place in the bonding. With the loss of such an attachment figure, we are likely to feel torn apart, as though the threads that wove our life together had unraveled. The sense of abandonment in loss is intense, and it may be a long time before the bereaved person shows any sign of wanting to explore or seek outward. We are preoccupied instead with refinding the particular other to whom we had been attached, and much of our behavior, conscious and unconscious, is in the service of trying to put right again that which has become so wrong.

Attachment, distinct from all the other forms and dimensions of relatedness, requires the physical existence of another person. The person to whom we are attached must be *there* somewhere. One can, for example, feel held or admired by an inner representation, but one cannot be *attached* to someone who is only internal. And attachment requires particularity. Another person, no matter how responsive or affectionate, cannot replace a lost attachment figure.

Although Bowlby limits his definition of attachment to relationships in which one person feels protected by someone who is stronger and wiser, most adult attachment relationships do not rely on protection. It appears that attachment after infancy grows beyond its initial, biological basis; it moves from seeking proximity for protection toward psychological proximity for emotional survival. In adulthood, attachment figures may be chosen for their availability rather than their capability. Even in childhood, attachments may form on the basis of responsiveness rather than protection. For example, in her autobiographically based book *Orphans* (1988) Eileen Simpson tells the poignant story of her childhood attachment to her sister, who was only ten months older. This attachment preserved them both through the upheavals of an orphaned childhood. Past childhood, people report attachments to many people who are not protectors, including intense attachments to one's own children. The unassuageable pain of the loss of a child attests to the extent to which children are attachment figures for their parents.

Weiss (1982) agrees that attachment to a peer in adulthood

usually develops without regard to that peer's perceived strength. Instead, an attachment peer may be perceived as fostering the individual's own capacities for mastering challenge. We take strength from our attachment figures not because they are strong but because their reliability, their "thereness," gives us strength. By their very existence, attachment figures become wellsprings of confidence.

As individual development proceeds, attachment can be maintained through more distant forms of communication. Because attachments are, in their essence, enduring structures, adult attachments can remain emotionally alive for years with no physical interaction. Attachments abide as a promise in time of need or as a template for the future. We have only to think of the attachments maintained by couples and families separated by war or the necessity of employment at long distance. We keep in touch through letters or, in the modern age, phone calls. And the figure of speech is psychologically exact: we keep "in touch," maintaining with symbols the connection (despite space) that bespeaks attachment.

Attachments to friends or relatives maintained at a distance seem to require physical presence if the relationship is endangered, however. Illness in one of the people, for example, will usually provoke a visit from the other. ("I needed to see that you were all right.") Similarly, an angry quarrel between long-distance lovers may arouse in each an urgent need to see the other, to reassure themselves that the attachment bond has not been damaged.

Attachment Pleasure and Affectional Bonds

Bowlby links attachment to the reduction of anxiety. In the early years, children separated from their mother are likely to protest, to try to regain contact. As we grow, "contact" is maintained through other forms of communication—forms that symbolize touch. This contact, which may occur only infrequently, reassures us that the attachment figure remains "there."

Unlike children, who seek contact with the attachment figure because the fact of separation produces anxiety, we as adults seek in our "secure base" the knowledge that the attachment figure is available should we become anxious. With development, then, attachment experience and behavior become more and more distinct from anxiety, and may become a source of pleasure in themselves.

Attachment pleasure is the joy inherent in the bond itself. The joy of feeling attached is in part a reflection of the conviction that if we are frightened, we will be responded to by the attachment figure. After infancy, however, it becomes more diffusely a pleasure of connection, of feeling not alone even if we are not in current or potential need.

Attachment evolves into an affectional bond (Ainsworth, 1989). In other words, the emotional experience of attachment is affection. Where attachment is intense, it may even be experienced as a quiet and deep form of love. Even when there is clearly a primary attachment figure—the person to whom we first turn when we are upset or frightened—most adults have a network of secondary attachment relationships as well. These are people who can be counted on to be responsive, people with whom affectional bonds are maintained as an aspect of enriching the emotional landscape of adulthood.

Weiss's (1982, 1987) studies of the unattached (that is, the unmarried) suggest that loneliness is the result of the lack of a primary attachment. Weiss views loneliness as separation distress without an object; thus the unattached person is, quite literally, suffering from the absence of an attachment figure. Because marriage promotes the proximity on which attachment rests, spouses are usually first candidates as attachment figures. But attachment can take complex forms as it weaves its way through the vicissitudes of adult life.

Tom's relational history is the closest to a "pure story" of attachment I've ever heard. His life has been marked by strong long-term attachments to others. His emotional life has been dominated by preserving these attachments, and his most intense grief has been the rupture of a relationship without his being able to say good-bye.

Tom's story is not typical, but it is a good illustration of some of the phenomenology of attachment in adult life. I present the entire relational picture so that we can view the way in which attachment systems intersect with other aspects of relatedness.

Tom

Of all those I interviewed, Tom drew one of the most peopled charts. (See Resource A in the back of the book). At each age, he showed many, many relationships and friends, drawn both individually and in groups. What is most striking about the pattern of his relationships is the continuity: people, once admitted into his emotional world, are not easily discharged. Tom's pattern is one of persisting attachment. There was an expansiveness and affection in Tom's voice as he described the people who have mattered to him. He wanted to tell me their stories too. It was clear that people captivate him.

As Tom remembers his life at age five, he was primarily involved with what he described as his "two mothers." His Aunt Gloria, his mother's unmarried older sister, lived with them until he was an adult. Tom carefully tried to draw them equidistant from him on his relational maps, not choosing between them as to their importance. Later in his life, he became more strongly attached to Gloria than to his mother, but as a child he cared for them equally. Gloria was more open and friendly than his mother—more like a friend herself. She had a black boyfriend, and the racial difference prevented them from marrying. They used to take young Tom along on car rides and to movies. He felt that she liked having him with her.

While Gloria was more adventurous, Tom's mother was more "at home." Tom's sister was born when he was about five, so his mother's attention was taken by the new baby. Tom remembers his mother as "nothing special—the usual things—I'm hungry. I would have gone to either one if I was hurt or sick; it didn't matter which one. At this age I broke my hand; I was hospitalized and operated on. I remember going to my mother. It was in the morning, and I remember rushing to my mother and she took me, but if Gloria had been home, I would have gone to her."

Tom remembers his father as being much less available during those early childhood years. He worked long hours and came home late, so tired that he would fall asleep in the living room. Tom could not remember very many interactions with him; it seemed to him that his father was often out of town to do a job.

Tom also remembers Vera, his kindergarten teacher. She was "nice, warm. I remember her with fond memories." The central people, then, for Tom, were warm, available women—people he felt he could turn to, who were "there" for him.

This left him free to turn his attention to his "group." Tom most remembers being outdoors playing with kids during his childhood. This was a happy, carefree time. There was a "secure base."

By age ten, Tom felt more of a relationship with his father. Perhaps, Tom suspects, it was easier for his father to have a relationship with someone who was not a baby. They used to talk about school. "He liked math and I was good at math, so we would discuss math problems. He used to be interested in what I was doing in school."

Tom remembers his mother as a nurturer in this phase of life. "She was less interested in what I did in school. I remember her as providing food, house activities. She would prepare the meals, clean the house and my room. We had interactions around those kinds of things more than other things." At this point, Aunt Gloria had become more like a friend, but Tom's memories of this period are vague. He feels that he was mostly involved with his friends, less interested in spending time with adults.

Tom found a group of classmates in school to whom he felt even closer than to the group of neighborhood kids. He spent most of his time with these friends, going to their homes or playing soccer behind the school. They also belonged to the Boy Scouts, and this group was the center of many of their activities.

Again Tom remembers a warm schoolteacher—a woman who had no special importance except as a source of warmth and affection. At this age, he remembers his first romantic kind of relationship, with Jeannie: "She was a girl from my class. We studied together, and I loved her in a certain childish way."

Friends became more distinct by age fifteen. Among those in Tom's class were several boys who became "best friends" at different times. Best friendship, in large part, turned on availability—who he sat next to most often, or who was in most of his classes. Among them, Tom was particularly fond of Sam, who was very bright and inventive. Their friendship began when Sam, returning after a year in another city, found himself behind in math class. Tom took

pleasure in helping him to catch up. Although Tom spent more
time with Sam than with others, he also spent a good deal of time
with his friends Robbie and Mark, studying together (or rebel-
liously not studying together). His relationships were defined
mainly by the fact of spending time together. Tom had no particular feelings of admiration for his friends, nor were these relationships of self-disclosure. Rather, the boys were buddies, special
companions, the "gang," the people who were there. Most were
people who had been there for some time.

Tom was hesitant about girls at age fifteen, but he had special feelings for Terry. They spent time together but did not formally "go out." Tom thought about her a lot, however, with the
first real stirrings of sexual feelings. Tom's family had faded largely
into the background by this point:

> I never spent much time at the house. I used to go, eat
> lunch, throw my things, go out. At that age, I was a
> discipline problem. If they had a rule, like that you
> couldn't play on the school field after school, I would
> do it anyway. Or I would cut classes to be with my
> friends or not do my homework. [Teachers] would call
> my mother and she would go and she would say,
> "What can I do?" I didn't like it, but it didn't bother
> me a lot. I was interested in my friends and social
> activities, sports, music. School didn't interest me at
> all.

Tom's parents seem to have been quite accepting and non-
intrusive. He remembers little effort on their part to discipline him,
despite his rebelliousness. Rather, they remained available and affectionate; they left him free to pursue his own path. "Our house
was very warm and very open. People could come to eat when they
wanted to. At this age, I didn't let my parents interfere with my
social activities. It was a standing joke at my house. They would ask
me, 'Where have you been?' and I would say, 'Here and there,' and
it became a joke. They would say, 'Oh, you've been here and
there.' "

There was one teacher, a math teacher, who made a strong impression on Tom as an adolescent:

> He was very young. I didn't like most of the teachers. He was almost like a friend. We used to go to his apartment, and for me he was an excellent teacher. From him, I realized what math was all about. He really tried to explain mathematics. I did work only in his class just because I liked him; he was more approachable, and he really loved the subject. I remember when he gave an exam and I wrote it in a lousy way, untidy, he wouldn't mark it. He said, "This is not the way you write," and he told me to take it home and write it the way I should, and then he marked it.

Tom seemed to sense that this teacher knew that there was more to him and asked him to express that.

Another teacher, Mr. Solomon, was Tom's nemesis. He always tried to control Tom with rigidity and rules, and he always failed. Tom disliked the feeling of tension with Mr. Solomon. He was used to easygoing affection and warmth in his relationships and did not know how to respond to Mr. Solomon's displeasure.

By age twenty, Tom had gone off to the local state university with Sam, Robbie, and Mark. They still stuck together for many activities—for example, they joined the same fraternity—but now they spent more time talking about their experiences and ideas. They stayed in touch with the other members of their hometown group during vacations. Tom also made some new friends who shared some of his new interests—especially his growing interest in chemistry.

Around this age, Tom had his first sexual relationship. Dana took the initiative with him and helped him overcome his uncertainty with girls. They were very close, but not for long. Although Tom was popular in the group and had many other girls with whom he was very friendly, he felt that "girls were not attracted to me. I wasn't very successful romantically. I didn't try very much— I was shy. With Dana, it was her idea: she took the initiative to make the relationship and to break the relationship. I missed her for some time afterward."

Laura was a female friend from high school to whom he used to talk about his personal feelings. "Well, not a lot about personal feelings at this age, but more than to anyone else."

Tom did not see his family very much during this time, but he wrote to them frequently and at least stopped at home for some time during vacations. They had, however, continued in psychological importance as a "base."

Tom met Rita in chemistry class, and they became friends. They studied together, spent a lot of time together, and after a time they became romantically involved. Unsure what the relationship meant to them, they broke up several times, but finally they decided that they felt better together, as a pair. "There are lots of things you do together in pairs, and she was my partner [in classes]. We did many things together. We weren't sure. We sort of tried, but then we broke up. We found we didn't feel very good without each other. I even had another relationship for a while. But we felt, both of us, that we wanted to be together, and so we married—just like a natural decision."

Tom did, however, maintain his connection to his large group of friends. Mark and Robbie had married, and now everyone would get together on weekends or holidays. Wives and girlfriends were simply integrated into the group. As had been his pattern in adolescence, everyone in the inner circle of attachments was important; the most important was the one he spent most time with, and this was in part a function of external factors. Tom needed a partner, and at this phase of his life, Rita was that partner.

Tom also found himself getting close to Ira—an old buddy from high school, but someone who had never had special status with him before. Ira and he discovered a strong mutual interest in country music, and sometimes Jerry, a new friend from English class, would join them. Another member of the old high school group who had joined the same fraternity also became an important companion at this time.

Yet another old high school friend appeared in math class and shared Tom's enthusiasm for math. At this time, Tom's father, who had meanwhile retired, decided to return to college, and the three of them took a differential equations class together and spent hours working on the problems.

Before he married, in between college and medical school, Tom lived with his Aunt Gloria, who had by this time moved into her own apartment. She shared with him the difficulties she had had in her interracial relationship. He talked about his hopes and dreams for his research. They became very close; Tom felt that he could confide in her, share his thoughts and inner feelings in a way he had not with anyone else. Although Tom continued to visit his family on holidays and school vacations, he did not feel very close to them.

In medical school, Tom found his most important mentor: George, an oncology researcher with whom he began an apprenticeship that lasted into his working career. "I learned a lot from him— more than in any formal studies. He gave me a lot of freedom to be responsible, to do things. His kind of supervision was very general. He let me have my own project, and I liked it. We started writing articles together. I learned a lot from him about how to write, how to publish, how to present things. We became friendly. We talked about—argued about—politics. Our research had some public exposure. We enjoyed debating with other people."

Age thirty found Tom and Rita with a one-year-old daughter. He was still connected to the same group of old friends. Sam and his family lived in the same neighborhood, and Robbie lived not far away; they visited frequently. Although Mark lived farther away, had gone into business, and held quite different values than Tom, they maintained their friendship nonetheless. They just tried to stay away from controversial topics.

There were now more ups and downs in the relationship with Rita. Always a moody person, she was increasingly tired, unwilling to go out, and emotionally withdrawn for long periods of time. Tom found it difficult when she closed up, made herself emotionally unavailable to him. Unable to talk together about what was going on between them, they would each retire into their own pursuits until she came out of her shell once again.

Now intensely involved in his own research projects, Tom found new friendships among his colleagues, with whom he spent an increasing amount of time. He found among them people he looked up to and admired; he enjoyed trading ideas with and learning from them.

The most painful moment of Tom's life came with the death of Aunt Gloria. She had moved to another city, and he had not seen her in nearly a year. When she came back reduced by cancer, he was shocked to see her withered and frail. He sat by her side for most of the week before she died and was glad of the opportunity to say good-bye. Although Gloria had not had a major role in his life for some years, she was the first loss among those to whom Tom was intensely attached, and he experienced her death as a loss of a part of himself.

Tom was a bit closer to his parents at this point, largely because of their shared interest in his daughter, Karen. Often they would keep Karen at their house while Tom and Rita went to conferences or pursued their social activities.

At midlife, about age thirty-five, Rita became more and more depressed and withdrawn, which was increasingly intolerable for Tom. Although he would not have been able to say this himself, his relational pattern was so weighted toward simple availability that this was the worst thing that Rita could do to him. Their inability to talk about problems pulled them farther and farther apart.

Tom became increasingly drawn to Mary, a research colleague who was very much available to him. As he experimented with her openness, he found a language to talk about feelings. But the prospect of enduring the pain, conflict, and tension of a divorce was repulsive to Tom. He feared hurting both Karen and Rita. He had never had much patience for discord and had kept his relationships smooth, even if that meant maintaining some emotional distance. But Rita's withdrawal from him left him feeling without a partner—a partner that he needed above all.

In this period of turmoil and anxiety, Tom turned to his high school friend Laura, who was also going through a life crisis. To her, he poured out his anguish and his fears. He shared none of his distress with his male friends, however, until he had made a decision. In his experience, it was with women that you could share your deepest feelings and concerns. Such problems did not belong with male friends—even friends as old and close as Robbie, Mark, and Sam.

In Mary, Tom found someone "more like me in her attitudes. We want to do the same things usually. She's much more independent than Rita. She's very professionally involved. She knows how to do things; she needs me as a partner, needs to talk to me about things. Rita was more dependent, and I didn't like it. That was more like a man/woman relationship, where she was more responsible for the household and I for the outside. With Mary, we're partners, and we both share everything." He adds, with a laugh, "She's even busier than I am." Tom seemed to have found in a woman what he had always valued in his male companions—someone who shared his interests and was available to him—but also someone in whom he could confide, a property for him that belonged exclusively to women.

Having made his decision to divorce Rita and marry Mary, Tom informed his friends and his colleagues at work. In time, all the relationships were put right again—including his relationships with Karen and Rita.

At forty, life and relationships were very stable. His marriage to Mary remained good, full of sharing. Karen remained close and visited often. Mark's wife became very ill during this time, so Tom spent extra time with Mark, supporting him through her death and his grieving. All the other old friends were still there as well, bound in an intricate pattern of bonding and togetherness, keeping up with each other, sharing special events, being available in times of need. Their lives seemed inextricably linked, even when the friends had few common current interests.

At this age, Tom really discovered his sister for the first time. As their parents aged, they shared an effort to see to their comfort. He had something in common with her at last.

Age forty-five was a time of losses. Karen was now across the country in college. Laura, who had become a less close friend after their life crises had passed, killed herself without explanation, leaving Tom pained at not being able to help or to say good-bye. Then, while Tom was presenting a paper out of the country, his father became ill. By the time he returned, his father was in a coma. "I just sat there for a couple of weeks near his bed. I used that time to think about him and separate. I admire him: he was a special man. Part of it is his representing the old generation. He was all his life a carpenter, but he knew much more than I did. Plus he was very modest, very shy—whatever he had, he was happy with." I asked Tom if he was like his father in any way, and he said, somewhat sadly, that he was not.

Several weeks later, George, Tom's former mentor and close colleague, died suddenly. Three important, sudden losses—and no opportunity to say good-bye. This left Tom's peopled world rent and violated. Meanwhile, his old friend Ira was becoming increasingly psychotic, despite Tom's efforts to help.

Tom's relationship with Mary continues to be stable and satisfying. They have together made some new friends. Despite the losses, there is still warmth and companionship in Tom's life. The network of attachments, diminished somewhat, remains vital.

Tom presents an unusual relational pattern, in that themes of attachment and availability are so much in the foreground. Tom seems not to use relationships for self-definition, nor does he orient himself to gaining others' approval. In addition, we hear little about mutual self-exploration or emotional neediness. Instead, Tom's interpersonal life has been marked by warmth and affection in relationship, availability, keeping in touch. Few people have so many lifelong friendships. Tom attaches to others loyally and deeply. Others are a secure base for him. They share his interests and enrich his life.

What we know of Tom's early life suggests that he was securely attached, certain of the availability and responsiveness of two "mothers." With a family that held him without impinging on him, Tom was free to use his attachments as a secure base from which to explore. He could always return home to the mother who made good things to eat and to the aunt-mother who provided stimulation and wanted him with her. Devoid of or denying emotional strain and conflict in the family, Tom does not seek emotional complexity in his later relationships. Instead, he wants people to be with, to attach to—not compulsively or desperately, but deeply and devotedly. He is ready to bear the pain of ultimate separations. He is available to people when they are in need and quick to respond to others' distress. But he wants people not to demand more of him emotionally than he is prepared to give.

For Tom, as Bowlby suggests, attachment relationships are a hub in his life, a wellspring from which he draws strength. His sense of others' availability to him and his way of interlinking lives teaches us something about the phenomenology of adolescent and adult attachment.

In addition, Tom's form of grieving shows the dark side of attachment. His grief reaction is neither "Things are falling apart" (when a holding other is lost) nor "How am I going to continue to be who I am?" (when a validating other is lost). Instead, loss leaves a hole where a link had been. Tom grieved intensely at the loss of his father—despite the fact that he had neither relied on his father nor identified with him. He sat by his father's bedside for weeks and thought about how their lives were linked, and he mourned that the tie had come to an end.

For Tom, the essence of bonding with others lies in their availability to fill his life, to keep him from aloneness. This core of attachment is present, to some extent, in all relational schemas, but it is often hidden behind or confounded with other ways of being together.

Chapter 5

Passionate Experience

*The absolute yearning of one human body for another and its
indifference to substitutes is one of life's major mysteries.*

—Iris Murdoch, *The Black Prince*

Relatedness in the service of passion is the story of arousal and
union. The passions are foreground phenomena. Unlike the quiet
togetherness of attachment or the invisible solidity of holding, the
passions take center stage: they are noisy and insistent. The passions
constitute intense experience—aspects of experience that are affectively charged, that claim our attention. Themes of passion and
passionate arousal are heard through most people's life stories,
sometimes dominant, sometimes counterpoint, sometimes barely
audible.

Psychoanalysis and the Passionate Experience

From a psychoanalytic point of view, all human connection is, at
its root, "passionate." We are *aroused* to interest in others because
of biological needs (although this connection may not be conscious
or experienced). Arousal results as powerful biological drives seek
gratification. In other words, we need others to satisfy our fundamental drives. Freud's view is quite extreme on this matter: we need
others *only* because of these powerful drives. Freud called these
pleasure-seeking needs "libidinal," and most of his theory is oriented to explaining how these needs change and are channeled
throughout life. From this vantage point, mothers are important as

feeders and as frustrators; fathers are important as authorities who curb our primitive impulses. Both parents are important as early first love objects—objects of one's first passionate/sexual desires, but objects who cannot, of course, be attained.

Much of psychoanalytic discourse has been devoted to an explication of the Oedipus complex, in which the dynamics of passionate desires, intense rivalry, and murderous hatred play themselves out in the family triangle. The early experience of sexual desire is presumed to be oedipal, and later experiences are revivals of this early passion play. Oedipal dilemmas are, by definition, not fully resolvable; thus they may be reenacted again and again.

Because of the enormous frustration that follows from first experiencing passionate desire in an impossible situation, distortions of personality development become inevitable. As a result, psychoanalytic inquiry has been primarily concerned with understanding the rechanneling of frustrated passionate wishes—repressed and rechanneled by social necessity into symptoms, sexual perversion, character pathology, or other forms of emotional disturbance.

Given its biological base, psychoanalysts regard sexual excitation in its various forms (oral, anal, and genital) as the currency of exchange in interpersonal relatedness. The energic model of psychic function posits that all energy is fundamentally libidinal—that is, lustful, pleasure-seeking.[1] It is the proscriptions of social life that make taboo these primitive urges. Thus most forms of relatedness are the result of compromise between instinct and frustration, desire and defense. Our interpersonal attachments are sublimated forms of drive-dominated investment in others.

Psychoanalysis, being a theory of the unconscious and internal rather than of the phenomenological and observable, has much greater explanatory power when dealing with the unusual and perverse than with the normative. But we have derived from its theoretical expanses a model of psychological maturity: Freud thought that the hallmark of developmental success was the attainment of adult genitality. What Freud meant by this was the successful formation of a dyadic relationship with another adult of the opposite sex with whom sexual gratification is both possible and mutual. Difficulties in forming such a relationship are thought to derive from unresolved early conflicts that make desire greedy or insatiable, envious or sadistic, or overwhelmed by doubt and feelings of genital inferiority.[2] Failure to give up pleasures of earlier stages can make adult love "immature" or can lead to deficiencies of genital performance, such as impotence or sexual unresponsiveness.[3]

As the British psychoanalyst Michael Balint (1953) points out, from psychoanalysis we know more about what mature love is not than what it is. We have, by now, some real understanding of the traumas and conflicts that lead to inhibition of the capacity for sexual encounter with an appropriate partner. We also understand much about the ways in which excessive guilt and inhibition can interfere with the experience of drive gratification in a relationship. But we are hard-pressed to describe within psychoanalytic metapsychology a "healthy" nonidealized adult heterosexual relationship.[4] While psychoanalysis has a well-articulated theory of drive gratification, it has relatively little to say about love.[5] Rather, it tends to assume that love is an emergent concomitant of well-satisfied drives.

While psychoanalysis helps us to better understand the passionate experience of men, it tends only to confuse things when women are under consideration. Oedipal phenomena are more clearly apparent in men; in women, the importance of the Oedipus complex—even its very existence—is under serious question (Simon, 1991). Arousal, the core of passion, is more physically based for men and more emotionally dominated for women. Men arrive at passionate love through sex, while women find passionate sex through love. The story of passion that begins with drive is therefore much more a male story than a female one.

With so much of what goes on in this realm unconscious, it is not surprising that we hear relatively little about pure drive gratification in the phenomenology of people's experience. Where it is most apparent is in reports of adolescent relatedness—the first coming to terms with oneself as a sexual being and the need for others for sexual exploration.

Pure genital sexuality, the psychoanalytic ideal, is, however, a kind of metaphorical fiction. M. Balint (1953) points out that its realization is present most commonly in animals. Where it is present in humans, it does not really qualify, in my opinion, as a form of relatedness. Occasionally, for example, men, in moments of candor, will confess to dread at the prospect of having to talk to the woman with whom they just casually had sex. In the film *When Harry Met Sally*, Harry says, "You have sex and the minute you finish, you know what goes through your mind? How long do I have to lie here and hold her before I can get up and go home? Is thirty seconds enough?" After satisfaction, the woman is of no further interest. Sexuality here is fully genital, but it is only barely interpersonal.

Genital love, as opposed to genital sexuality, is sexual desire fused with tenderness, mutuality, and/or attachment so that sexual experience occurs in the context of other relational factors. Where this is most clearly present in relational phenomenology is in the expression of the wish for "union" or oneness, which is the quintessence of the sexual experience.

Touch and Union

Touching is the earliest form of contact. Pleasures in being stroked and fondled are among the first sensations of infancy, and they continue throughout life. Through tickling, rubbing, and patting, the infant experiences pleasurable skin contact as an expression of affection. Skin-to-skin contact is as close as we can come to obliterating the physical boundaries between us, to make what we love and value a part of ourselves.

When we feel drawn toward someone or something, our basic impulse is to touch it, to be in physical contact, to overcome separateness tactilely. Recently, while snorkeling in a beautiful reef, I found myself in the midst of a school of large, brightly colored parrot fish. Transported by delight, I responded primitively and automatically by trying to embrace one of them. This had the opposite effect, of course—which I could have anticipated intellectually—of driving them away. Wired into our biological program is the wish to clasp to ourselves what brings us pleasure and to find pleasure in the clasping.

In sexual contact, touching and intimate touching are the essence of the transaction. Only in sexuality are we given license to touch another person freely and expressively, as though the other's body were our own. And only in sexuality may we touch and be touched intimately, entrusting what is most private to the access of the other. In sexual behavior, physical boundaries between self and other are set aside. In the giving and receiving of touch, the distinctions between donor and recipient are blurred. Kinesthetic sensations in touching are always mutual.

Sexuality plays a central role in most intimate relationships, because the mutual exchange of intense physical pleasure and responsiveness is the most powerful medium for the interplay of connection, apartness, and reconnection. The space between you and me can disappear. Or we can work to keep it open to whatever distance we need.

Issues of touching, because of their connection with body boundaries, are frequently sources of conflict between lovers. It is not unusual clinically to see couples who have made a battleground over who can touch who where and in what way. He, for example, wants access to her breasts, but she says she cannot bear to be touched there. She wants him to have oral contact with her genitals, but he finds this kind of closeness repulsive. In sexual relating, rules are set about how much of the body self is given over to the other, and for what purpose.

When we can touch another, we can feel less separate. In giving and receiving physical pleasure, we can open ourselves to another person who is open to us. In sharing orgasm, we can, for a moment, be united in a state of oceanic boundarylessness—at one.

Sexual desire is perhaps the most powerful of magnets that draw people to one another. The search for a sexual partner dominates most people's relational stories from adolescence onward. Where this is a passionate search (and it is not always), desire is experienced as a wish for union.

The fantasy of union or fusion is first recorded in Plato's *Symposium*. Here Aristophanes is given to tell the myth of a whole human being with two faces, four arms, four legs, and two genital organs. Zeus, fearing the creature's power, tears it in two, and each remaining person is fated to wander the earth in search of its other half.

Whenever one has the good fortune to encounter his
own actual other half, affection and kinship and love

combined inspire in him an emotion which is quite overwhelming, and such a pair practically refuse ever to be separated even for a moment. It is people like these who form lifelong partnerships, although they would find it difficult to say what they hope to gain from one another's society. No one can suppose that it is mere physical enjoyment which causes the one to take such intense delight in the company of the other. It is clear that the soul of each has some other longing which it cannot express, but can only surmise and obscurely hint at. Suppose Hephaestus with his tools were to visit them as they lie together, and stand over them and ask: "What is it, mortals, that you hope to gain from one another?" Suppose too that when they could not answer he repeated his question in these terms: "Is the object of your desire to be always together as much as possible, and never to be separated from one another day or night? If that is what you want, I am ready to melt and weld you together, so that, instead of two, you shall be one flesh; as long as you live you shall live a common life, and when you die, you shall suffer a common death, and be still one, not two, even in the next world. Would such a fate as this content you, and satisfy your longings?" We know what their answer would be; no one would refuse the offer; it would be plain that this is what everybody wants, and everybody would regard it as the precise expression of the desire which he had long felt but had been unable to formulate, that he should melt into his beloved and that henceforth they should be one being instead of two. The reason is that this was our primitive condition when we were wholes, and love is simply the name for the desire and pursuit of the whole [Plato, 1951, p. 53].

This fantasy has enormous emotional power and speaks to a deep yearning in each of us to find completion, to merge with what is missing in us, to seek and possess the Other.

Psychoanalysis has tended to understand this wish for union as a wish to reexperience a very primitive mother-infant union. Margaret Mahler's (1975) notions of symbiosis, of undifferentiated experience, mark the earliest phase of human life—a phase that is never fully given up and mourned. "The whole literature of the world, from love songs to philosophy and, indeed, theology, bears witness to the pain of tolerating this separation of subject from object, and to the supreme bliss which is invariably experienced as the disappearance of this separation and as a reestablishment of the mystic union between subject and object" (Balint, 1952b, p. 27). Always we long to return to that union of selves that we knew before we had to recognize our separateness. And in adult interpersonal life, such union becomes possible, however fleetingly, only in passionate sexual love.

The early developmental phase of psychic oneness (Mahler's symbiosis) has been characterized by other psychoanalysts as a phase before reality testing. In early infancy, babies assume that their interests and their mother's interests are identical: the mother must not want anything that will run counter to the interests of the infant (A. Balint, 1953). This pleasurable state of harmony is what is sought again and again in later life. We long for the sense that the Other wants what we want, identically and in the same moment. The pathos of this wish is sung in the sad refrain of the song, "Send in the Clowns": "I thought that you'd want what I want. Sorry, my dear."

This intense desire for merger, for harmony of interests, and for oneness has been viewed by psychoanalysts alternatively as a pathological regressive need and as a healthy capacity to achieve union without fear of merger. The healthy adult must be able both to tolerate separateness and to be open to intimacy. How this need for union is evaluated in the individual case depends much on the circumstances of the individual (and on the worldview of the psychoanalyst). Kernberg (1980), for example, takes a step beyond other psychoanalysts by giving the urge to union and transcendence precedence over sexual gratification as the central force of sexual passion.

Because Freud's legacy did not include a clear image of healthy adult relatedness, psychoanalysts ever since have discussed these phenomena only in the most abstruse terms. Most simply assume that when oedipal issues are adequately "resolved," an adaptive and gratifying sexual relationship will follow. M. Balint (1953) is one of the few psychoanalysts to give serious attention to how people go about creating this intricate form of intimate interaction. As adults, our needs are too complex for us to achieve union without much preparatory work. In order to engage in harmonious sexual love, partners must undergo what Balint calls "the work of conquest"—the process of discovering how to satisfy as many of each other's needs as possible. Far from the automatic sexual union of animals, humans

> are not only expected to give our partner as much as we can bear, but even to enjoy giving it, while not suffering too much under the necessarily not quite complete satisfaction of our own wishes. All this must go on all the time both before and after genital gratification for as long as the love relation itself lasts. . . . This work causes considerable strain on the mental apparatus, and only a healthy ego is able to bear it. Still, it cannot be relaxed till just before the orgasm. Then, however, the happy confidence emerges that everything in the world is now all right, all individual needs are satisfied, all individual differences sunk, only one—identical—wish has remained in which the whole universe submerges, and both subject and partner become one in the mystical union [p. 116].

The need to take account of the other's needs and wishes is, however, a socially imposed necessity, a form of delay and frustration. The wish for union, as it is experienced, is a wish for possession of the other. Powerful urges to engulf, to penetrate, to devour, to contain, to own, and to control accompany the wish to merge. This gives rise to the intense jealousies and rage over frustration that color passionate relationships.

Passionate union must also involve union with otherness. That which is not-self becomes, momentarily, part of the self. Here paradox prevails. Only because of a morphological difference is heterosexuality possible; yet its object is to obviate that difference. At the height of sexual arousal is the experience of oneness and sameness, yet one sex can never know what the other's experience is really like. Nor can any person fully know any other person. Again and again in passionate love, the mystery of otherness is solved, only to find its riddles still unanswered. Union is achieved, difference is overcome—and yet we are still left to wander the world as separate selves.

People experience wishes for union in widely varying ways. Some find such wishes, with the threat of loss of identity, terrifying, so they disown them. For many people, such wishes are experienced only indirectly, through identification with literature, theater, and movies, which frequently take the quest for union as their theme. Other people, at the opposite extreme, actively seek such experiences of union in their relational lives and feel whole only when in a passionate merger with an Other.

Where intense sexual union is unavailable or feared, people often seek some other form of intense connection to others. Passion exists as much in its intensity as in its form of expression. Friendship, for example, can be passionate and asexual at the same time. Carol Smith-Rosenberg (1975), who wrote about passionate friendship among women in nineteenth-century America, documented the emotional intensity and romantic tenderness that was present in the spiritual love between women of that time. Kept in gender-segregated social networks, women expressed to each other the same longings for reunion and intense needs for one another that the twentieth-century mind thinks of as concomitants of sexual involvement.

In one form or another, people seek some kind of intense connection with others. Here the nature of the connection may be less important than its strength of feeling. Fairbairn (1954), who starts from the premise that libido is object-seeking rather than pleasure-seeking, demonstrates that both pleasure and pain are channels to the object. We can feel intensely connected to each other through hurt, anxiety, or hate as well as through pleasure. And some of our most intense relationships are marked by strong ambivalence, which is an alternation of these intense feeling states. Interpersonal conflict itself can be arousing, which is why lovemaking between long-time lovers is often best after a fight.

The need for intensity in relatedness explains in part why people stay in painful relationships. Often it is the conflict that is arousing and makes the person feel connected to another. The fear is not of pain but of emotional deadness. The battered woman who tries to explain that her husband hits her because he loves her is communicating her understanding that at least he feels strongly toward her. He is not indifferent, which is what would be unbearable. In these instances, to be hurt physically as the result of someone's strong feelings, however sadistic, is to feel intensely connected; and that is better than to be someone who evokes no response at all.

Falling in Love

Falling in love is a unique experience, not on a continuum with other ways of being. It is, in a sense, a separate plane of relatedness—one that only some people have experienced. A wild bird that no one can tame, sings Carmen, this form of love is a mysterious and lawless state of being that no one can adequately explain or predict.

Because falling in love is passionate in its intensity and its quest for union, it must be taken up in a discussion of passionate experience. It is impenetrable, however, because—by its very nature—it stands apart from reason. Shakespeare likened falling in love to being anointed with love drops. Mythology and history link falling in love to magic. Potions and powders and spells produce the soul-wrenching state of focus on a very particular Other. The person who is in love feels possessed. Here is Dickens's description of the experience, in Pip's words: "I loved [Estella] simply because I found her irresistible. Once for all; I knew to my sorrow, often and often, if not always, that I loved her against reason, against promise, against peace, against hope, against happiness, against all discouragement that could be. Once for all; I loved her none the less because I knew it, and it had no more influence in restraining me, than if I had devoutly believed her to be human perfection" (1861, p. 195).

Falling in love has been much maligned in the psychoanalytic literature. It is viewed most frequently as a form of temporary psychosis or as an addictive state (M. Balint, 1953). It is the irrationality of falling in love—against reason, against peace, as Dickens puts it—that has made the experience difficult to place in a rational theory of human development. Ethel Person (1988) has recently taken issue with these views and attempted to restore the understanding of falling in love as an aspect of healthy development. One of her major themes is the role of falling in love as an energizer of life, a catalyst to self-development. Here there develops an important contradiction with classical psychoanalytic reasoning. Gratification—in this case, sexual gratification—should produce a state of quiescence, of satiation. On the contrary, however, the intensity of the state of being in love, even where there is powerful and frequent sexual satisfaction, tends to produce a general excitation that spills out into other pursuits, leads to new interests, causes a general vitality that paints the world in Technicolor. Falling in love, merging with another, produces paradoxically a heightening of the experience of self.[6] Self-transcendence and self-awareness are both outgrowths of the experience of falling in love.

Falling in love represents, above all, hope. As Bion (1961) points out, the defense of pairing in groups has less to do with sexuality and more to do with messianic group fantasies. In creating a sexual pair, the group keeps alive the messianic hope of redemption from its conflicts and inevitable death. In a state of being-in-love, the fevered expectation is the reunion with that which has been lost, the repair of that which has been wounded, the entry into a state of ecstatic fusion with the life force itself. This is why falling in love is so often experienced as a form of rebirth and the loss of love as a loss of hope.

We are drawn in our fantasies and inner lives to images of the transcendent and promises of renewal. The appeal of old-fashioned love stories (such as *Moonstruck*) never wanes even for jaded modern audiences. We never tire of sharing in the fantasy that true love found will lead to eternal bliss. Nor do we ever tire of weeping cathartically at the tragedies of love lost, which form the very core of literature, theater, and opera.

All this, however, stands somewhat apart from the essence of relatedness, although the hopefulness embodied in falling in love is part of what powers the effort to love over time. But in order for relationships to be lasting, the other relational dimensions, such as attachment, empathy, mutuality, and validation, must also play a part. Passion alone does not sustain.

The Greeks, who were the primary source of most of our mythology of passionate love and falling in love, did not attempt to make a connection between falling in love and the love that endures. Their interest was more in the consequences of the intensity of passionate desire—desire that drove people to violent or heroic actions. Wars are fought for the "having" of a loved one; rivalry in love is sufficient motivation for bloodshed. Yet the only Greek story of ongoing, sustained, and ever-renewing love describes the love of a mother for her child in the myth of Demeter and Persephone.

The Greeks did not aspire to explain why one person was chosen over another, either (except for Beauty). Eros (Cupid) was invoked as a random or mischievous force that set in motion the passions of falling in love. With Freud came the first real effort at explanation of the choice of the loved object.

Freud taught that all finding is a *re*finding. With this concept, he felt able to explain what no one else could explain before: why certain people are chosen to be fallen in love with. Rather than the randomness of Cupid's arrows, Freud believed that unconscious factors do the choosing, selecting on the basis of similarity to the childhood parent of the opposite sex, the first object of passionate love.

Psychoanalysis, to the extent that it can explain states of falling in love at all, does so on the basis of the Oedipus complex. Children intuitively sense an exciting, gratifying, and mysterious link between the parents—a link from which they are excluded— and this forms the basis of a sexualized fantasy life. Adolescent falling in love is a quest for these mysterious gratifying experiences (Kernberg, 1980). Postadolescent falling in love is understood to be a reedition of a childhood falling in love, only this time with a nonincestuous object whose connection to the original object is repressed. The data base psychoanalysis uses to come to this conclusion is the experience of transference love, which is assumed to be the same as falling-in-love experiences in real life. This is a dubious supposition, however, given that the psychoanalytic situation is one designed to foster regression and to allow for the projection of internal and infantile relational modes.[7]

Exclusive attention to the analysis of the regressive, repetitive elements of falling in love overlooks the essential core of the experience, which is as a container of hope and futurity. While falling in love always contains some elements of reexperience in its repetition of gratifying elements in the relation with the opposite-sex parent of childhood, it always contains new elements as well. Falling in love promises rebirth. In the sense of newness of the world and all that it contains, the person "in love" feels "brand new," able to experience a region of existence unimaginable beforehand. One never falls in love in the same way twice.

Falling in love can change one's life even beyond the relationship, awakening novel thoughts, feelings, and goals (Csikszentmihalyi, 1980). As many poets have suggested, falling in love may be a key to new worlds, new organizations of experience. Those I interviewed who had had a falling-in-love experience tended to emphasize its self-transforming meaning in their lives. Merger and identification with the passionately loved other brought into their lives new interests and new aspects of self.

The need to be fallen in love with, the wish to be the object of passionate desire, has its own complex history, much less explicated. Historically, this need has been assigned to women. Medieval courtly love, for example, was the province of men. A woman could accept or reject the knight who paid court to her, to be sure, but there was no focus on how she experienced him or what she desired. Psychoanalysis has similarly assumed that while men strive to love, women yearn to be loved (and will consequently love whoever seems to love her).

In literature, women who love actively take enormous risks. Where they allow expression to their passionate desire and it is not reciprocated, their despair leads them to suicide. The great (active rather than passive) female lovers—Anna Karenina, Emma Bovary, Madame Butterfly—all die of their passion. A woman cannot survive an unfulfilled passion in this view. Therefore, the cultural mythology seems to say to a woman, better wait to be sought, await a declaration of love from a man before allowing awareness of one's own feelings.

And there are advantages to being the loved one, to be sure. As the object of passionate desire, each person is utterly special, particular. Although we are very particular in other forms of love, we are never so particularized as when we are the object of someone else's passionate love. Most people are attached to several people. We have mutuality and empathy with many others. But never do we receive so much attention and so much intense focus as when we are passionately loved. The flowers received, the love poems written are all means of attesting to the exclusive attention and emotional intensity bestowed on the beloved. Only in the brief, dimly remembered period of early infancy, when we were the object of our mother's preoccupation, were we so much the focus of the psychological world of another. There is no greater form of narcissistic gratification.

In the striving for particularity, Freud saw the jealousies of the oedipal period, the wish to be solely loved by the parent of the opposite sex, and the rivalries of the pre-oedipal period in the wish to be the only child. From a more existential point of view, being the object of such love testifies to our uniqueness and special worth. It says that we cannot be replaced by another, that we are, in that sense, protected against both anonymity and death (Yalom, 1980). The idea of "forever" is always a part of passionate love. Our union, this feeling of one for the other, will be eternal. To be in love is to join the immortal gods.

Growing into Love

Falling-in-love experiences were in fact rare among the ordinary people I interviewed. Marriage was most often undertaken on pragmatic and affectionate grounds rather than passionate ones. Elena, for example, spoke of how her marriage to Jeremy was based on her experience of him as caring and warm. She said that she did not experience with him that "crazy, sick" feeling she had had with men she had loved before him.

Where women I interviewed reported passionate involvements with men, those involvements tended not to be with their husbands. Molly, for example, interviewed at age seventy-five, had had a fifty-year-long affair with David, a man whom she loved but chose not to marry. Although he excited her in every way, both with his knowledge and his lovemaking, Molly believed that his narcissistic lack of concern for others made him unlikely to be a good husband or father. Molly married a loyal, rather unexciting, somewhat depressed man instead—a man whom she enjoyed nurturing—but she secretly continued her relationship with David. Even after her husband had died and her children were grown, Molly still did not wish to marry David. Although she continued to feel passionately toward him, she was still put off by his selfishness and incapacity for true mutuality. Nevertheless, Molly emphasized the riches that David brought into her life, in the form of music, theater, intellectual stimulation, and sex. Although he caused her conflict and pain over the years, he enlivened her life.

Among those I interviewed, women appeared to be more reality-oriented than men in their relationships. They tended to pay attention to emotional responsiveness and mutuality, to base relationships on empathy and interaction, and to resist idealizations and the irrationalities that underlie the falling-in-love experience. These women's lives were often transformed by loving but seldom by falling in love.

These same women, however, were very likely to maintain long-term fantasy experiences of passion or romance and to find such fantasizing gratifying. Nancy, at age forty-eight, spoke with intense feeling about Steve, the "love of my live," whom she fell in love with while in college. "I was obsessed by him. Where I went was colored by whether I thought he would be there. What I wore was determined by whether I thought I'd be seeing him that day." They had a long, conflicted relationship, and Nancy never felt that she had a safe bond with him. He always treated her ambivalently, sometimes doing insanely romantic things and sometimes disappearing from her life for a time. Nancy "created" herself in order to appeal to him. She read the books that interested him, bought the music he liked to listen to. Nancy remembers herself as constantly anxious, in a state of what she called "delicious agony." "My heart would break over and over again. He would look at me intensely with those marvelous eyes and then ignore me." For nearly twenty-five years, through a marriage and a divorce and many other lovers, Nancy has not passed a day without thinking about Steve, without reveling once more in the intense passion she experienced with him and wondering at some level if someday, somehow, she might encounter him yet again.

Even when fantasies are unlikely to be transformed into real experience, the tension around their possibility provides an enlivening form of excitement. In these fantasies, women are more likely to imagine themselves as the object of desire than as the one who desires. For some women, being intensely desired *is* the experience of passion.

Adolescent girls are generally introduced to sexuality through awareness of themselves as objects of masculine interest. They are aroused by being noticed, by being wanted, which in turn leads them to strive to be even more so. This stands in strong contrast to the boy's initiation into sexuality, which is genital, visible, direct, and insistent. The boy is clear on what he is experiencing and what he wants. For the girl, sexual awakening is diffuse, emotional, nongenital, and responsive to others' interest. She is ushered into womanhood by an upsurge of romantic fantasy.

Women's experience of themselves as objects of men's desire often supersedes awareness of their own desires. As Gilligan and Stern (1988) point out, male definitions of love relationships often leave women disconnected from their own experience of desire. In the myth of Psyche and Eros, Psyche is forbidden to look at her lover, to know anything of who he is. She must content herself with being desired—and treated well—in darkness. As in this myth, women struggle against the dark, where they are prohibited from direct perception of their own feelings; they focus instead on being appealing in hopes of being loved. Anxious lest they not be chosen, they have little chance to experience themselves as doing the choosing.

Fantasy therefore becomes a realm in which a woman is free to have complete control—to be chosen or to choose. Women also enliven themselves by experiencing passionate intensity vicariously. Soap operas and romance novels, largely female in their audience, provide a channel for this kind of vicarious passionate experience while women attend in reality to the more mundane and less intense forms of interpersonal life (Radway, 1984). Men, by contrast, when aroused to passion, are more directly in need of gratification, more likely to experience passion in action.

Adolescent Roots of Sex and Love

Whatever unconscious residues of the Oedipus complex of childhood shape preparedness for adult sexuality, adolescent experience has powerful and largely unacknowledged effects on how sexuality is integrated into adult experience. The striking differences between the genders in their early experience of sexuality phrases the developmental problems quite distinctively and sets the stage for the never-ending "battle between the sexes."

For the boy, sexuality comes upon him unbidden, as an urgent physical demand. He experiences frequent erections, even when he is unaware that he is thinking about sex. He is physiologically made to be aroused by visual stimuli, by which he is surrounded. He may ejaculate in his sleep. Although he can masturbate and must come to terms with whatever anxiety and guilt he may have about masturbation, he is also aware that his physiological arousal seeks an Other for its satisfaction. Early- and middle-adolescent male fantasies represent girls or women as objects of gratification; boys think about "fucking" as a pleasurable activity using a female body as equipment. If we listen to the conversation of adolescent boys, this is what their joking and teasing (and their anxieties) are about. With time, boys are socialized into an awareness that finding a sexual object is more complicated, that they must, in Balint's phrase, do the work of conquest in order to achieve sexual gratification. (This work of conquest is culture-specific. Part of the male protest against women's liberation has been that the rules of this conquest have changed so much.)

By late adolescence or early adulthood, the young man has more or less achieved a capacity to integrate his sexual feelings with more affectionate ones. Although the earlier pure-sex, woman-as-object feelings never fully disappear, the psychologically healthy man is able to love a woman who sexually arouses him and to be sexually aroused by a woman he loves. In passionate desire, the wish for possession and union is fused with sexual arousal.

Female development follows a very different pathway to the

same end. The early-adolescent girl's first awareness of sexuality is in vaguely erotic stirrings. She may begin thinking about how it might be to be "liked" by a boy and have fantasies about being sought after, admired, perhaps kissed. She may think romantically about a particular boy and want to be special to him. Adolescent girls spend a great deal of time together talking about and trying to understand love. But the early-adolescent girl will remain for a long time repulsed by (though curious about) the idea of genital contact. Finally, with socialization, she is able to integrate genital sensation with the romantic feelings that flood her. In the age before our current cultural preoccupation with sex, many adolescent girls were taught to masturbate by their boyfriends. They had not known it was possible. (Now women are just as likely to be taught to masturbate by their therapists.) The relative infrequency of adolescent female masturbation despite the erotic striving of this period demonstrates that female adolescent sexuality is fantasy-dominated and emotion-laden. Only with time does the adolescent girl learn to integrate physical desire with her yearnings for love. In passionate desire, she has achieved this end, wanting a union and possession that is also sexual. But, as Ann Landers has demonstrated, many women remain focused on the tender and romantic in their love relationships and would be happy to forgo genital contact ("Sex vs. Hugs . . . ," 1985).

Women's postliberation sexual behavior has made it difficult to assess anymore what is fundamental to female sexuality. Many women have experimented with male attitudes toward sexuality as they have experimented with other male attitudes. Some women have demonstrated that they, too, can objectify the Other and "use" men for sexual gratification. Women have tried to demonstrate that they, too, can take the initiative and be "casual" about sex.

My clinical, research, and life experiences lead me to disbelieve the depth of any of this, however. One research participant, for example, reported that after her divorce she began having sex with everyone she went out with. She thought of herself as in need of sexual gratification, so she made use of whoever was available. But she discovered that these experiences were hollow and not what she wanted: "I can produce better orgasms by myself. What I really wanted was to have sex with someone I loved."

The femme fatale in the movie *Fatal Attraction* approaches the hero in the "modern" spirit of a liberated woman, seducing him with imaginative and highly erotic sexual activity. But it turns out that sex is not what she really wants. She wants a committed relationship with him; she wants a family. "You know the rules," this already married man tells her. But, the movie seems to say, they are his rules, not hers.

That the two sexes come to the same integration by such different roads defines the ongoing tension between them. Women feel mystified and chagrined at the male focus on "pure sex," which has never been part of their own experience. Men cannot fully understand the emotional cloaks in which women wish to dress sexuality.

One forty-year-old widowed woman patient reported breaking up a possible romantic relationship when the man who was courting her declared, "I really want to go to bed with you. I love sex." Another woman told of how she had dated a man who had obviously learned that he must please women sexually. In the midst of their first intercourse, he asked her, "On a scale of 1 to 10, how excited are you?" She found his instrumental approach to sex so unromantic that she never saw him again.

Men, on the other hand, complain of their perplexity about what a woman wants. They are likely to feel manipulated by a woman who asks a lot of them in other arenas but withholds sex. A male patient with a sexually inhibited wife protested, "Here I just bought her a $400,000 house for which I work night and day, and I don't even get to screw!"

Adult Sex and Love

Of orgasmic experience, pure sexual satisfaction, the people I interviewed had little to say, although many mentioned that sex was or was not satisfactory in their marital relationship. Where sex was highly satisfactory, people tended to report greater affection and tenderness. The number of asexual or relatively asexual marriages in this study (as well as in my practice) is somewhat surprising, given the focus on sex in our society. Asexuality in marriage seems to be the last of the well-kept shameful secrets. In many marriages, by what appears to be somewhat mutual consent, sex simply drops off or disappears altogether. Passion is perhaps more mythologized and fantasized about than lived.

The most passionate relationships that people described were on the way to or outside of marriage. But even here, sexual gratification was but one of many factors of importance in the relationship.

In most heterosexual relationships, however committed, however unromantic and nonmysterious, there nevertheless appear to remain moments of passion. There is a continuum here, for which intensity and union form one pole and inhibition and lifelessness form the other. People content themselves with relationships all along this scale. To a few it is given to find their "other halves"; most do their best to fit together imperfectly.

Although falling-in-love experiences were far from universal among those who shared their relational histories with me, the quest for particularity and specialness through love was part of each person's story. People may not expect to be the object of passionate love, but they do wish to feel chosen, to feel like a priority to someone. People speak of wanting to "come first," to feel that someone is focusing at least some of his or her attention on them, courting them, trying to please them.

We are a culture that has come to distrust falling-in-love experiences, although in some other ages they have had an association with enduring and sustained love. In the 1950s, one of the most popular songs celebrated the idea that "love and marriage go together like a horse and carriage." Yet in the late 1980s, a male friend of mine could remark with great feeling about a mutual acquaintance, "I was once in love with her for a whole day." In an age that knows little socially enforced sexual inhibition, the connections between passionate desire, falling in love, and sustained love become tenuous and confusing.

We know that there are clear cultural aspects to the expression of sexual and romantic feelings: how and toward whom love is expressed is transmitted culturally. The notion of love as a basis for marriage, on which our current theory of family relationship is based, is a recent social idea. As recently as the nineteenth century, passionate affection centered legitimately on same-sex relationships. Romantic love was invented to express mainly unfulfillable desires of unmarried troubadours for married women. And sexual behavior, in a short space of time, has gone from being approved of only in marriage or committed relationships to relatively free expression as a form of recreation. But the human propensities for union and intensity, for the merging that is possible only in sexuality, for particularity and specialness—these needs are fundamental and universal, although their expression and satisfaction may change with the cultural winds.

The connections among these life-changing feelings and powerful states are a source of ongoing struggle and conflict in human experience. All lovers, whether they come together for gratification of sexual desire or whether they fall in love, whether they plan to stay together for a night or forever, must in some way think through the relationship between sexual passion and love. The problem for psychological theory recapitulates the struggle of the lovers. Freud did not have a theory of love, and confusion has resulted from the effort of theorists to deduce adult love from the achievement of genitality and from the Oedipus complex. As we have seen, genitality alone does not amount to what is usually meant by sustained, adult "happy" love, and most writers who try to make it do so slip in other dimensions of relatedness, as though mutuality, empathy, sharing, and cooperation somehow derived from or were concomitant with the fickle but potent forces of sexual arousal.

Paul

Paul grew up on a farm with his mother, father, and grandfather. Paul's charts, like those of Tom (whose life was discussed in the previous chapter) are in Resource A at the back of the book. Thinking back to age five, Paul remembers his grandfather most clearly. "I spent a lot of time on my grandfather's lap, just being there with him. He was not very warm or expressive, but he was there." His mother and father were also "there"—reassuring. "I felt taken care of," remembers Paul, but he has no specific memories of his parents from this age. Paul recalls that the focus at home was on getting the farm work done. The adults were hardworking, and he remembers playing around them as they worked.

Paul soon had siblings. He remembers them as being important when he was between the ages of five and ten. "I remember my sister, just over a year old, at the top of a slide laughing. I'm down at the bottom as her big brother to catch her. She died of pneumonia shortly after, at eighteen months old. I was five and a half." Paul's brother was also important to him at this age. "I had to take care of him. He was three years younger. I couldn't run off and leave him alone, though I tried to. I remember putting him on my bike to take him places and cursing under my breath the whole way. He was too much younger than I to be a playmate." Paul's cousin, one year older, lived down the road; they were together a lot. They burned down haystacks together, roamed the woods, went bicycle riding, explored their world, went to the swimming hole. "We were insurance for each other. If one had difficulty, the other was around to holler."

Paul can see his mother and father clearly in memories of age ten. He remembers them packing a picnic basket, for example. "They are just there; they are a team, function well together, take good care of me." His grandfather had died by then, but Paul does not remember a sense of loss.

Paul also remembers Mrs. Moore, his teacher in the one-room schoolhouse across the road from the farm. "She took good care of my academic life. I was a 'star'; school success was an important part of my life. She helped me: put me in positions where I could learn, let me work with the older kids where I could learn more."

By age fifteen, Paul had gone off to boarding school on a scholarship. Most important to him at this age was a group of boys who were his schoolmates. Because they all lived together, they felt like his family. "I was a very small kid," admits Paul, and his size shaped his adolescence. Always the youngest in his class, he was a late maturer as well. As a result, he could not keep up with the other boys in sports. To compensate, Paul developed his musical talent. He was good at this and thus received a lot of recognition, but he still longed for the masculine prowess of the other boys.

Two of his male friends from this time stand out in importance. One was Bill, his roommate, whose family became a kind of second family. The second, George, was someone Paul admired. He ran track with him and did other sports. Their bond was firmed when they learned that they both came from small towns: "We understood one another. Also, he was big and tall. I loved being associated with someone who was big and tall."

A "group of females" was next in importance at this time. When Paul started growing into a tall, attractive young man at age sixteen, he began playing sports more earnestly, and he also dated "town girls." "I was exploring like crazy. I had had no opportunities with girls when I was a small little jerk and felt like an outcast." Mainly, he wanted to be physically close; he enjoyed the sensual pleasure of nearness and touching. Not interested in the girls as people, he did not want to spend time with them just to talk. "I didn't offer much to the relationships. I was fickle, wanted to have several relationships."

Paul omitted his parents from his age-fifteen drawing (and thereafter until age forty-five). Asked about this, he replied, "Who needs them? I left home. When I came home in summer, I no longer worked on the farm; I worked at the country club. I felt much smarter than my uneducated father. I didn't even go to them for money."

Age twenty found Paul in medical school, working hard. He was with some students from his prep school, and although he was not particularly close to any one of them, he had a sense of belonging to a group, of having grown up with them. He got along all right with his roommates, but he shared little with them. At this age, Paul was pulling apart from male friends. He was working a lot, "going my own way, living my life by myself, studying, earning money."

Women, on the other hand, still interested Paul. He was still exploring sexual relationships with different women, but this was a side of himself he never talked about with anyone. This was a private realm—one of secret thrills and somewhat forbidden excitements. Paul was, however, hesitant with the women he really admired, fearful of their rejection. "Inside, I still felt like the little jerk from Hicksville."

Paul had met Helen in college and had heard from mutual

friends that she liked him. Paul describes her as not special in any way. "She was not my dream, but she was achievable and her father was a doctor, so she would be a 'good choice.'" Paul was ambivalent about the relationship for some time. "I broke off with her so many times, but I came back because she made sense and she knew what was 'right': she knew what was socially right and could keep me out of sexual trouble, so she was a good choice—a good, pragmatic choice." He came to the conclusion that "being in love was probably a fiction. Helen would say that I wanted too much from a relationship and that life really didn't include being in love. She persuaded me that people don't have relationships that are wonderful, they have relationships that work. I felt very grown up to be accepting this and concluding that Helen was pragmatically a very good wife for me. We got married after my second year of medical school."

At age twenty-five, Paul was just starting out in general practice in the town where Helen was raised, and they had two children. In his diagram, Paul drew the children attached to Helen, with all three of them distant from him. "I was there to earn a living, and she was there to take care of them. I was proud of the way she did things. She was a good doctor's wife. We treated each other nicely. Sex was largely disappointing and infrequent."

Of his children, Paul says, "They're mine, but they're really hers. I dove into my job and was away a lot. I was such a young doctor, felt there was so much to learn. I was doing additional training in the city, traveled to seminars. I *visited* my home."

Paul's patients were also important to him at this time, though not as individuals. "They were there for me to nurture, care about"—ways of relating that were missing from his personal relationships.

At age thirty, there were few relational changes, except that Paul now had four children. "We were a picture-book family," but there was little emotional involvement. One of his patients, Edie, was of special interest to him. "Nothing happened, but I fantasized about her a lot, wondered what it would be like to be married to her, imagined sleeping with her."

An important relationship appeared at age thirty-five: Paul grew close to Ned, a doctor he worked with in the city. They went to meetings together; their families spent time together and went camping together. Ned was one of the few men in Paul's life with whom he felt he could share who he was, although he grew very slowly into this. He liked Ned and was pleased that Ned saw something in him to value.

Paul found himself fantasizing more and more about other women. "I was so often alone with [my patients]. I could get some satisfaction from being close to them. I could touch them and get away with it. Even with Ned's wife, I was imagining what it would be like to be married to her; I was wanting more."

As Paul turned forty and his children grew into adolescence, he felt more of a relationship with them. He could talk to them about common interests, take them on camping trips, play tennis with them. He continued to be interested in trying to share himself with others, experimenting with being honest with people, but that was difficult. He was able to share ideas and values with John, a tennis buddy, but he could never really find a way to share himself.

Unable to find the kind of connection he longed for with his male friends, Paul again sought what he needed from women. By age forty-five, Paul was separated from Helen and living with Marlene, who changed his life in many ways. She had been a patient with common interests, and Paul found her irresistible. At first, he just enjoyed spending time with her, enjoyed having wonderful sex; then she became much more to him. Paul was flooded by a rush of emotion as he began talking about what Marlene meant to him. When he could speak again, he said simply, "It's nice to feel prized and cherished." In short, Paul had fallen in love. "It's nice to share, to find somebody you think fills all those fantasies and find out it's not just a made-up story."

Marlene helped him to reconnect with his parents:

Through Marlene, I learned to appreciate them. My parents had always come to visit, but Helen didn't like my mother, and I had always been ashamed of them. Marlene prizes my parents. I'm free to enjoy them for who they are and see them for their strengths and weaknesses. I didn't like the "hickness" of them, but now I see the strength they have. They were there all the time: in spite of the shit I gave them, they kept coming. I found everybody again, even the ghosts of my grandparents. I value them now. I wish I could tell them that.

Paul's brother, whom he resented having to take care of in childhood, had never been part of Paul's emotional life. Now, however, he became a close friend. "We do good talking. I really love his wife. She is like a sister to me. We see each other and our families often now."

Ned and John remained important as supportive friends, and Mark became a new friend because of his support. Because Paul's separation from Helen had caused a great scandal and he felt ostracized, he was deeply grateful toward those who were there for him, who tried to understand and did not judge him.

His relationship with Helen at this age was openly hostile. Full of rage, she refused to talk to him and put their children in the middle. The children remained loyal to their mother, causing Paul to mourn the relationship he had never really had with them.

At Paul's current age, fifty, he is enjoying marriage with Marlene and the new, more open relationships he has made. He continues to feel new bonds of connection with the people in his life, and he still feels prized. The only problem is the tension caused by Marlene's children, who get in the way of their being just a couple. But Paul looks forward to the time, not too far off, when he can be alone with her and they can together savor what he feels is his boundless good fortune to have found her.

Paul has been most intensely drawn to people by his drives; that is his pattern of relatedness. Throughout most of his life, he was only marginally invested in people: he got along with others but did not entrust much of himself to them. His parents of childhood were shadowy figures who "took care" of him but offered him little emotionally. He shared activities with friends and seemed to establish relationships of mutual helping, but he felt little about other people beyond his immediate practical need of them.

The loss of his sister in childhood seemed to instill a need to undo his helplessness. The memory of being a big brother and catching her on the slide is a clear statement of his wish to protect her. His choice of medicine as a career was very likely in part an effort to be able to conquer the illness that he was unable to save his baby sister from. Perhaps the trauma of this early loss and the subsequent loss of his grandfather curtailed Paul's ability to invest emotionally in others. His solution seems to have resided in an identification as a "helper"—an early identification rooted more in a defense against powerlessness and guilt than enjoyment of helpful interaction with others.

After partially overcoming his shame about being short, young, and a "hick," Paul hesitantly approached women with his sexuality as an adolescent. He was interested in the dynamics of his own arousal as well as in his capacity to conquer. Still, this appears to be the first time in his life that he felt directly stirred by other people. But Paul backed off even from his sexuality, fearing that it would lead him away from the social acceptability that was at the center of the identity he wanted. Because Paul wanted above all not to be a "hick," he observed the social forms, trying to accept the idea that whatever dreams he had of passionate union were fairy tales. He lost himself in work, at which he was very successful, and occasionally gave way to fantasy about other women and surreptitious touches. Paul was, in Thoreau's phrase, living a life of quiet desperation. Not until midlife, after tentatively opening himself emotionally in relationships with men, did Paul dare allow his passion expression.

Paul's relationship with Marlene became life-transforming. His sense of passionate involvement, of union with her, of being prized by her, acted as a catalyst for Paul's capacity to relate to people in general. He developed relationships within his family for the first time in his life; he became close to male friends, because he could allow himself to need them. Paul's world burst into a bloom of others.

Paul is an example of the life-enhancing, self-transcending power of passionate love. Allowing himself to feel the force of his wishes for union and possession opened the way to other experiences in relatedness. Through passion, he discovered pleasure in others and joy in relatedness. Now he suffers the pain of knowing what he has lost: the years of emptiness, the hollow, tense, guilt-ridden relationships with his children. Yet Paul is transformed.

In feeling prized and cherished, he has found his tears and his compassion.

For Paul the transcendent (and therefore most potent) aspect of passionate experience was found in the discovery of a desired other who chose—and cherished—him. That experience is common to others I interviewed as well. Frances, age sixty, married for forty years to an alcoholic, has had a secret affair for eight years with her minister. They have sexual contact only once or twice a year, but her knowledge of his interest in her, his desire for her, and the risks he has taken for her gilds her life in specialness and makes her glow with energy to pursue her activities.

Daniel, age forty, married for fifteen years, had a brief affair with Linda, his wife's best friend, after discovering his wife's affair with a friend of his. He and his wife used these experiences to explore and reignite their marriage, renewing their bond to each other. But Daniel continues to meet Linda occasionally, "just to talk. She's crazy about me. She wants to run away with me. Sometimes we kiss and hug and share good memories. For me, it's like being in a good book, the warmth and the excitement. But it's got nothing to do with real life. It's some kind of excitement from time to time—for a day or for hours, not beyond." The passions are capricious. They do not preserve, but they ignite.

Specialness and closeness expressed in the (however transient) exclusivity of passionate sexual intimacy are central elements of what Plato's lovers "desired" of each other. Being "united" and therefore prized as a part of the Other, more than sexual gratification, seems to be the piece of the early oedipal situation that continues to cry out for realization; it seems to be the piece that is closest to consciousness, at least. In finding one's "other half," even in largely fantastic relationships such as the one Daniel describes, is the realization of one's own uniqueness. In this way, passion defines the extreme of individuation even as it represents the most intense form of union.

Passionate experience exists on its own plane of relatedness, set apart from the other dimensions but connecting and intersecting them in intricate ways. How these levels of fantasy and desire get represented and integrated with "real" experience is often the most vital narrative, the emotional heartbeat, of people's lives.

Chapter 6

Eye-to-Eye Validation

*And of all these facts and feelings the strongest of all was the
need to be known for her true self and recognized.*

—Carson McCullers, *The Member of the Wedding*

Held securely, the infant gazes into the mother's eyes and has the
experience of being looked at as well. The "good-enough" mother
gazing at her baby is, at least much of the time, gazing with joy and
possessiveness, with love and satisfaction. She likely smiles. The
baby, in response, internalizes a sense of connection beyond that of
being held. The baby feels held in a different way—with emotional
ties rather than physical support. Those ties give the baby the sense
of producing emotional meaning in the world, of having an effect
on the other. This is the realm of emotional exchange across space,
of validation and empathy, of finding ourselves reflected in others
and anchoring ourselves in our effects on them. In discovering that
others respond to us, we affirm that we ourselves are really here.

In eye-to-eye relating is the recognition that we have meaning to others, that we exist for them. Beyond that, we discover that
aspects of our existence provoke feelings in others—feelings about
and in response to what we are and what we do. We discover that
some responses from others are pleasurable to us—gleams, smiles,
beams—and that others are not—abstractedness, frowns, coolness.
Through this modality of connection, we locate ourselves with
other people in increasingly complex ways across the life cycle.

The "Gleam in the Eye"

Throughout life, we read our meaning for others in the look in their eyes.[1] These looks are far beyond words: eyes speak more profoundly than language the tenor of relatedness. They express, surely and absolutely, how much and in what way we matter to the Other. Words may lie; eyes cannot.

And what we read is a calibration of mattering to which we respond in a profound and authentic way. We come to know the soul-enriching joy of feeling wanted, sought, of producing joy in the Other; we also come to know the despair of finding blankness, distance, and inattention in the eyes of the Other.

In a most basic way, the (m)Other infuses in the infant a will to live, a will to selfhood, by providing emotional responsiveness (Guntrip, 1971; Winnicott, 1971).[2] What we see, first and fundamentally, in the eyes that look back is that our existence is (or is not) valued in the (m)Other's eyes. If we are fortunate, we read in the language of eyes that it is right and good that we are here. As infants, once we have discovered, however dimly, that others exist, the gleam in our mother's eye reflects the essential goodness of our being and forms the core of our sense of specialness.

Throughout life, we value ourselves to the extent that we can believe that we really matter—vitally—to someone else. And this sense always remains in eyes. The psychologist Zick Rubin (1973), for example, found that one can distinguish people who are in love from people who like each other by the time they spend just looking deeply into each other's eyes. The look of love is a look of intense valuation, of being prized and cherished, of being special. At the wedding of a friend of mine, as the groom watched his bride approach him at the altar, I heard a middle-aged woman behind me sigh and say to the woman next to her, "Never in my whole life has anyone ever looked at me the way he just looked at her." In her voice were intense pain, sadness, envy, and regret. Never, she seemed to be saying, has anyone ever wanted me so much—not sexual wanting, not attachment, just simple *valuing*.

The need to matter in the eyes of the other has psychological significance as an aspect of forming a sense of self in relation to the world. On an existential plane, the sense of mattering to another becomes an early form of locating the self. To young children, the necessity of existence is their necessity to one or both parents. "You don't even care if I exist" is the expression of hostility and despair often uttered by depressed people who have lost the sense that their existence is justified by their value to another.

The first eye-to-eye responses are unconditional. The infant brings joy not for doing anything, just for being. The mother, in her primary preoccupation with her infant, welcomes the baby's needs and wishes and, in bringing the baby what it needs, provides also a sense of well-being and goodness.[3] The (m)Other communicates, "I am happy that you are here." Sullivan (1953) suggests that the tender appreciation conveyed by the mother to her infant is the earliest root of self-esteem.

As we grow and develop, we never cease to need this unconditional, simple valuing in another's eyes. Amid the bustle and conflicting demands of adult life, however, we may see it less frequently. One place we may observe gleams in eyes is at airports. Like sequential lights flickering on, eyes in turn illuminate in the waiting crowd as valued others emerge from the airplane. This is an unconditional response: it says, "it is a pleasure to see you. You are a person whose existence brings joy to me." The eyes that light up single someone out of the anonymity of the human procession. Our attachment to life is to these human others who gleam at us. These are moments that, when we are the person who is sought, enrich our lives. They are moments to cherish, because they represent a fleeting respite from the greater complexities of eye-to-eye relating that characterize the majority of our interactions with others.

We need to feel invited to be in this world. To mean something to someone else justifies our existence in an important way. I think that this is why adopted children seek so hard after their birth parents. They seem to want to know who, in however accidental a way, wanted them here, brought them here. This is also why children who think that their parents wanted to abort them have so much trouble in life. They feel like eternal party-crashers, attenders without an invitation. "No one wants you here" is what heartless children say to one another. It is perhaps the cruelest of statements.

One of our deepest needs is the will to matter. In her novel *The Mind-Body Problem*, the philosopher Rebecca Goldstein says, "To matter. Not to be as naught. Is there any will deeper than that? It's not just unqualified will, as Schopenhauer would have it, that makes us what we are; nor is it the will to power, Nietzsche, but something deeper, of which the will to power is a manifestation. We want power because we want to matter" (1983, p. 212).

This need to matter, to be simply valued by another, has only recently been conceptualized within object-relational thinking. It was emphasized by nearly all the research subjects, however. Important people from childhood were often remembered in terms of having "made a fuss" over them, made them a priority. What was important was to feel that they really counted with someone who loved them just for their existence.

Knowing Who We Are

With adequate responsiveness, infants develop a will to selfhood and embark on a lifelong quest to discover their own nature, to express themselves. Here the need is of an Other to know what one is about. By becoming real to another we become real to ourselves. Eye-to-eye contact with a responsive other gives us confidence in our own experience, allows us to feel validated in who we are, and shapes what we come to believe about ourselves.

Buber (1965) points out that it is uniquely human to require this kind of confirmation: "An animal does not need to be confirmed, for it is what it is unquestionably. It is different with man: Sent forth from the natural domain of species into the hazard of the solitary category, surrounded by the air of a chaos which came into being with him, secretly and bashfully he watches for a Yes which allows him to be and which can come to him only from one human person to another" (p. 17).

The "good-enough" mother, in responding to her infant's needs for food, for holding, for soothing, for company, and for stimulation, is not only responding to the need itself but is confirming for the child that what is inside (as need) reverberates outside (as response). Thus the infant has the experience of being acknowledged, of being a self with attributes and capacities.

All of this takes place over a long period of time, of course, during which the infant only gradually learns about selfhood. In the beginning, there is some sense of blissful union with the Other, a merger in which all is satisfied and joyful without boundaries. But as the infant gradually integrates an awareness that others not only exist but have their own experience, eye-to-eye relating takes over as a process of discovering what is self. Our need for validation requires that the interpersonal world around us confirm that we are (externally) what we feel ourselves to be internally. Although validation is not a necessity for survival in the way that holding is, it determines the quality of selfhood the individual will have. Guntrip (1971) makes the point that the experience of genuine personal selfhood is so crucial that survival is hardly worthwhile without it.

There are mothers who are instinctively adept at empathic eye-to-eye contact. When the baby points to a toy horse hanging from the crib, such a mother says joyfully, "Yes, you see a horse," mirroring the baby's perception. She carries the baby to it, and the baby bats it with her hand. Again, joyfully, the mother says, "Yes, you can make the horse move."

The baby is now eight years old. She is in school, playing soccer with her friends. The soccer ball is coming toward her, the goalie. She reaches for it, but misjudges. It goes by to score the goal for the opposing team. "You're a stupid klutz," says her best friend. "That ball came right toward you."

The girl gives up on athletics, grows up some more, and decides to become a psychologist. In presenting her first therapy session to her supervisor, she describes the patient, a woman who speaks of her pain in her relationship with her drug-addicted boyfriend and of her inability to separate from him. The student therapist then describes how she reflected to the patient the intense tie she feels to her boyfriend, her wish for him to be more predictable. The supervisor comments to the student, "You were really able to hear her yearning for him to change." Yes, that's what I did, thinks the student. I did something that makes sense to my supervisor— something a real therapist might do.

This is a thumbnail developmental history of eye-to-eye contact, a process that has its roots in infancy but grows through complex elaborations across the life cycle. At each stage, the development of the self is framed and shaped in the mirrors that others provide.

Much of what we do (or ought to do) as therapists is eye to eye; that is, we recognize our patients as who they are, knowing with them what they think and what they feel so that they in turn become more able to think what they think and to feel what they feel and thereby integrate themselves. Carl Rogers (1951) built his whole system of therapy on unconditional positive regard and empathic listening, conditions necessary to promoting psychological and emotional growth. For many patients, that is *all* that is needed.

In eye-to-eye relatedness, the stream of relational development and the stream of development toward separateness converge.[4] Being responded to empathically not only connects us to the person who is responding to us but also firms our sense of ourselves. We need others to help us to be more separate from them—more ourselves. We can be sure we are what we are only when there is someone else there to know with us what and who we are. "Feeling real," says Winnicott, "is more than existing; it is finding a way to exist as oneself and to relate to objects as oneself and to have a self into which to retreat for relaxation" (1971, p. 117). Winnicott believes that the essence of psychotherapy is giving the patient back what he brings. Only through such mirroring can the patient come to feel real. Self psychologists, doing psychotherapy from an empathically responsive stance, repeatedly note the decrease of tension and anxiety in their patients just as a result of feeling understood (Kohut, 1977; Schwaber, 1980; Lindon, 1991).

We have recently learned, as theorists, that the responsiveness of the environment may be the most important aspect of healthy development. The self grows only in the context of interpersonal nutrients, and its course of growth is framed within the confines of the personalities of the people already there.

When we look into other people's eyes, we see them looking at us. Much happens in this eye-to-eye contact. One aspect of our looking is to find in others' eyes a mirror of our own experience; we see aspects we know of ourselves that are known by others. We learn about ourselves and learn to organize ourselves through the experience of our wishes, feelings, and thoughts and through the reactions that we stir in others. Because children are still in an early reality-testing phase, and because parents have so much power in children's lives, children are very susceptible to confusing their own perceptions of what emanates from themselves with their parents' interpretations, demands, and projections about what is and should be there.

In order for the healthy self to develop, the child needs adequate mirroring from those people who feel near enough to himself that they feel almost like part of the self (Kohut's selfobject). The child reaches for the toy bear. "You want the bear," says the attuned mother. The child hugs and strokes the bear. "Yes, it's soft," says the mother. In mirroring, someone is so much with us that he or she is practically in us.

When we are empathically responded to, we feel affirmed as that which we are. Buber stresses this concept as "imagining the real," which is a form of deeply knowing the other's existence and participating with the other where he or she is. This need to be known, to have our experience articulated and recognized by someone else, is a profound and basic one.

We are perhaps most aware of this process when it fails. When someone is developing well, the empathic nutrients that sustain the emerging self become as invisible as the air that sustains the physical self. When such nutrients are not available, however, we begin to see an array of emotional disorders related to a self that cannot cohere.

We often see patients with what I think of as "wanting" disorders (although they are usually classified as problems of narcissism). These are people who have lost the capacity to want. One such patient was raised by a mother who told her what she wanted. My patient, as a little girl, would reach for the ice cream. "You don't want that," said her mother. "You've had enough. You're full." My patient, uncertain (as all children are), relied on her mother's reality testing for most things. Here, then, she was left with confusion about which was more real: her own perception of her hunger and the appeal of the ice cream or her mother's conviction that she was full and did not want it. This woman grew up with intense confusion about her own needs and interests and came to therapy in late adolescence in an extreme state of identity diffusion.

Another patient spent a year of therapy trying to learn about what she wanted. Did she want to be married to her husband, or did she prefer to be with her lover? Her question to me was what she *should* want, what was *right* to want. As I worked with her, I came to understand that she had no referents for the term *want* as something that originated in her. My focus, as a therapist, was to try to help her learn about what she deeply wanted. But she reacted with bafflement to variants of this question, because *want* was always preceded by *should*. Once I asked her what she did when she went shopping—how she chose which sweater to buy, for example. Simple, she said. She went with a friend and asked the friend which looked better.

In order to learn to know what we want and what is inside of us, someone has to be available to recognize it with us—but *not* to confuse us with what it is that they think we *ought* to want or what it is *they* want or feel. Kohut (1977) places mirroring at the center of his theory of the requirements for the development of a healthy self. A mirroring other (or selfobject) confirms us in what we are, accepting the feelings and perceptions that emanate from inside us as what they are. For Kohut, empathy—the accepting, confirming, and understanding human echo—is a psychological necessity of life. He suggests that empathy may constitute an even more powerful psychological bond between people than the sublimated sexuality of love.

Those parts of ourselves that are not adequately mirrored are split off from the personality. We keep these parts of ourselves secret and private, or we repress them altogether. This, in Kohut's view, is the origin of narcissistic disorders. What cannot be mirrored becomes tinged with shame. Fantasies and wishes to be grand and very special, wishes to be wonderful and joyously welcomed, form the nucleus of striving and initiative. These, however, are especially vulnerable to inadequate mirroring. For fear of making fools of ourselves, we do not let anyone know about our dreams.

The need for empathic responsiveness is, in infancy and childhood, critical to the structuralization and formation of the self. What is adequately mirrored becomes, in time, a part of psychic organization—a more or less certain region of self that we feel is really and truly us. People who have had good-enough empathic response will feel integrated and whole; their world will feel "in tune" with them most of the time. When they are disconfirmed or misunderstood, they will be able to restore equilibrium without too much distress, having internalized enough previous experience to absorb what might come. But at times of change or crisis, needs for a responsive echo will become central once again. When we try something new, for example, we are once again pure, unknown, and vulnerable. During developmental periods of transition, validation is most necessary. One such time is the adolescent passage, when restructuring of the self is the primary developmental task. At this stage, the question "Who am I?" is in part a question about who will know the self that the adolescents feel that they are. Who will be able to know about and bear with them their new emotions? Who will be able to know what is inside of them? This is the origin of the heartfelt battle cry of adolescence: "You don't understand me." (And often people really don't.)

Looking back on his adolescence, Warren, a forty-year-old interviewee, spoke with gratitude about Bonnie, a neighbor his parents' age who "introduced me to myself." And "introduction to oneself" is a perfectly precise way to describe the phenomenology of eye-to-eye empathic responsiveness. In Warren's community, every male was supposed to be "macho" and good at sports. "I was thinking a lot about life and death, writing songs and poems secretly, and this wasn't something I could discuss with the guys on the football team. The conversations I had with Bonnie were the first I ever had with a grown-up person about serious things, and she helped me see it wasn't a problem to have these feelings, which I had thought it was. Anything tender or anything about feelings, you had to hide it or ignore it. With her, I didn't have to."

Similarly, Gerald remembered that it was a friend of his parents who first took his political ideas seriously. "He really seemed interested in what I had to say," said Gerald, who felt that he was being taken for a "mature person" instead of a kid for the first time.

Even as the self firms in adulthood, we continue to need others to acknowledge us as who we are. Even the most integrated personalities, taken out of a responsive, acknowledging environment, will tend to fragment in the absence of validating response (Wolf, 1980).

The persisting need for empathy not only serves structure

and growth but also sustains us through whatever frustrations and disappointments there may be. The feeling of being understood empowers our coping mechanisms. The simple fact of someone else knowing what we are going through gives us courage to go on. Repeatedly, people within the research study emphasized the importance of empathic others as central ties in their lives. Desires to be understood were expressed more poignantly than any others. Beyond sex, beyond fears of loss and abandonment, wishes simply to be known and accepted seemed to be closest to the core of what people wanted from each other.

Melanie spoke of a painful adolescence: she had felt awkward and alone, set apart from her less inhibited, more adventurous peers and distant from her mother, who was preoccupied with a handicapped younger child. Melanie grew tearful thinking and talking about her mother. "She took care of us, but it was a different kind of caring. I could never talk to her or anything like that. She was busy trying to take care of the house, and I got to help with that—we had moved a lot." Melanie was terrified of her violent father, although he could be quite tender when she was sick. The most important person throughout her life was her Aunt Lydia, who—just nine years older than she—always seemed to understand her. "There wasn't much she could do about any of it, but she was supportive, believed in me, was never critical, just there—really my anchor. I could go there after school, and I could tell her things. When my minister began doing weird [sexual] stuff with me, Lydia was the only person I felt I could talk to about it. I didn't know how to feel about it."

The most connected, related people in the interview group all seemed to have had such people whom they could rely on for empathic response. Melanie's descriptions of Lydia suggest that Lydia was an intuitively caring and responsive person with a bountiful capacity for empathy. Other subjects in the sample, however, seemed able to "create" an empathic person from an uncritical available one. Helen, for example, always felt that her silent grandfather "understood" her. He hardly ever spoke, but she believed that he knew what she felt.

Wilma, an eighteen-year-old patient of mine, wanted to be in therapy but found it almost impossible to talk to me. So great was her conviction that no one could ever understand her that she was utterly paralyzed about sharing her inner experiences. Wilma was the unwanted child of hard-driving, embattled professional parents who were eager to develop her sports talent into a tennis championship. Practicing many hours a day, she felt that she existed only to win.

Wilma seemed not to have a language for any of her inner experiences, except that she noticed she was very depressed and isolated. Having given up tennis, much to her parents' dismay, she had no idea how to envision a life for herself. Wilma came to her therapy hours and looked at me, stared at me, as though I were perhaps a tennis opponent. It was extremely difficult to begin the hours. She felt herself empty, with nothing to say, and she experienced my questions and efforts to be empathic as attacks. With much time, she gradually began to perceive that I was attempting to know how she felt, from her inside perspective. Once I asked her if she had ever felt understood. With much shame, she told me about her cat, which she often felt really knew and could understand her pain. Her memory of this cat and her ability to share this memory with me marked the beginning of her emergence from her depression.

The feeling of not being understood is one of the most painful in human experience. Sullivan (1953) believed that not to be understood was tantamount to ceasing to exist, to the destruction of the self. Despite friends and lovers, despite attachments to others and embeddedness in a human network, we may nevertheless feel painfully not understood. The success of psychotherapy in our culture rests largely on its provision of empathy (despite the theoretical and technical disguises that empathy sometimes wears). We are never so vulnerable as when we risk an aspect of the core of ourselves to the glare of misunderstanding. We are never so whole as when we feel understood.

The need to be known and thereby affirmed is fundamental. Yet, paradoxically, we can never be fully known. No one will ever completely understand how it is to be who we are. The need for empathy, then, is an effort to escape our separateness and bridge the space between. Let us return for a moment to Warren's experience. He found, once validated in his experiences by Bonnie, that he was able to have many other confidants. As he grew into adulthood, he found many other people with whom he could discuss his innermost thoughts. He liked to talk to others deeply—about the meaning of life, about what was important and what was not, what was right and wrong. What was most important to him was having people he could really open up with, and he treasured those with whom he was able to have such conversations. In general, he found intimacy easier with women, but he had close moments with men friends as well.

In reflecting on his life, however, Warren said with much pain and regret,

> But it's never happened that I had a 100 percent connection. I always had the feeling there was a limit, that that's all the intimacy I could get, and that's it. With a woman it has been easier, but I couldn't say that I could be total. Most of the time, I would be feeling something I have to hold back. There's a kind of a black hole inside me from a long time ago which tells me that I'm different, and it's bad to be different. I open it from time to time and discover things about myself and share them with others; but still I hold back, because I'm afraid that what I have there is so different that it won't be okay. I fear that it wouldn't be understood. I couldn't explain it to myself, so how could I explain it to other people?

Warren dealt with his need to try to express this inchoate part of himself by writing poems, songs, and stories. At age twenty, he gave a set of his poems to his closest friend with great trepidation. Several days later, his friend returned the poems, telling him, "They're absolutely wonderful, but I didn't understand them." Warren felt crushed and began to despair that anyone would fully and completely understand the "black hole" inside of him.

Warren was somewhat unusual among the research participants in putting authors and other heroes on his relational chart. He spent a great deal of time with Nietzsche, he explained, and sometimes he felt more understood reading the great philosophers and poets than talking with real people. Somehow they were able to articulate thoughts that he had but could not express; for him, as for many others, this was a powerful (though indirect) form of empathy.

Universally, then, at the far end of eye-to-eye experience is a "black hole" that others cannot enter. We can be seen and validated intensely and well, but never completely. Total understanding is, for some, an ideal (though never in fact reachable) goal; they make an ongoing effort to overcome the ultimate aloneness of being trapped inescapably in our own experience.

Being Known by Others

Keeping ourselves together and integrated is, as we have seen, a formidable task—one requiring the assistance of others to mirror and validate us. Beyond this emotional responsiveness and empathy, there is another kind of knowing: a knowing that is more cognitive, more reactive to our whole being and to our capacities. When others "know" us, they also store for us a record of our identity. Sometimes this is painful, as when others remember us as incompetent children and remind us of our former inadequacy. If we are haunted by past identities, we may wish to get away from people and places where we are "known" in order to begin again, hoping to be "known" by different parts of ourselves. At other times, however, people "knowing" us is a comfort. People keep for us aspects of our real selves, and in expecting us to be who we are, shield us against periods of identity loss ("Remember yourself!").

Linda was devastated after her husband, Harvey, left her for another woman. Only her sense of responsibility to her infant son kept her from suicide. She felt that she had devoted her whole self to her husband, and she felt both abandoned and annihilated by her loss of him. She felt that all that she had been had been entwined with him; when she looked in the mirror, she saw nothing at all. Psychotherapy offered her little comfort or solace. In despair, not knowing what else to do, she accepted an invitation to visit two old friends from high school who lived in a different state. Although they had met Harvey, they had not known him well. Being with them—with people who had known her before her marriage—led her to realize, to know deeply, that she had had a self before she knew Harvey. She told me later how strange it was to have people talking to her about things that did not involve Harvey. She remembered how it was to *be* and to *experience* before she even knew him. Her old friends seemed to assume that she was still a person—the Linda she had always been—instead of a discarded half of a broken couple. They had (unwittingly, perhaps) recorded for her and played back an old self. By seeing this old self in their mirror, Linda could reexperience this self, this pre-Harvey self, and could thereby envision a self and a life after Harvey as well.

In others' eyes, we may also find selves that are just a step *ahead* of where we are: a confirmation of the self that we are becoming but are not sure we are—yet. People may induce us to be a little more than what we are by "seeing" us just a bit in the future. This is often a part of what good therapists succeed in doing. It is what people mean when they say that someone "believed in me."

I recall intensely the moment when I crossed the first bridge toward knowing myself as a "real" psychologist. It was a simple moment really. One of the senior staff members of the clinic where I was an intern approached me after a meeting, smiled brightly, and said, "I have an adolescent case that you might be interested in treating." I knew that she was talking to me, yet I had to fight hard the impulse to look behind me. She *couldn't* be talking to me. Could it be that she regarded me as competent enough or grown-up enough to "treat a case"? Feeling like an imposter, I had to respond appropriately, *as though* I were the person she thought I was, taking on the mantle, knowing that I would have to learn to carry it. And this was just the first of many such moments. It did not settle things; there was no magic in it. After twenty-five years of practice, I still struggle with whether I am really up to the task, and I need to see myself still in other' eyes in order to know.

Who we are in others' eyes affects our sense of our own reality—who we are in our own eyes. If we are not psychotic, we need others to validate our experience of ourselves and, beyond that, to offer us sometimes a better version of ourselves than we know ourselves to be.

Eye-to-Eye Acceptance and Rejection

The eyes that look at us can also misapprehend; they can see in us what is not there or can impose on us aspects of self that are not natively our own. The eyes that see us can reject what we are and compel us to be otherwise. Winnicott (1965c) called our attention to the false self that develops when children forego their own nature in order to please their parents. That false self is an effort to find favor, quite literally, in someone else's eyes. The child may attempt to become what someone else wants him to be, to think, to feel, even to want. The press and demands of the environment work against being able to match spontaneous inner experience with a welcoming response in the interpersonal world. As a result, the developing child represses what feels genuine and real and molds himself to well-socialized acceptability. When one acts only in reaction to another's demands or wishes, one develops as an extension of the environment rather than unfolds from one's own core.

The "trueness" or "falseness" of the self that develops is a function of the acceptance that the growing child finds in the world. Moving out of the unconditional love of infancy (which was there if the child was fortunate) where the infant matters just for existing, the child discovers that love and acceptance have terms and conditions. In others' eyes, we learn to read what is valued and what is not. We learn that there are limits to what we can express of ourselves. We learn that the love of the world does not evolve from our *being* but is predicated on what we *do*.

Beyond knowing that we are, beyond being able to empathically understand our communications, other people also regard us through their own eyes, evaluating us, deciding if we are all right with them. In the experience of eye-to-eye acceptance, we find ourselves approved of, with varying degrees of enthusiasm, not only for our being but for our doing—our expression of ourselves, which is also important. (Mattering is "I see *that* you are, and that brings me joy." Acceptance is "I see *what* you are, and I value you for that.") We learn as babies that, although we may be fundamentally valued by someone, some of our activities bring pleasure and smiles while others bring frowns and reproval.

Once babies become cognitively able to make the link between actions and the (m)Other's response, they can wonder about the meaning of the mother's approval or disapproval. The interpretation of this all-important communication becomes central to personality development. Some children are more able than others to distinguish between "I don't like what you're doing" and "I don't like you"; and some mothers are better at communicating this than others, of course. If children are able to make this distinction, they can decide whether or not to modify the unpopular behavior. But some children can manage only the other interpretation: "When mother looks angry, hollers, hits, and withdraws affection and smiling eyes, that must mean that I'm bad." Repeated instances of rejection can thus be seriously damaging to self-esteem.

More lethal still, the interpretation of disapproval may endanger connection on other relational dimensions as well: "Mother dislikes me, so she may leave me" or "Mother is angry and will not feed me" or "The world is too fragile to contain my impulses, and I may destroy it if I'm not careful." Rejection—the loss of eye-to-eye approval—necessitates whatever coping resources or defenses the individual can muster. Pathological defenses in this domain become the root of many emotionally troubled states in adulthood.

As we grow, the locus of eye-to-eye experience shifts to ever-widening circles as we learn what meaning we have to increasing numbers of others who see us from outside. We learn, however painfully, that we are imperfect. We are judged cute or smart or funny or musical or aggressive or slow-learning or funny-looking or unlikable. We may try to match these judgments against something that we experience in ourselves, trying to see whether they are modifiable. Often, however, if people do not experience themselves as aggressive or slow-learning or unlikable, they simply feel labeled, unmirrored. Then they must learn either to live in an irrational world or to absorb the label, however misapplied, into themselves.

Until the middle of childhood, children take for granted that they are who they are and that others are how they ought to be. It is not until age seven or eight that children begin to conceptualize the differences among themselves and to categorize each other. They find that some are better in school, some better in sports, some prettier, some braver. They learn that they are being identified by the world around them. These perceptions, too, must be integrated into the sense of self (or sometimes warded off).

The peer group of adolescence has been of interest to psychology in terms of its role in helping the adolescent separate from the family of origin. In the theory of adolescence, peers have been seen to provide "ego support" to the adolescent who is detaching from dependence on the parents. But the eye-to-eye role of peers has been largely overlooked. The investment of adolescents with peers serves the purpose of finding a place with the contemporaries with whom life will be spent. Toward the end of childhood, growing people begin to learn about how they will be identified by an often merciless group of judges who notice—and harshly comment on—whatever they say or wear, people they see, and whatever tastes and personal preferences are visible to them.[5] "That sweater is geeky." "How can you be friends with such a twerp?" "Don't act like a nerd." Judgments such as these are the stuff of young people's conversation. Never are people more unforgiving mirrors for each other than in youth. Never are people so controlling of one another.

The outcome of this painful phase of development is a sense of how one is "seen" by others. The developing person learns about his or her worth, who he or she is, in others' eyes.

Jill, a thirty-year-old unmarried waitress, told of being "devastated" in adolescence when a boy who dated her a couple of times began dating someone else. She concluded that she must be a "creep." She lost all confidence in herself until, two years later, another boy, to her great surprise, "picked me over one of my friends." These experiences seem to have had little to do with passion or attachment or mutuality. Rather, they were part of Jill's efforts to learn about her value in the marketplace of heterosexual selection.

Rejection, the negative pole of eye-to-eye acceptance, is a terribly painful state against which people build complex defenses. To be rejected is to be negatively valued—although, in some instances, this may be preferable to having no account at all. Being ignored is not to be seen by others, to be of no value to them. Being an object of scorn or hatred is at least to have presence. But such experiences of rejection often invoke self-hatred and uncontrollable aggression. Fears of rejection are often great enough that people will learn to contort themselves far from their inner predilections, to eschew individuality in favor of safe and acceptable conformity.

As people tell their relational histories, themes of acceptance and rejection reverberate louder than just about all other relational themes. Claire, for example, described all of her relationships as a quest to find someone somewhere who would fully accept her exactly as she is—something she was finally able to find in her current husband. What she emphasized as important in her marriage was neither physical attraction nor mutual interests. Primary to Claire was the sense that her husband was someone she was all right with, no matter what. This gave her the freedom to pursue her high-risk career in a venture-capital firm, to decide not to have children, and to be herself as fully as possible. She felt that she could always count on her husband to accept her and value her, unquestioningly and unconditionally. How different this felt to Claire from everyone else in her life: everyone else seemed to have expectations of her, to love her with strings attached.

Other people tell painful stories of nonacceptance, of feeling that who they are is not valued by spouses or friends. Poignant stories of efforts to be acknowledged and valued by parents often end with either resignation or rage. Sometimes, however, they have happy endings. Barbara told of how she sought throughout her life to have her uneducated mother value her intellectual achievements. When she wanted to go to college, her mother thought it a waste of money, so Barbara paid her own way through a state university. At graduation, her mother said only, "Now are you going to get married?"

Barbara worked in advertising for several years, until one day she ran into a former classmate who was finishing her doctorate in literature, the field that Barbara had majored in. This old friend reported that something Barbara had once said in a class had sparked her thesis investigation. Meditating on her friend's image of her as an insightful literary critic, Barbara decided to return to graduate school herself. Her mother was uncomprehending; she could not imagine why Barbara would waste her time and money and forgo marriage just to stay a student and sit in musty libraries. But when Barbara finished her doctoral work and gave her mother a bound copy of her thesis, she saw a light in her mother's eyes that she had never seen before. Through tears, her mother looked at her and said, "So *this* is what you have been doing all these years—writing a book. *A book!*" and hugged her. A book was something concrete that her mother could understand. Finally, there was a link of understanding—and acceptance—between them.

Parents are certainly the first and central figures with whom a sense of self-esteem and acceptability must be consolidated. Yet agemates offer another and often more exacting set of hurdles that must be traversed. Most of my research participants spontaneously narrated an account of how they were viewed by their peers at various stages. This served to sketch the backdrop against which their development took place. Men almost universally reported their size: being short is a serious developmental deficit for a boy, largely because athletic prowess is essential for achieving an adequate social rank. For girls, shyness and overweight are similar handicaps to feeling accepted. Accumulated rejections by peers for whatever reason lead to the expectation of continued rejection and may produce serious withdrawal from others. Not surprisingly, those in my survey who felt essentially accepted by at least some of their agemates told very different life stories from those who did not.

Where the negative pole of attachment is loss of the all-important Other, in eye-to-eye relatedness we fear losing the *love* of the Other. Our need in eye-to-eye relatedness is not just for the Other's presence but for his or her admiration, understanding, or approval.

In the narrative of research subjects' lives, the tension and interest around eye-to-eye recognition and acceptance is at its height from age ten through early adulthood. As I have noted, this is a time for discovering how we are seen by others: which views of us from others are idiosyncratic and which predictable. We also explore which aspects of the self are malleable and which are fixed. A boy may learn, for example, that although Georgie down the street says that he is a pimply faced creep with the cooties, most people think that he is reasonably attractive. Similarly, a girl may learn that no matter how much time she spends on her hair and how expensive the makeup she buys, she will never be responded to as a raving beauty.

By the time people reach age twenty-five or so, they seem to have accumulated enough experiences in reality to know about how smart, attractive, likable, funny, competitive, hostile, and so on they will appear to others. They have made their own acquaintance and take themselves more for granted. They have also largely come to appreciate the fact that people can have relational needs met—

needs for empathy, resonance, affection, attachment, and so on—even if they are not especially smart, attractive, or likable. They have, in a sense, come full circle in finding at least some people who will take them as they are.

John, an extremely handsome young male patient with a fragile self and bizarre obsessive-compulsive symptoms, found it terribly painful to be with people. His tension with others was so great that he could not relax. He feared particularly the attentions of women and the competitiveness of men. His first encounters with others were stiff and distant, and he realized that people therefore regarded him as strange. Unable to modify his "strange" behavior, he was finally able to live with their view of him; he came to recognize that people regarded him as strange because he behaved in a strange way. This in turn allowed him to behave a little less strangely with them.

Another patient, fifteen-year-old Stephanie, always wore a large-brimmed cowboy hat. After I got to know her, I was able to ask why she wore the hat. She said that it was easy to explain: people made fun of her for wearing the hat. But that way, when people made fun of her, she knew that it was because of the hat.

The worst fear for both John and Stephanie was to be rejected for something inexplicable—to feel simply, profoundly, and irreparably unacceptable. The experience of rejection becomes more manageable, however, when we can place it in a context in which our whole self is not being rejected or in which the rejection results from an incapacity in the other person rather than in the self. Cognitive restructuring therapies operate strongly on this theme, reinterpreting rejections to preserve a sense of the self's intrinsic worth.

Shame is the result of putting forward some valued part of ourselves and seeing revulsion in another's eyes. At the far end of shame is the experience of annihilation, which is, more generally, the negative pole of eye-to-eye experience. The unmirrored self fragments. In its failure to maintain its cohesion, it confronts the dangers of annihilation. Thus empathic, valuing, and accepting eye-to-eye responses of others are essential emotional nutrients; without them we cannot be.

Joan

The middle of three sisters who were a year apart in age, Joan grew up in a small town in a close family, surrounded by a large extended family. Joan's mother put a lot of energy into entertaining the children, taking them to plays and movies, reading them stories, involving them in projects and games. By contrast, Joan's father was largely absent. He was very busy, rushing from one job and responsibility to the next, with little time to be with his children. Joan's grandmother, who lived nearby, always seemed happy when she and her sisters came over to spend time with her.

Joan felt that she and her sisters grew up as a group and were treated as a group. But Joan, looking back, felt that she, more than they, needed to have her parents' interest and affection. "I seemed to be more interested in being close to both my parents and finding ways in which I could get their attention and find things of common interest with them. I tried to be like them so I could find common things. They always used to say I was the good girl who never gave them any trouble. I was the pleaser; they were satisfied with me."

Joan always felt secure that there were caring people nearby. There were always aunts and uncles and cousins available to be with when her parents were busy. There were many homes where she could go to watch television, stay for dinner, play, or just spend time. Joan felt welcomed and free to roam. When her parents traveled, it was easy for her to stay with other relatives or with her friends' families.

Competitive with her sisters for her parents' love, Joan did not feel close to them. Even as young as age five, she preferred to play with her own friends. Trying as hard as she could to ignore her sisters, Joan attempted to be a leader among her friends and organize activities with and for them. She thinks of herself at around this age as trying to be like an adult; she would try to be the helper of the kindergarten teacher and the one among the class who could be relied upon to be responsible.

Drawing her life at age ten, Joan featured a "boyfriend" who had become important to her at age eight. He was from her class at school, and "we considered ourselves like a couple, really good friends. We even thought we would get married, like a dream. We really felt we were in love." Joan remembers her longing at this age to be part of the adult world, and having a boy to be with in a special way made her feel grown-up.

Going to school in this small community, she felt very much a part of her class. But it was hard to feel close to any specific person when there was so much of a group feeling. She took part in lots of activities with her group, including Scouts, church, extracurricular classes, and trips and outings on weekends. Of this small, bucolic environment, Joan said, "I always felt it was an ideal setting, thought it was wonderful to be with friends and cousins doing interesting things together. When we were together, it would be a warm feeling of togetherness, but there wasn't the distinction of talking about personal things, like my relations with the family. It wouldn't seem appropriate to share feelings with them."

Around this time, age ten, Joan began to sense some reserve in herself toward her family. She felt that the expression of affection did not come freely to her. She had a sense of wanting to be close to her parents but felt that it was hard for all of them to really let themselves experience the closeness.

> I was closer to the kids my age. That took a lot of my attention. My family got to be farther in focus. Usually my parents were very busy and into other things, and I didn't really feel their presence with me. I guess I just gave up, didn't feel it was possible any more. I was aware of the gap between how I would have wanted the relationship to be and how it was. I felt that there was some kind of distance between me and them. If I tried to talk to my mother, she wasn't really with me. She was spacing out. With my father, we would usually talk about intellectual things, and I also felt that he is not really aware of what is happening to me in other parts of my life. I tried to be accepted by him, did things to be closer to him. I looked up to him. My parents were very proud of me. They weren't aware of my difficulties. They didn't really know me.

Even her grandmother was by now at a greater distance. "She was better for younger children. As we grew older, she had a hard time relating to us. I wasn't drawn to her so much any more."

With her extended family, Joan was also feeling more hesitant and distant. "I didn't feel as comfortable to go to their houses. I was more self-conscious and shy, felt maybe I wasn't so accepted there: like not being so sure if they liked me or not—if they really wanted me there."

Even by age ten, Joan had a strong sense of how she was expected to be and felt unable to "express fears or the dark things about me. I always felt I had to be strong and appropriate, and there were sides I couldn't show. I couldn't act silly. I was very serious."

In the midst of her adolescence, at age fifteen, Joan found herself increasingly critical of her mother. She felt that her mother was too different, too spontaneous. She wanted her to care more about what people thought, as Joan did, and not dress in unusual outfits or act so much like a teenager herself. Joan tried to be close to her older sister at this time, but their competition got in the way. She felt vulnerable and felt that her sister criticized her and put her down.

For the first time, Joan began having trouble with her schoolwork. The math had gotten beyond her, but she feared to let anyone know. When she could no longer hide her failing grades, she confided in her father and was glad to find him supportive of her. "For the first time, I felt that I could express my weaknesses a little bit. I felt I could be accepted even though I have all those faults."

Joan was closest during this time to two boys. With Ned, a friend three years older who had moved to another state, she felt safe to confide some of her estrangement from her family. She could "open up" some to Ned. In the safe and passionate relationship that they created together, mostly in letters, they fantasized about the relationship they were having and agonized about missing each other. (They saw each other only rarely.) Joan could talk to Ned because he was an outsider and far enough away that she could risk sharing more of her inner self.

Joan's other close friend was Ralph, with whom she had her first sexual relationship. They had fun together, but the relationship was mostly physical. He was from a lower social class and adored her. It was nice to be with him, because he completely accepted her; she was able to feel free and comfortable.

By age twenty, off at college, Joan found herself part of several different groups of friends. She joined a commune with some of the people she had grown up with, trying to make a safe environment with lots of sharing in the shadow of a large, impersonal state university. Again Joan emerged a leader, but she did not feel particularly close to anyone. She was responsible, looked to as someone who could take care of things, but she feared to show her "darker" side to anyone. People relied on her, counted on her strength and competence; they were blind to the conflict and pain that flickered beneath her polished surface.

Joan was able to find some closeness with Mel, who seemed patient enough to try to know her. She felt able to open up to him some, but he finally left the commune and went in search of himself elsewhere. Joan then turned to Larry, although she did not feel as comfortable with him. Larry "wasn't open himself. He had a hard time expressing feelings and really talking about things. But I felt that he was interested in me and wanted to be close and really put energy into maintaining the relationship."

Although far away at college, Joan worked hard to maintain contact with the people she had grown up with. "We really had to work to keep these relationships going. There was this deep feeling of connection with the people at home, because we grew up together and had been through everything together; so there was a feeling of commitment. I had a strong feeling of being connected to a group and having closer people around me when I went home. Being with these old friends met a strong social need, even though I couldn't talk to them about my new experiences or what I had been feeling."

When she was home for vacations, Joan tried again to be closer to her father. "I still looked up to him and gave him a lot of credit for his work. My own interests in computers were close to his, so we had many things in common. I tried to include him in my life in many things and get closer to him. It worked, but I always felt frustrated that we weren't close enough. He was interested but still very busy with what he was doing, so he couldn't really be there when I needed him. I had a hard time really expressing myself with him.''

Joan sensed her mother, on the other hand, trying to be closer to her, but she said that her mother "didn't really know how to relate to me. She didn't feel comfortable next to me. She was into herself with the different problems she had, couldn't really come out of herself. She seemed not to be so much in touch with reality. She was always very idealistic, and she didn't see problems. If I tried to tell her about a problem, or about any of my fears or doubts, she would be shocked and get really depressed.''

Joan's main focus in life by age twenty-five was to try to develop more personal relationships with people. She was building a thriving career as a computer programmer but felt that her main business in life was trying to develop herself as a person. Surrounded by people, she still felt isolated.

Henry, her most recent boyfriend, had helped her learn to come out of the shell that she felt imprisoned her. "He was very different from my father—very easygoing, more spontaneous, not as intellectual or serious. I felt I could really feel free with him and express myself pretty much, even though I always had a sense of wanting the relationship to be more than what it was. I felt he knew me, at least better than anyone else ever had, and I wanted to matter more to him. We were lovers and friends, but he didn't want any kind of a commitment." When Henry was offered a job in another city, Joan felt that she had to learn to live alone. The challenge was to tolerate the end of the closeness with Henry without retreating into her shell.

For the first time, Joan began to have emotionally close relationships with women friends. She joined a religious group and found a few friends with whom she could share feelings and experiences, although she continued to struggle with her tendency to hold herself back and feel unfree in a relationship, still fearing to express herself emotionally. Through her increasing awareness of herself and through close relationships with other people, Joan began to see her mother more clearly. She began to fill in the spaces that had always made her mother seem so vacant and began to form a more mature picture of who her mother really was. In doing this, Joan began to feel more "known" to her mother as well.

As Joan became more able to articulate her experience of distance from others, she found that her younger sister felt much the same way she did. This discovery of a common struggle brought them together, and they began to explore the similarities in their personalities and early histories. This shared inner search brought them together for the first time in their lives, and Joan now regards her younger sister as her best friend.

Together, she and her sister have begun to approach their father to talk about how they have all come to feel so far from each other emotionally. "We started talking about very personal things, including our relationship and what has happened through the years. I started seeing him more as an equal, stopped looking up to him, and we became friends. I started seeing many things in our personalities that are similar."

Joan discusses all the other friends and people in her life in terms of how well they know her and how much of herself she can express with them. Nell, a woman she works closely with, is important because "I feel very open and natural—can be myself without a need to judge myself for things. She accepts me, and that helps me really accept myself as I am." She continues to feel frustrated in her distant relationship with her older sister. "I really wish I could make her understand how I see things, but we don't see each other very much."

Of Marty, a friend from her computer consultation group, she says, "I can share with him things that happen to me—things I'm concerned with and things he's concerned with in his family. I used to have fantasies about him, but now we know it's a brother-sister relationship."

With Don, her occasional lover, "It's a very open kind of relationship. I can express my feelings. We get into a lot of arguments and can get closer from it. We can feel close physically; we just share things together." With Ben, a friend from her religious group, she has a strong friendship. "I feel close to him spiritually. We just feel that we know each other—really *clearly*—like we can really see each other and talk about things that touch us deeply."

At age twenty-six, then, Joan is intensely involved in trying to bring her real self to her relationships with others, to be seen and recognized, to take the risk of revealing herself and being known. Growing up in what appears to have been a relational environment of security and attachment, Joan purchased a "special" place in the family at the price of becoming a "pleaser," as she put it. She learned to be an exceptionally good girl, burying all that might not be so acceptable and lovable in herself. In her eagerness to be other than part of a group of sisters, Joan hurried herself to be "grown-up" and join her parents. To do this, she had to disavow her silliness and immaturity—all the feelings that are natural to a child, to which a child is entitled. But early on, when she began to sense that she had left an important part of herself behind, she began to struggle with when and if she dared risk her success as an admired leader, exemplary daughter, and outstanding student by exposing what she felt to be the "darker" parts of herself. Since then, Joan has begun connecting to others based on the degree to which she feels that they are people who can accept and respond to the more emotional and thus more vulnerable and "real" parts of herself. She intensely needs people to validate her inner experiences rather than just to expect her to do what she is supposed to do. She needs people who will mirror and hear her rather than "space out" (as she felt her mother did). She wants, however ambivalently, people to "know" her.

Like many other people, especially many young people, Joan focuses on others to see herself in their eyes, hoping to find in their acceptance of her a path to acceptance of herself. Easily finding a place in a group, feeling part of a group, Joan hopes to see in others the secret of her own uniqueness but fears being too unique, too different. The problem, then, of being for others versus being herself with others dominates Joan's odyssey of connection to others.

Transparency: An Excess of Being Known

Although most people who have not been too traumatized by rejection or injury strive for more and more communication of self with the interpersonal world, there is still often a need to reserve a part of ourselves as secret and private—or at least to know that we *can*. "There's something I've never told you," my patients tell me defiantly when they feel that they are too much known, too unseparate, when they are fearful that there is too little space between us. Laing (1965) points out that at the far edge of being known are the dangers of too-fragile boundaries. If those boundaries are breached, the self is vulnerable to invasion or engulfment. As autonomous selves, we wish to choose how much of ourselves we will share with those who matter to us. Being seen when we do not want to be feels like invasion or control.

Louisa, a research participant and thirty-year-old social worker, grew up with the fantasy that her mother was omniscient, knew all her secrets. One day in first grade, she skipped school with a friend, only to have her mother greet her hours later with an angry question about her activities. This felt to Louisa like evidence of her mother's capacity to "see through" her, and she felt helpless, unsure how to feel really separate from her mother. This fantasy of her mother left Louisa with a lifelong struggle about how to guard her privacy. She hesitated to tell others more about herself than they "needed to know" and learned to be close to others by being the person other people brought their problems to. But when it came to saying anything about herself, she would become frightened, unable to share any but the most superficial details. When I interviewed Louisa, she began the meeting by bursting into tears. She had agreed to be interviewed as a first step in trying to talk about herself, as a way of trying to get the courage to see a therapist.

People without a firm sense of self, for whom empathic responsiveness was absent or problematic from the beginning, must struggle very hard to be able to experience empathy in later stages of development. For such people, being known is likely to seem hostile or dangerous. Not having firm boundaries of self and other across which eye-to-eye experience can take place, they feel without skin.

My "silent" patient, Wilma—once she became able to talk to me—told me how it had felt to her all those silent months. At times she had wished I was like her cat, able to understand her without her saying anything at all. But at the same time, that prospect terrified her. If I could know all her thoughts without her saying anything, she would have no defense against me: I would take her over (as her parents had), and she would be like my puppet, without a self.

The experience of transparency is an experience of loss of control about what "shows." Although this is most often found in borderline or psychotic states, it is also a piece of nonpsychotic relational development. Fears of being naked and on display—caught "with one's pants down," open to the derision of unempathic eyes—disrupt our connections to others and lead us to wish to cover ourselves and hide what may be vulnerable. Eye-to-eye contact must be calibrated and appropriate; too much can be as painful as too little. Sometimes we need to hide.

Chapter 7

Idealization and Identification

I should never have believed it if anyone had told me I could love like this," he said. "It is not like anything I ever felt before. The whole world is divided into two halves for me now: one is she, and there all is joy, hope, light; the other is where she is not, and there all is gloom and darkness.

—Leo Tolstoy, *War and Peace*

Idealization is an internal process that draws us toward others in an effort to possess them or their qualities. We may wish to possess people externally, by controlling or "owning" them in some way, or we may be content to identify with them: to "have" them internally, as people we carry with us or try to become like. The domain of idealization in relatedness begins developmentally with the recognition that those others whom we have discovered, who have their own (shareable) experience, have qualities and capabilities that differ from our own. With adequate cognitive maturation, awareness of the self and of others leads inevitably to comparison and to the further awareness that others have attributes that we ourselves do not.

When we idealize others, we locate in them qualities that we wish to own for ourselves. Our concern here is not with the qualities that we do possess (as in eye-to-eye relatedness); nor are we concerned with drive gratification or attachment. Rather, our longing is toward possession of that which is outside of ourselves that appears far grander than what we know ourselves to be.

All writers about love and about relatedness have commented on the human tendency to idealize, and they have remarked on our need for others at various periods of our life to embody or personify our idealizations.[1] Other people represent for us what may be possible, what we might strive toward. Since ancient times, love has been defined as a longing for perfection (Singer, 1987).

The Nature of Idealization

Although the experience of idealization can take many forms, the core of this domain is expressed by the wish to follow someone into new, perhaps dimly perceived realities and to in some way enlarge the self with the substance of another. We may look to others to expand our awareness, we may wish for some kind of possession of another's perfection, or we may consciously identify with and try to become like someone we admire. Each of these experiences involves focus on qualities in others that lead to modifications in the self. In this form of relatedness, people profoundly move us and shape us—but in a very different way from those relational modes we have already considered.

Idealization tends to involve internal links—inner conversations with people who are important to us. We may be deeply connected to our important, idealized others without seeking proximity to them, or we may intensely desire physical closeness. The phenomenology of idealization is not always observable, nor is it predictable. Idealization comprises a savoring of others in which we review and replay them in fantasy, imagining the self linked to them and to their perfection. Again there is paradox here, for we grope toward what must remain out of our reach. To attain an idealized other is to lose him or her—at least as an *idealizable* other. Many a lover has found that the loved one's perfection pales with his or her availability. Successfully identifying with the aspects that we admire in someone may also mean the end of the (external) relationship. Thus many people report "growing out" of relationships with mentors and leaders and lovers once their capacities have been internalized.

Idealization is necessary to growth. Only when idealization is present is there a joyous sense of vista and motion, or transcendence of the boundaries of self and limitation.

Idealization and Perfection

Deep in our mythology and in our individual psyches is an image of omnipotent perfection, in which one can do and have everything one might wish. Our developmental theories start with an image of infantile omnipotence, a fantasy-dominated period in which infants harbor the conviction that they can command perfect attention and perfect satiety. Although one cannot verify through any empirical means that the human begins life with this experience of perfection—an experience which is soon lost—this idea is the starting point for all theories of narcissism and relatedness. It is also the starting point for the dominant mythology of our cultural origin: in the beginning was the perfection of Eden. There was Paradise, and inevitably it was lost. The image of lost paradise, which echoes deeply at archetypal levels, has psychic roots that seem to reach to our earliest awareness.

We begin in infancy with a primitive and pervasive experience of power, having the illusion of commanding the world. But this early period of infantile omnipotence rapidly gives way to a recognition of the limits of the self. One is not only *not* the one in control of all the good things that happen, there is another being who controls these things. The long period of dependency in childhood gives humans extended time to experience existence among those who are stronger, more agile, more knowledgeable, and more competent. We spend many years surrounded by danger and mystery in the presence of those who seem to know how to keep safe and who have plumbed the enigmas of how things work. We rue our own inadequacy but rest secure in the capacity of others. We may not be omnipotent, but *they* are; and someday (we hope) we, too, will be all-powerful.

Alecia, a forty-five-year-old teacher and mother of three, spoke sadly of how, in the "old days" of her childhood, grown-ups were really grown-ups. They knew how to do things; they were certain and in charge. Now that generation is dying, and there will be no more grown-ups. Certainly Alecia herself has never felt that she was as "grown-up" as her parents seemed to be.

The desire for the Other in this form of relatedness is for those powers and attributes that we do not have but long to have, and this longing comes to form the nucleus of our ambitions. That the adult can do what the child cannot becomes a source of both frustration and possibility. Although the child may feel small, there is a thrill in reaching toward those who offer themselves for idealization. "Now *I* will try to do that . . . someday."[2]

From the child's point of view, the problem becomes one of how to participate in and possess parental omnipotence. One possibility is to attempt to please or to unite with parents in order to participate in their powers or to have control of them. Another route is through identification, taking in the image of the parents as an ideal that forms the template of the child's growth. Children consciously strive to become like their parents (and others), to do the admirable things that they can do. Learning, in this way, becomes a form of love.

As development proceeds, the parents are less and less idealized. The young person, usually at adolescence, strives to come to terms with having real rather than ideal parents but searches for others who seem to possess the idealized qualities that the parents once exemplified. Adolescents may "fall in love" with a new hero in the yearning to possess for themselves the grandeur of the Other. To be in the presence of an idealized other is exciting, because it promises the possibility of once more being united with the fantasy of perfection.

Idealization is sometimes intense, and it may or may not be blended with passionate desire as well. Most contemporary psychoanalytic writers (Viederman, 1988; Bergmann, 1987) emphasize the idealizing aspects of falling in love. The beloved is a representation of the idealized parents of childhood, embodying all that is desirable and perfect. Ethel Person (1988) goes beyond this in pointing out that some people are indeed more idealizable than others, and that idealization, while far from reality in its one-sided affect, is often nevertheless based on some actual attributes of the loved Other.

Heinz Kohut's fresh approach to the understanding of idealizing phenomena in psychotherapy was derived from his observation of his patients' idealizing transferences (1977). He began to see that his patients' belief in the perfection of their analyst were not simply defenses against rage or defenses against castration fears. Nor, he learned, was it useful to call his patients' attention to their lack of reality testing by pointing out his actual lack of perfection. Kohut understood that his patients' belief in his perfection was often necessary to their process of organizing an adequate sense of self. The self is partly a product of ambition and dreams, and these are morsels that people absorb through contact with others. We orient and integrate ourselves in part through our experiences with idealizable others—people whom Kohut terms "idealizable selfobjects." His terminology indicates that such people are people who embody our ideals and inform our own ambitions, their importance residing in the space between us—part self and part other.

These idealized others who shape our life are therefore part real and part imaginary. Arthur was the most important man in Eve's life. He was her French professor in college, and she fell in love with him the moment he walked into the classroom. He seemed like a Greek god. His mind, his body, his style, his sophistication— all seemed to embody a perfection that Eve had never known in real life. Desperate to win him, she became his star pupil. She made a dramatic suicide gesture when she finally had to realize that he was gay and therefore unwinnable.

Nevertheless, Arthur changed Eve's life inexorably, as she made efforts to possess him in whatever other ways she could. They had a great friendship, and he was an ardent supporter of her work and her talents. She felt that he was her champion and master. He got her excited about literature and encouraged her to work toward a doctorate. Eve followed Arthur's example and advice: she applied to a graduate program in French literature at Stanford and was awarded a major fellowship. All the while that she studied, although she was physically far from him, she felt very close to him. As the years passed and Eve saw Arthur less and less, she nevertheless continued to think of him and to imagine talking to him every day. In fact, her fantasy life with Arthur has continued throughout her life. She tells him (in her imagination) about how she is and what she is doing, making her own experience more real to herself.

Captured by the intellectual dazzle, the sophistication, and the glamour that Arthur put before her, Eve wanted to own him in some way. As so often happens, Eve experienced and expressed this wish as sexual desire, as a wish to "have" him sexually. But with such access blocked by his lack of sexual interest in her, she began to identify with him instead, to organize her own talents and energies toward as much union with him as possible. Identification thus became another way to have Arthur inside of her. Embodying her vision of perfection, Arthur formed the core of Eve's adult ideals.

Idealization, therefore, affords two interpersonal responses. Either we try to possess and control the idealized person or we try, through identification, to become like that person.

Idealization and Romance

The desire to possess the idealized Other is the core of romantic love. Although sexual passion can get attached to this impulse in complicated ways, sexuality is often the means of possession rather than the nature of the impulse itself. Conversely, some of the most intense romantic (idealized) relationships are never consummated. What is central to desire in this context is the belief that our loved object is ideal and the wish to own this idealization for oneself.

In classical psychoanalytic thought, these desires have their roots in the oedipal desire for possession of the idealized parent—a desire for *exclusive* possession, to own completely all of what is perfect. Throughout life, however, others (beyond our parents) seem idealized to us, and we may find ourselves wishing to "have" them. In possessing these perfect others, we ourselves will be aggrandized, linked to flawlessness and superiority, at one with the gods. (Greek mythology frequently takes up this fantasy of becoming one of the Immortals—a fantasy endemic to all aspects of human achievement.)

Well beyond the Oedipus complex, idealization is a response to our own vulnerability and lack of knowledge: we need to believe that someone else has the mastery that we ourselves lack. Grace, a violinist patient of mine, spoke of her sense that her music professors were like the gods on Olympus—people larger than life whom she could never join. Yet she felt that if she could form a special bond with them, really *matter* to one of them, she would be on an intermediate plane, linked to the greatness that she dreamed of. The way to attract their attention, of course, was to practice the violin diligently. Grace used her idealization as a way of bridging to and bringing forth her own skill, but the intensity of her idealization kept her from ever feeling good enough. She preserved her ideali-

zation at the price of intense envy (which she could not admit) and
a strong sense of inferiority. In Grace's case, idealization both mo-
tivated and thwarted her. Year later, as an acclaimed violinist, she
always played her recitals "for" Professor Milton—who, in her imagination, always found her music less than perfect.

Idealization, then, is a relational process fraught with danger
as well as possibility. While it enlivens the self, it requires the ability to admire without too much envy and to be vulnerable without
too much shame.

In romantic expression lies the greatest hope of actual *possession* of an idealized Other. Romeo is smitten by Juliet's perfection, as are all lovers as they first behold the romanticized Other.
But again a paradox: although the desire may be for sexual union,
idealization—which is the foundation of romance—necessitates distance. The great (idealizing) romantic poetry, the poetry of chivalry
and courtly love, was, after all, written by men for married women
with whom there was no hope of sexual union. And, in their re-
moteness and disdain for their admirers, the ladies may have been
attempting to conceal the fact of their imperfection (Singer, 1987).

When we idealize others, we are ourselves elevated by contact
with them or symbols of them. We must have heroes, and we long
for connection with them. But unlike the actual proximity we seek
to attachment figures, there is often a kind of magical aspect to the
links we have to those we idealize. Bits of them take on special
meaning; our existence with them is on a special plane. We treasure
aspects of them as symbols of our connection to what is larger than
ourselves. In the beautiful contemporary film *Manon of the Spring*,
the hero spends his life secretly loving a very beautiful (idealized)
woman with whom he had a brief affair in his youth. Feeling that
she abandoned him, he never loves another. All he has left of her
is her comb, which he cherishes as a totem, a symbol of the most
intense connection he made in his life. In a very powerful final
scene, he dies with this comb in his hand. The comb, which represents his idealization (now two generations old), has given meaning to his life. It is a symbol of his encounter with Beauty, a token
of his taste of Love—his (experienced) finest moment.

Similarly, adolescents may feel aggrandized by mere contact
with their idols. "He looked at me" or "He touched me"—the teen-

ager feels blessed and often energized and empowered. We treasure our symbols of contact with idealized others as testaments to our own specialness or as harbingers of its possibility. (I have a letter from Kohut that I revere in this way.)

We need heroes and we need to be close to them. This dual need shapes our lives in powerful ways. It leads some people into cults or attracts them to charismatic leaders who they believe are larger than life. They subordinate their own initiative and desires in order to serve the leader, in the hope of creating a magical connection between them and their hero.

Passionate idealization forms a core theme for only some people; not everyone has had clear heroes. We are still unable to tell why idealization should be such an intense organizing theme for some and only a minor subtheme for others. For some, idealizations are mired in complex and conflictual psychological processes, interred beneath guilt or shame or muted by the anxiety and dread of too-painful longing. Other people temper idealization with admiration and maintain an important and enriching connection to those they term "models."

The Nature of Identification

Another avenue to possession of idealized others is through identification. We can "own" our admired and valued others by becoming like them. Thus others come to serve as blueprints for aspects of the self. Viewing others in an idealized way motivates our own resources; it makes us able to learn.

There is an enormous psychoanalytic literature on identification, because Freud was much taken with the importance of this mechanism both as a form of defense and as an aspect of normal development. His interest was primarily in the role of identification in the growth of the superego as a resolution of the Oedipus complex. As a form of relatedness, however, identification is not defensive but expansive. Because we admire, we attempt to imitate or own a particular quality.

Conscious forms of identification begin with feelings of admiration. There are, of course, many other routes to and forms of identification, and these identifications may in fact serve other aspects of relatedness (such as preservation of an inner sense of connection to feel held or validated, for example). But identification can be a form of relatedness in its own right when we seek to maintain connection with and to value someone whose qualities we seek to absorb into ourselves. Nicholas, a twenty-three-year-old carpenter whom I interviewed, felt distant from his father. They rarely spoke, but Nicholas admired his father's ability to do anything with his hands. Nicholas dreamed of having that kind of competence, that kind of hands.

Admiration and efforts to emulate form a central aspect of people's experience of others. Not surprisingly, then, it was rare for research subjects not to include in their relational spaces at least one person who was important as an object of identification. A number of subjects even included people whom they did not know—people whose writings or achievements were so important to their sense of purpose in life that they sometimes overshadowed ongoing real relationships. One thirty-five-year-old man spoke of having his most intense conversations during two years of his late adolescence with D. H. Lawrence.

Adolescent and young adult subjects, still sifting through the possibilities for their own identities, are most likely to highlight this dimension. Older adult subjects, retrospectively, are often able to see identifications that they were unaware of at the time. Many subjects say, for example, that they became more like one or the other parent than they had realized or intended to.

Conversely, however, identifications frequently melt with time. It is the fate of a successful identification to be integrated into the personality—its source faded and blurred, its final form so much edited that it is no longer solely the attribute of either the donor or the self. To describe this joint creation, mixed like paint colors in the space between, we speak of "influence" rather than identification.

Stimulation and Growth

One of the most common experiences that the research subjects reported in vital encounters with others was that of feeling stimulated, of having their awareness expanded. They talked of people who offered them something of interest or novelty that led to an enlarged experience of themselves.

When we think of postinfancy growth and development, we tend to think of expanding capacity in *abstract* terms. In fact, however, much of our learning takes place within relationships, through the direct efforts of one person to make available to another the opportunity to learn.

People (maybe especially women) move along in the world through relational connections. When we ask people about the history of the development of an interest or skill, they usually mention a *person* at the root of it. People bring to each other something new.

Mothers, of course, do this automatically with their babies. They show the babies new objects and sights. They read to them and try to expand their world. They take them for walks and outings to show them what is interesting in the world. A baby's reaction to this novelty is usually joyfulness and gratitude. Throughout life, as people continue to offer us new sights, sounds, and experiences, they become vehicles to the new as they activate our desires and lead us to reach.

Sue, a twenty-one-year-old research participant, lived with her grandparents during the week until she was eleven. She spent weekends with her mother, who worked in another town to support her after they were abandoned by Sue's father. She began her life narrative with reminiscences about her grandparents, and she organized her memory of their relationship in terms of their taking her places.

> They always did a lot of things with me. They were always out doing things and always took me with them. Always took me along—camping, out to dinner, swimming. I was probably a little closer to my grandmother, because she was the one who told my grandfather, "We're going here or there," and my grandfather would go along. My grandmother taught me how to whittle. I loved to sit with her and do this, and to this day I can whittle the most amazing animals. My grandfather used to play math games with me, and that's where I think I learned to love math.

Sue contrasts this experience of her grandparents with how she felt with her mother. When she saw her mother, now remarried, on weekends, she slept on a fold-out couch in the small living room. Often while she was visiting, her mother and her stepfather would go out, "dropping me off at someone's house so they could go. I hated her for doing that."

Sue's memory of "doing things" with her grandparents, then, exists on several dimensions. It is clearly a memory of being wanted—eye-to-eye mattering to someone who wanted her with them instead of dropping her off. But that it focuses on *activities* also speaks to the stimulation dimension. Sue's grandparents were offering her avenues to development of her own capacities. And indeed, Sue's life continues to be filled with activity, purpose, and people who light new paths for her.

We learn from each other. We bring into close contact what each of us carries of the world. In doing so, we represent possibility.

Allison

Allison grew up as the oldest of six girls. Although she remembers her mother as overburdened with housework, child care, and a difficult financial situation, her mother was the center of the family, taking good care of her and her sisters. "She was there all the time. I remember meals, walks in the garden. She was there. I remember her wearing a white uniform at home. She was functioning as a mother. She was a basis for the trust and feeling of security."

Allison's father, a government official involved in international affairs, was often absent. "I admired him. He gave me a lot of intellectual stimulation and challenges. He taught me to read early and talked to me seriously. When I was six, he left for a whole year. I remember missing him, admiring him for the important work he was doing, and I remember my mother's aggravation at being left alone to cope with all the problems."

At age ten, much of Allison's time was taken up with having to help with the care of her five younger sisters. Her primary job was to help the older ones with homework. Allison was "the smart one" of the group, which won her father's special attention. "He sometimes took me to his office and gave me work to do and then took me out to lunch at a restaurant. He was proud of me, of my knowledge, of my understanding. Sometimes he would boast about me and make me answer questions in front of the people he worked with. He was so smart and so important then. I idolized him. He introduced me to a love of history."

Allison's mother still seemed to her to have a great deal of work and responsibility all the time. She was always worrying a lot, always taking care of the children and any members of her extended family who seemed to need help. Allison saw her mother's role in her own family of origin as the one who took care of everyone else. This family had had more than its share of sickness and death, and Allison's mother was always having to figure out how to solve all the problems. "Often she seemed resentful and bitter that my father didn't help her more. I don't ever remember her laughing or playing with us. Once I remember an old girlfriend of hers from high school visiting us. She told me that my mother was so intelligent and had so much potential, and it amazed me. She never helped with my homework or did anything intellectual with me. She solved all the problems to keep us eating well and dressed well. I didn't want to be like her."

Partly because of her father's connections, Allison won a scholarship to a "classy, snobbish private school," where she became the best student in her class. She was very achievement-oriented and used school to escape from the sense of gloom and pressure at home. She also escaped to the home of Jessica, her best friend, with whom she could share confidences and talk about what she felt.

At age fifteen, Allison thought a great deal about how she was similar to and different from everyone she knew. She felt critical of her sisters, for example, for not being as conscientious about schoolwork as she, but she also admired them for their gaiety and funlovingness. She and Jessica had more and more profound, soul-searching conversations late into the night, especially about "how the two of us are different from everyone else we know."

Around this time, Allison's mother decided to return to school.

She lost weight and changed tremendously. She went back to books that I didn't even know she had. My father and I mobilized around her to support her. She worried that she had forgotten everything. We encouraged her, made her promises to help in taking care of things. My father amazed me in how much he supported that. She was proud of what she was doing. She trained as a high school science teacher. She would leave me instructions about lunch, and we all took turns with the chores. We all started to share the cooking and shopping. I was so happy she changed and was happier. I was very proud of her. She started to buy things with her own money—house decorations, clothes. I remember her pride in making her own money. She could feel free in allowing herself to do things she couldn't do before. I started to see that she has brains and knows a lot.

Still, Allison continued to idealize her father. "I felt afraid of his very clear values. To me, he was someone who knew exactly what was right and wrong. I didn't always agree, but I wasn't strong enough to confront him. So I started to hide things and only to share things we agreed about, which was in my intellectual world. I began to keep him at a safe distance in my life."

Allison had a boyfriend at this time, to the consternation of her very conservative father. She appreciated her mother's greater openmindedness; she felt that she did not have to hide her actions as much from her mother as she did from her father. When Allison and Tim used to sneak away to his house and explore sex, she felt very sinful and excited. At the same time, though, she was deeply involved in fantasies of love with a boy who hardly noticed her. This kept her from feeling that she really loved Tim, but she had a special bond with him in terms of the discoveries they were making together and the activities they shared.

Allison tried to confide in Jessica about her relationship with Tim, but Jessica, who did not have a boyfriend, did not approve of her sexual activity. Feeling torn, Allison endured a painful time. "Jessica was more important for my soul, but I needed Tim too. I was between all these people but not fully with any one of them."

Another important person at this time was Allison's history

teacher. Only five years older than she, this teacher told Allison and her classmates stories of life at the university, with which Allison was "fascinated." "She was a model for me and also gave me time, books, advice, encouragement."

There were many other friends, teachers, and groups who filled Allison's very active and rich high school life, but she recalls most at this age the people who offered her models for how she might be. One group that she was involved in, a political group, offered her a link to her father's work. "It was like a branch of him."

When at age twenty, at the university, Allison found people from diverse backgrounds, she felt emancipated from the narrow, rigid value system of her family. "I was shy and different. I was from the old world, and they were the new." Living at the university, she resented her parents' restriction of her freedom, and she struggled with them over rules that they made for her. She finally broke from them by falling in love with Juan, a Puerto Rican classmate who could not have been more different from her family (except that he, too, was an intellectual who, like Allison's father, seemed to know quite clearly what he was about).

With her new involvement with Juan, Allison cut herself off from her old identity and everyone who had mattered to her previously. Jessica had married someone from their hometown by then and could not share Allison's new ways of thinking. Allison and Juan, intensely in love, felt sufficient unto themselves; they seemed to satisfy all of each other's needs. "I was good for Juan and he was good for me, and that was it."

They continued to study together, now in graduate school in history, and they eventually married. When Allison was twenty-five, their son was born, and she viewed him as "a concrete materialization of the dream, of the love, of the change, of my new identity. I had so many expectations of him." The only other important person in Allison's life at this period was her dissertation supervisor and mentor. "We had a good relationship, because my work was always very important to me. My work was around him. He taught me, and I learned a lot. My self-esteem came from his praise."

By the age of thirty, some of Allison's idealizations had faded. With great difficulty, she had come to terms with the fact that their son, Johnny, was not the son they had hoped for. Reckless and physical, he showed little interest in learning to read. He was aggressive, not cuddly. "He was difficult. I didn't understand him. I demanded a lot from him, and I was disappointed in him. I was aware of it, but I couldn't change. Juan felt the same way. We comforted each other. We had wanted him to be bigger than life, and he wasn't."

She and Juan had their first fights over how to raise Johnny. "I learned that nothing is perfect, but the great thing is to solve problems, not to avoid them. We learned to take ourselves less seriously and with more humor. We stopped thinking we were so unique. When our daughter was born, we were able to take things easier. I didn't have to fight so much anymore or to prove so much. My relationship with my daughter was healthier: I could accept her for what she is."

Less exclusive now in her relationship with Juan, she began to "let some other people in." She developed some close friendships with other women, and she and Juan together formed friendships with other couples. These other relationships stretched the tight shell that she and Juan had had, but she was pleased that he was able to accept her connection to others.

Not until age thirty-five was Allison ready to reestablish a relationship with her parents. Able at last to relate to them differently, they all found a way to accept one another. "They no longer tried to boss me or tell me what to do. We're friends. My father was very proud of my career, and he and Juan found a lot to discuss. Being a parent myself gave me a lot in common with my mother. I began to see them as interesting people to talk to without having to accept their opinions."

Working hard on her studies of women in history, she worried often that she was not a good enough mother and spent too little time with her children. At this point, Allison's students began to be important in her life. She enjoyed helping them over their own struggles and encouraging them. "Emotionally, I get a lot of satisfaction from helping people and teaching people and learning from them. I feel a lot about them. They are a part of my life, although no one in particular."

This was a stable time in Allison's life. She felt natural and spontaneous with her daughter, despite ongoing conflict and tension with her son. She had also deepened her relationships with three women friends, and they had become interested in feminist issues. They developed their sense of being women together and shared a sense of injustice about how they were discriminated against academically because of their gender. One of her friends was a poet, and through her poetry the four friends began to discuss deeper and deeper levels of their lives.

By age forty, Allison had been offered and had accepted the presidency of the college at which she had taught for many years. "I began to feel at this age like I was the mother of everybody. I had a very rich life. I was in the position of giving, and I enjoyed this. I felt that I had tremendous resources and strength. Before, I had always felt that what was important was in terms of my achievements, but now it began to feel like it was in my personality, my strength to support other people and to love other people."

Only Allison's son continued to resist her love. Unable to reach him, she continued to be pained that he did not share or even admit his problems to her or Juan. The other relationships in her life stayed stable and satisfying, however: she and Juan remained intimate friends and lovers, and her women friends offered welcome respite from the rigors of her now public persona.

The nadir of this period was the illness of her mother.

> She became fragile and more emotional, and we began to talk more openly. My sisters and I took turns sitting with her when she didn't feel well. She told me about her life, her childhood, and her family, and we developed a sort of feminine bond. I managed to draw her into my feminist awareness, and we became much closer than we had been for years. I began to see her as someone who was much more worthwhile than I had considered her before.
>
> I felt resentful toward my father for not being a good caretaker of my mother. When she didn't feel well, he lost patience and I felt it was not right; but I felt it as a shortcoming that he couldn't help. He couldn't stand sick people or weak people. I talk with my father about politics, about my work, and about

public problems, but my mother is more like an intimate friend. And I feel like I've developed a loyalty to women which is quite different from the relationships I have with men. Although with my husband it's an excellent relationship, it's on a different level. I have a sense of superiority about being a woman, a sense of looking down on men and how limited they are in how deeply they can feel.

By the time Allison was forty-five, her mother had died, but Allison still represented her on her relational diagram.

I came to idealize my mother. She became for me much more of a model than she was when she was alive. There was so much she did for people, so much she offered them. She was a strong person, overcame so many difficulties. I began to see my father as weaker than she was. As a widower, he was so helpless without her. I became the support to my father, cooking for him, taking him places. He is now an old person, and the balance has changed. It's not always easy to take care of him.

Allison began to share this burden with her sisters, whom she grew close to after all these years. "I discovered that these women whom I have disregarded all these years are altruistic and less self-centered than I, and I started to like them. There is a growing closeness between me and my sisters, and our children have started to grow close. Now my nuclear family extends in a much more meaningful way."

Within the tapestry of Allison's complex and multifaceted life are woven many idealizations and identifications that serve her lifelong effort to decide the terms on which she wishes to live. At its simplest level, her history can be seen as a quest to integrate conflicting identifications with her mother and her father. In her early years, Allison had an intense identification with her consciously adored father, and this formed the core of her intellectual ambitions. Disparaging the overworked, depressing life of her mother, Allison placed value on the life of the mind and on public, "important" work. She hated the caretaking role that she was forced to assume with her sisters, and she devalued her mother's caretaking of everyone else. She could value a relationship with her mother only when her mother joined her as a struggling student. Yet by midlife, Allison experienced her public, prominent role as university president in terms of being "a mother of everyone."

We can trace some of the myriad threads of identification that she has woven into a way of living. Along with her conscious identifications and admirations (which are many), she has had to fuse and come to terms with unconscious and latent identifications. In the process of forming her own identity, Allison made use of part identifications with others who embodied other integrations, other ways of valuing. She looked to her high school history teacher, who was both an intellectual (a historian) and a caretaker (a teacher), but she thought *consciously* only of the more striving, intellectual side of her.

In the process of adolescent transition while at the university, Allison found other people to embody new values and ideals. Juan represented different, radical political values and freer social and sexual behavior. Allison joined him in that new framework, forging a new identity. She found another professor to admire—one who personified her intellectual ideal, and she worked with him toward that end. Then, having succeeded occupationally, she returned to her disowned identification with her mother.

The maze of frustration with her son led Allison to discover the real challenges of mothering. This, together with her growing closeness to other women, brought Allison to value caretaking in a new way. As a mature woman, Allison discovered her own mother as her hero.

Allison's pattern throughout her life has been that of idealization, identification, and then an effort to come to terms with inevitable disillusionment. Her vision of others as embodying a kind of perfection has powered her efforts in their direction. Once she has attained their level, awash in reality, she has then had to work to reintegrate a sense of herself and of others. Allison's is not a story of angry disillusionment, however. For her, disillusionment resulted in integration, a search for new ideals, and continual growth. She always looked to others to stretch her, to help her find in herself what she had not had access to before. Her wish throughout her life was to enrich and transcend herself; at this point, the core of her life is to offer this to others. Having absorbed so much from others, she feels able to be "the mother of everybody."

Counteridentification

Any discussion of identification would be incomplete without a consideration of counteridentification: the wish *not* to become like. This wish was expressed by a great many of the research subjects. Whatever was traumatic or unfulfilling about the important others of our childhood is likely to become devalued, and we make a great conscious effort to avoid acquiring or expressing this trait. But counteridentification is a highly complex process—and often a pernicious one; people must frequently do battle with strong unconscious identifications that are consciously disowned. Much as people are traumatized by childhood abuse, it is nevertheless the abused child who often becomes the abusing parent.

Unconscious identifications, consciously disowned, may lie dormant until they are afforded a different role in the personality. Allison, for example, remembers strongly wanting not to be like her mother, and she avoided caretaking roles for many years. If we had interviewed her at age twenty, we would have been impressed by her strong negative identification with her mother and with the role reversal that seemed to have taken place in the relationship. At the time, Allison wanted nothing to do with being an overworked woman who took care of everyone. Yet through a tortuous process of growth and change over the subsequent twenty years, Allison not only realized this disavowed identification but came to idealize it.

Identifications (and counteridentifications), then, have intricate histories of their own. Some identifications are dormant; these serve well at some periods of life and not others. Counteridentifications may be powerful as ways of defining the self in contradistinction to someone else. Ella, for example, is devoting her life to creating a family unlike the one her self-centered, neglectful parents provided her. She wants to be a good mother and to give her children everything she never had. She maintains an ambivalent connection to her parents as a way of reassuring herself that she is unlike them. Positive or negative, our connections to other people catalogue possibility.

Counteridentification can, however, be an intense form of connection. Our need to be unlike someone is a way of carrying that person's image through life. We are as closely tied to people when we cannot bear finding them in ourselves as when that is what we most wish to do.

Disillusionment, Distance, and Defense

All idealizations ultimately fail, because all heroes are found, in the end, to be only real. Yet the relational experience of disillusionment, the negative pole of idealization, involves a despairing withdrawal from others. Without a belief that someone, somewhere, sometime could embody one's ideals, hope is impossible and becoming itself is impeded.

Healthy living requires a balance between reality and idealization. We can feel very empty without heroes. In our hyperrealistic, cynical age, it is easy to lose respect for idealizing processes, to mock those who admire. Yet our increasing experience with idealization as a form of love and connection shows us the ways in which it can empower people to act in their own behalf. The Wizard of Oz is everywhere in life, a venerated Other who *seems* powerful but whose real power lies in making it possible for us to find ourselves and our own resources.

We always need to maintain a piece of what Kohut calls the "old infantile delusion of others' omnipotence despite the repeated frustrations and failures that teach us the limits of our own and others' power" (Tolpin, 1980). When we are unable to find new people to venerate and idealize, we are likely to sink into a form of narcissistic depression—to become bitter, hopeless, and unable to act (Josselson, 1986). Other people provide our link to a sense of meaning in life.

Idealization can also be used as a way of relating to people at an emotional distance. Several interviewees in this study (uniquely male) spoke of people primarily in terms of the ideologies or ways of life they represented. Saul, a bright and very sensitive thirty-year-old, responded to people with intrigue about the values they embodied. His most spontaneous and intense emotional expression during the interview was in remembering his first-grade teacher (the only person he mentioned having loved). He said, "I loved her. I felt that I wanted her to be my mother. I felt, 'How interesting you are, and how much knowledge you have.' My mother was not so bright and shiny like that. She couldn't answer my questions." I asked Saul more about what he wanted of this teacher, and he made it clear that he wanted her intelligence rather than her affection. "I feel she was giving me her mind and her strength. I wanted to come home to her each day and have more of all she offered. I think she liked me, but I admired her more than she had a special feeling toward me."

Throughout his life, Saul tended to connect to people by admiring or being drawn to their ideas. He made little distinction on his relational chart between people he discussed ideas with and authors whom he read. All were important in shaping his ideas, in helping him to think about the question that troubled him most: how he ought to live. His quest was for someone with something "really fundamental to tell me. I needed a structure for the world." Although he had a girlfriend at one point, he took little initiative toward her; instead, he found himself fitting into her plans for him. When she left him, he felt little loss. His emotional life with others was in the realm of intellect; he was looking for answers to his tortured questions about life, and for someone who could help him find those answers.

Idealization was Saul's primary form of relatedness from childhood on. Although we could comment on the relative absence of other forms of relatedness in his life and on his tendency to relate to others only at an emotional distance, it is important to recognize also the way in which purely idealizing tendencies have kept him connected to the flow of human interaction.

Chapter 8

Mutuality and Resonance

And we'll live,
and pray, and sing, and tell old tales, and laugh
At gilded butterflies, and hear poor rogues
Talk of court news; and we'll talk with them too
Who loses, and who wins; who's in, who's out;
And take upon 's the mystery of things.

—William Shakespeare, *King Lear*

Mutuality is emotionally being with another, joining in. In mutuality, we resonate with one another. (*Mutuality* describes the process; *resonance* describes the emotional experience.) Like two instruments whose notes form a chord, we together create something greater than our own experience. We share, we cooperate, we play. We find ourselves in another and another in ourselves. Of all of the dimensions of relatedness, mutuality is at once the most commonly experienced, the most humanly rewarding, and the hardest to talk about.

Mutuality occurs *between* selves, and this is part of why language falters. Anyone who has seriously addressed this space between loses articulateness and begins to create hyphenated words (Miller, 1986). Thus Buber creates the "I-Thou" (1958), Miller speaks of the "self-in-relation," and Stern (1985) postulates a state of "being-with." Because our language tends to make assignments to me or to you, we lack the discourse of *we*. Yet mutuality is a joint creation, maintained by mutually held mental states. In thinking about mutuality, we must remember that it always occurs in the space between people, as a product of both of them, with each

148

individual contributing to, participating in, and taking from it. In mutuality, then, it is the *we* that is centrally important.

The Quest for Mutuality

In our quest for mutuality, we learn which aspects of our subjective experience are shareable and which are not. We learn how and when it is pleasurable to share ourselves and to share another's self and how and when it is better to remain behind our own barriers. In this dimension are needs for companionship: walking side by side with someone, playing together, "hanging out," "talking to."

Although this is an important dimension of human development and experience, I think that it is the least theoretically explored and understood. Yet how rapidly our patients begin to improve when they become able just to be with others, swapping stories, experiencing a communion of selves that has no goal. How often is our own experience made fuller by sharing it with another.

Mutuality exists on a continuum from simple companionship to an intermingling of souls. Nothing in mutuality is *for* anything but the simple pleasure of resonance itself. Why mutuality should be pleasurable remains obscure, since it is not reducible to drive or instinct.[1] Rather, mutuality appears to be the expression of our fundamentally social nature—an evolutionary predisposition, human and emergent, simply to "be with" others.[2]

After the great discoveries of infancy—that there are others and that others have their own experience separate from ours—is the further realization that experience can be shared. Infants from seven to nine months old begin to seek to share their experience of events and things by trying to direct the focus of another's attention to the focus of their own. They learn to point and to follow the line of another's pointing (Stern, 1985). Their wish is not "Look *at* me" but "Look at something else *with* me"—a whole new realm of experiencing life and relatedness. By being able to share the focus of attention on something other than the self, the baby becomes capable of transcending egocentrism and participating in a new form of relatedness.[3]

Stern's recognition of the importance of the emerging capacity for shared focusing leads us to a new appreciation of what takes place in the earliest relationships. When a baby who is carried to the window points to a squirrel on the tree branch outside, several things are taking place at once: holding (his mother is carrying him), attachment (his mother is with him), and validation (he is confirmed in what he sees, and maybe he even senses that his mother thinks he is clever for having noticed the squirrel). But the central aspect of the interaction is not these things—not "how clever I am for seeing the squirrel: I am good"—but rather, "I want you to be seeing the squirrel too; I want us to be seeing the squirrel together." Issues of "good me" and "bad mother" are far in the background, as is concern about self-other differentiation. What is foremost experientially is "I see the squirrel and I feel you seeing the squirrel and I feel you knowing that I see the squirrel and I am enchanted and you are enchanted and each is more enchanted because the other is too—and it all feels very special."

Infant research demonstrates that infants become aware of the mother's experience and aware of its match to their own (Stern, 1985). Although we know that this awareness becomes *possible* with cognitive maturation, we do not know why it becomes *pleasurable*. We *do* know that the need for mutuality is present early, however, and remains a powerful motivator throughout life.

Mutuality is a pure form of communion with another person. Either we see what another is doing (physically, emotionally, or metaphorically) and try to orient our own experience—either actually or vicariously—or we allow another to join us in what we are doing. Such joining can occur on either a small or a grand scale. At the simplest level, we often feel a bond with someone who is merely *doing* what we are doing. Because the other is engaged in the same activity at the same moment, we may assume a similarity of psychological state. A stranger and I are both looking at a painting, for example. In this moment of (assumed) resonance, I might initiate a conversation. "Isn't that a beautiful painting!" is a different comment if I say it to someone than if I think it to myself. I am alone able to appreciate the painting. Appreciating it *with* someone is a very different experience. At the other extreme of resonance, looking at the same painting with a close friend, I might find that her associations to the painting match mine or that her thoughts about it spark in me a new and deeper appreciation, both of the painting and of her.

Because emotional attunement is part of empathy as well as mutuality, these two dimensions may seem to shade into one another. Empathy, however, is more of a one-way street (although *mutual* empathy is certainly possible). In empathic responsiveness, one person is taking in, holding, and perhaps reflecting the experience of another, putting aside her own reactions and experience. In mutuality, both people are participating in each other's experience, each recognizing the experience of the other and adding to it. In empathy, the experience is "I know how you're feeling" or "I feel that you know how I'm feeling." In mutuality, there is a different experience of communion, of feeling *together*: "We had a wonderful time," "We had a good talk," "We both know what it is to lose a loved one," or even an involved, eager, "And what happened next?" Resonance is also different from validation (which, like empathy, is an eye-to-eye experience). In validation, I look to you to confirm for me some aspect of myself so that I can have greater certainty about my own qualities; in resonance, I take what I know of myself (and of you) and extend it to join with what you know of yourself (and of me) so that we can experience what we know of each other and how those parts of each of us join together. Although I may have a (not unpleasant) awareness that my knowledge of myself and of you may well be reshaped by our interchange, reshaping is not its aim.

Because mutuality represents the continuum of shareable experience, mutuality becomes the glue that binds us to one another in the human condition. Culture is the monument of mutuality, the record of what we share together. Culture not only channels our drives, as Freud would have it, but allows us a means to speak our inner truth and link it to the truth of another. Culture, like play, exists in the space between us that is neither solely inner reality nor objectively "there." It is a product of our mutual creativity.

Although there are ways in which we are trapped inside our own uniqueness—monads without windows, as Leibniz pessimistically viewed us—we are creatures who protest our isolation and seek each other out. To know that someone else—*anyone* else—has had my experience means that I am not alone. To be alone with an awful secret and the belief that only I have this feeling, fear, or fact to live with is the most excruciating form of isolation. This is like the terror, so often a theme of science fiction, of being the only person among a group of (even kindly) aliens. One's physical needs may be met, one may even be treated gently, but mutuality is impossible. Then, as the science fiction unfolds, something usually occurs to make resonance possible, and this development is always deeply stirring (in life as well as fiction). Witness the moving moment in the film *E.T.* when the alien and the boy stretch their fingers toward each other and make contact for the first time.

At the opposite pole of isolation lies the danger of so much interconnection that the boundary of the self is lost. At this extreme, experience is not only shareable but completely available. When the self is unbounded in this way, we lose a sense of ownership of our experience. While under certain circumstances this can be pleasurable, it can also be frightening and even dangerous (if we are not certain that those boundaries can be reestablished). At its extreme, the experience of complete existence in the space between is psychosis.

Mutuality and resonance, in their many forms, are the stuff of most human exchange. We chat pleasantly about the weather, share a joke we heard with our hairdresser, pass an hour over coffee gossiping with a friend. These mostly unremarkable events soon fade into the dustbin of memory, yet without them life is apt to feel empty and cold.

Among all the relationships that people in the research study described, more were mutuality-based than anything else. Yet this is the dimension that we can conceptualize the least. How, for example, can we be rigorously precise about what is meant by a "sense of connection" to another person?

Jean Baker Miller and her research group at the Stone Center have been at the forefront of efforts to try to understand and discuss the role of mutuality in psychological health. For them, "mutual empathy" is central to all psychological development. Janet Surrey (1987) describes mutual empathy (the equivalent of mutuality) as an experience of "being with" and "being seen" by another while "seeing" the other and sensing the other "feeling seen." The outcome of this seeing and being seen is true psychological connection that empowers growth. As in the scene from *E.T.*, when we (mutually) touch someone, we become energized. We experience a surge of vitality; we feel better about ourselves; we become more able to act; we are more likely to reach toward others.

Miller (1986, 1988) stresses that mutual interchange with others is essential for psychological growth. Because interaction in a framework of emotional connection stimulates energy and vision and the will to act, mutuality is empowering (Surrey, 1987). Intellectual development, too, often takes place through mutual empathy and shared understanding, as connected rather than rote learning (Belenky, Clinchy, Goldberger, and Tarule, 1986). Yet our culture has led us not to attend to these interchanges; they are non-events (Miller, 1986; Surrey, 1987; Belenky, Clinchy, Goldberger, and Tarule, 1986). Responsiveness to and with others, which has often been the province of women, is not viewed as *activity* in our patriarchal culture.

Even in this discussion of mutuality, I inevitably focus on the higher orders of resonance—those that are remarkable because they are intense or special in some way. It is unlikely that many of the research participants had either the time or the inclination to draw even a fraction of their experiences of "being with" others. Asked if there were important people in her life whom she had not discussed, Glenda, a research interviewee, echoed Miller's point. She was overwhelmed by the question, well aware of how important is her contact with many, many people. "So many people have been important. I could sit on a train and have a conversation with a person for ten minutes, and I'll remember what I've learned from them forever after—people who come into my life and don't stay and yet they've touched me deeply. People whose names I don't even know, people I've seen on TV who've said something that struck a note, somebody I talked to for ten or fifteen minutes can change my life." Tolstoy (1930) thought that such communication—touching others—was the ultimate function of art.

"All real living is meeting," wrote Buber (1958, p. 11). And the essence of meeting is authentic participation in one another's lives. Within mutuality are infinite shadings and gradations that are part of our affective knowledge of others, and there are as many nuances of authenticity. Our experience of this meeting is organized beyond cognition, in the realm of something closer to affective or intuitive knowledge.

Resonance cannot be delineated precisely from the outside, because it involves an experienced affective joining. When people deeply resonate with each other, they feel as though they were thinking together or feeling together or coping together: their thoughts, affects, associations, and awareness are linked in such a way that they become part of an ongoing stream of experience. (Brainstorming sessions and encounter groups are efforts to schedule resonant exchange.) The deeper the resonance, the more relaxed is the boundary between self and other, the more each person is fully (but not completely) in the space between.

We "know" when someone is listening politely as opposed to really listening to us, even though overt behavior may be precisely the same. We "know" when someone is really resonating with us, sharing experience rather than passively attending. "You aren't listening to me," says one. "Yes, I am," says the other. Both people are speaking truth about their experience, but at issue is how *much* of the self is listening.

These are dimensions of experience that are beyond ordinary logic. We do not reason out the other's intentions or mental state. Rather, we feel it, intuitively, as a sense of "presence." Resonant talk flows seamlessly—feelings and words, ideas and fantasies intermingling. Resonant talk is absorbing; both people are fully present. It is these nuances of mutuality that make it such a rich, but elusive, subject of inquiry.

Developmental Origins of Mutuality

Research into infancy and early childhood processes suggests that mutuality has its origins in the earliest phases of life.

Affective Attunement

The first evidence of mutuality exists in the affect attunement of mother and child. Stern (1985) presents evidence that infants are sensitive to the affective "match" of the mother's response to their experience. When that response is "off" in intensity or rhythm infants stop what they are doing and look disturbed and confused. Similarly, infants can tune in to the mother's affective state; they are aware not only of what the mother is doing but with what affect she is doing it. This affective relatedness occurs before language and continues after. Although nonverbal attunement becomes overshadowed by language and verbal exchange, it continues nonetheless. It is on this stream of fundamental intersubjectivity that mutuality lies; it predates and is beyond language. As adults, we continue to be aware of nonverbal behavior and to communicate with each other wordlessly, but we are less likely to *conceptualize* this form of communication. It is very difficult to conceptualize in ordinary language what is beyond words. We can, however, allude to these processes.

Example: I sit in a lecture hall and become progressively more exasperated with what the speaker is saying. I look over at my close friend, and with our eyes we comment on our shared contempt for the discussion.

Example 2: I walk along the beach with a close friend. Though we do not speak, we are deeply in touch with each other. When we talk later, we find that we were thinking the same thoughts.

Language itself is a mutuality-based form of discourse, and it can be used to increase resonance or curtail it. The closer we are to someone, the fewer words we have to use to get our meaning across. As a form of sharing meaning in agreed-upon ways, language offers another way of being together. (For example, we often refer to those with whom we feel resonant as "speaking our language.")

We can well understand language cognitively without resonating with it affectively. Sometimes we read or hear words that move us profoundly—words that "go through us" just as a high note shatters crystal. Poets often use language resonantly, to affectively join us to their experience and truth. Language can, however, also be used as a defense, as when someone either intellectualizes in order not to feel or speaks in order to keep distance from someone else.

Rapprochement

Like affective attunement, rapprochement is a process that brings the self to the boundary with the other and integrates the meaning of the relationship with the development of the self. One of

Mahler's (1975) greatest contributions to the understanding of the separation-individuation phase of development is a schematization of the processes and stages through which an early sense of selfhood is consolidated. The young child (eighteen months), newly hatched from symbiosis, enjoys a love affair with the world, practicing new motor skills, feeling omnipotent, exploring the world. Awareness of separateness from the mother, however, gives way to a new need for her—the stage of *rapprochement*. But how shall we understand this return to the mother? Mahler, given her interest in separation and individuation, sees this rapprochement as being in the interests of refueling—getting both new energy, as it were, for the continued exploration of the world and reassurance of the mother's continued presence. Relationship is thus linked to the child's separation from the mother; relational fuel, according to this analysis, is necessary for selfhood.

Yet another way of looking at the rapprochement phase would be to recognize the child's interest in bringing the mother along, joining her to the new discoveries. Children who are moving forward into the world want to "inject" their experiences into the mother, not necessarily for validation but to keep her resonant with them. "Come along, let me show you what I found." And even if the mother does not come or look or join, in fantasy the toddler has linked together self, mother, and the new experience. Join with me. Participate with me. It is for these experiences that we do not yet have adequate concepts.

In adulthood, the paradoxes of the rapprochement phase continue as developmental challenges: how to experience our selfhood with the others who are important to us and at the same time take part in their selfhood, participating together in this space between. We must take time for the unpressured telling of our stories, one to the other: "This has been my experience. . . . Let me show you."

Mutuality is sometimes on a collision course with attachments, as we find our explorations of our world moving us away from those to whom we are attached, or as they grow away from us, unwilling or unable to include us. We describe as "keeping up with" people our efforts to maintain our sense of existing side by side. In a relationship of mutuality, we may not be emotionally absent for too long or the "with" experience vanishes. The "work" in an ongoing relationship is often that of staying resonant, of keeping up with those who are important to us lest we get "out of tune" with each other.

Expressions of Mutuality

Mutuality can consist of a variety of relational aspects, either singly or in combination. Several are discussed below.

Companionship

With its focus on early experience in the family as formative in personality development, psychology has long given scant attention to companionship. Complex experiences in this domain are simply grouped under the umbrella category of relationships with "peers," which are understood as homogeneous entities opposite to parents.

I found it interesting that most of the people I interviewed who were not psychologically sophisticated generally began their discussion of the most important people in their lives with those with whom they felt mutual. They began with their companions—people they enjoyed being with, spent time with, had fun with. Fun involves, among other things, affective matching—in other words, resonance in joyful arousal.

From early in childhood, children are fascinated with other children. Play is at first parallel, then mutual. And as every parent discovers, no one can play with a child like another child. Agemates offer each other mutual responsiveness that cannot be matched by someone of another developmental level. Children invent games among themselves that are incomprehensible to the adult. Yet the children experience resonance among themselves: they are sharing deeply, involved in what each contributes to the activity, able to enter into a mutually created world. Children's play is spontaneous; it "flows." At the same time, children are learning about shared activity, incorporating *both* people into the action. Eventually, they discover that they can do this more easily with some than with others, and they begin to have preferred playmates on the basis of this mutuality.

Winnicott (1971) has written about the "potential space" that is the milieu of play. This potential space exists between fantasy and reality, between objectivity and subjectivity, as an "intermediate area" in which we can relax the strain of objective perception. Here we may imagine together. Here we may visit and share our all-important illusions. A truly intimate companion is someone with whom we can voyage to this potential space.

We never outgrow our need for playmates, although opportunities to play may become scarce in the seriousness of adult life. Still, we always need someone with whom we can relax our boundaries, put off our public masks, and allow our invention, silliness, fantasies, and puckishness to find expression—in the full expectation that our playmate will respond in kind.

One of the great pleasures in life is laughing together with someone. (Psychoanalysis might translate this into sexual, orgasmic terms, but I do not think such translation is necessary.) Laughter is a visible, audible emotional resonance. And the joy of laughter is heightened by mutuality. If we come across a funny cartoon while alone, our impulse is to share it with someone who will experience it as we did.

One of the reasons that it is so hard to study relatedness is that if we interview people about their relationships, especially their companionate relationships, they are likely to tell us that what they do together is "have fun." They have a difficult time articulating that fun, however, because it is not external and not internal; it exists in the space between, in the mutuality between the companions. Two adolescents, for example, find it "fun" to go to the mall together and "hang out." Their parents are mystified. What could be the fun in spending a beautiful day inside a mall watching other adolescents stroll by?

In describing their companionate relationships, the people whom I interviewed stressed not the activity itself but the togetherness. "We caught salamanders together." "We rode our bikes together around the reservoir." "We were in each other's houses." In short, we were a *we*.

Winnicott points out that in mutuality, people are both being found and created by the other. Certainly, we often must search to find those with whom we can resonate, but we must also have the capacity to make resonant use of people who are there. Some people are lonely because they are without emotionally compatible companions; others do not know how to experience and respond to the attempts at mutuality from others.

The Emergent We

Related to, but not identical with, companionship is the emergent *we*. Here experience is enriched simply because it occurs in tandem. We feel empowered, larger than self, participant in something that could not have been created alone. A team effort often exceeds any individual effort. And the joyous sense of "We won!" is a very different experience from the triumphal sense of "I won!" The orchestra creating music, the theater troupe putting on a play, the political group effecting change—all these are more than the sum of the component *I*'s; and the sense of being a piece fitted together into a larger whole is a part of the experience of each person.

I love to watch pair ice skating for the opportunity to participate vicariously in this kind of mutuality. There is something exhilarating about the seamless precision of two bodies moving in such unison, creating exquisite forms that overshadow what either skater could achieve alone. And yet there are bits of this togetherness all around us—in the momentary flashes, the "clicks," the comings-together of our efforts that catch fire. And in these comings-together, we know (together) with deep conviction that whatever it was that we made happen was not because of you or because of me, but because of *us*.

Sharing

With language development, mutuality becomes more deeply possible through verbal exchange. With words, we can know about what is inside one another and we can locate intersections of our experience and being. We use words to look for the resonances, the points at which our experience overlaps or is the same or can echo. We try to connect what is inside one to what is inside the other, bridging the space between us in what Buber (1965) calls "genuine conversation."

Sharing involves an intermingling of selves at an emotional level, from the most superficial to the most profound. It is a form of mutuality that does not necessarily involve companionship. I have been profoundly moved by moments with near-strangers, and I have had no more than superficial exchanges with people who are my frequent companions.

Among the research participants, sharing was the aspect of mutuality most prized and emphasized. Again, though, it was hard for people to articulate beyond their highly valued experience of having someone to "talk to." And this seems to be as far as language goes on this dimension. Talk to about what? About everything. "This was someone I could *really* talk to," said my interviewees. The implication here is that such sharing is not for validation but for catharsis and connection. For many, this was the highest form of valuing.

When mutuality is at its highest resonance, we feel that we have a soulmate. With this very special other person, we can fully know and be known. Our own experience is enhanced by sharing it with this chosen friend, and our lives are enlarged by participating in their experience. Meghan talked of having "gone through" a rape with her closest friend. Although it was a painful, awful time, she felt enriched by joining her friend so intensely. Her anger, fear, and pain were so strong that the traumatic event might just as well have happened to her.

The other side of sharing is the capacity to be moved, the capacity to receive and experience the feelings of the other. (Being moved, I think, has less of a self-other boundary than does empathy, which takes in the other's experience but does not join it with one's own feeling; but being moved and empathy are certainly on a continuum.) When we have participated in the sharing of self and other, we say that we feel "close." How close we feel is a function of how deep, central, and important is the sharing.

Stewart, a research participant, told about a colleague—also his best friend—with whom he has written two books. "We think so much together that when I look back, I can't tell which part I have written and which part was his. Even with what I am writing now. The ideas are so much both of ours that I would not feel right if I did not put his name on the article as well." Stewart is describing a soulmate, someone with whom the meeting of the minds is so harmonious that the boundaries between them become irrelevant. Aristotle used this as his paradigm of friendship: "a single soul dwelling in two bodies" (Diogenes, 1925, p. 20).

Twinship fantasies are common in human development. The longing for a twin is the longing for one who is totally resonant, who can be "with" in all one's crevices and hidden places. Kohut (1984) understood this need for twinship as a need to feel human among humans, as a sign of our basic alikeness. We learn that experience is fuller when it is echoed in another—in fact, not just echoed but fully reverberated. Then it is not our own experience coming back (as in empathy) but our own experience belonging to another as well, who declares, "I, too . . . " (or better yet, does not have to declare it; it is known).

In psychotherapy, one of the most therapeutic of experiences is the discovery that others, too. . . . Others, too, have felt the same way, have had the same doubts, fears, inadequacies. "I learned that I am not the only one who . . . " is often the first thing that people value about their therapeutic experience.

Particularly at adolescence, the need to find oneself in another becomes paramount. Not surprisingly, then, many writers have noted the upsurge in importance of the best friend at this stage (Deutsch, 1944; Youniss, 1980; Sullivan, 1953). With the growing (cognitive) recognition of the differences among people and the increasing (emotional) complexity of experience, the young person feels an intense need to feel "like" someone else. Intimate adolescent friendship thus involves deeper and more total confidences than at any other time of life. So much of the developing self is new and frightening; the only reassurance is that someone else is on the same path. Perhaps, then, as Kohut suggests, that path is indeed the path of the human condition.

Just as no one can play with a child like another child, no one can be present for an adolescent like another adolescent. Especially in sharing the dawn of sexuality, in trying to imagine being "grown-up," adolescents need each other. Theirs is a land of excitement and confusion that adults can (perhaps) remember but cannot revisit.

The striving for social position and the terrible judgments

wrought on adolescents by each other also drive young people (particularly girls) in search of a compatriot—someone with whom to share the daily agonies. This sharing of "growing pains" brings adolescents together in a new form of mutuality, which—if they are fortunate—will be found and renewed in other life transitions. In old age, those who are best adjusted are those who have a confidant; and this confidant is just as likely to be a friend as a spouse, at least among women (Lee, 1988).

The capacity to turn to others for mutual confirmation, for exploration of possibility, for feeling not alone in the face of challenge or trauma—this becomes predictive of mental health throughout life.[4] Like companionship, sharing is a side-by-side experience. We muddle jointly through life, laughing together our joy and crying together our tears.

Frequently, our experience is enriched by telling it to someone else, as though the experience itself were more real in the sharing than in the experiencing. How often do we respond to an event not affectively but with a mental "Wait till I tell _____ about this!" It is though we will wait and *really* have our experience during the telling.

During a week I spent on a Caribbean island, I asked Anthony, the aging island native who ran the water-sports equipment shop, to review sailing principles with me. Used to the peculiarities of vacationers, he went out with me in a Sunfish. Soon we came upon a windsurfer who was stranded, unable to sail his board back. With no motorboat available to help him, Anthony decided to try to tow the sailboard on the Sunfish, a fairly ambitious project even if I had been skilled enough to sail the Sunfish properly (which I was not). It took us nearly half an hour of trial and error to get the board and its sail positioned so that they did not interfere with the sailing of the Sunfish—and to get everything else to work right as well. Anthony swore colorfully most of the way, the object of his invective being the windsurfer who had not known how to get home on his own. As we approached shore, I said to him gleefully, "You did it!" Anthony exclaimed with much feeling, "Oh, this will be something to tell the priest!"

I do not know if Anthony really did tell the priest, but as I thought about his exclamation back on the beach, I felt an appreciation for the ways in which the space between us—whatever that ought to be called—anchors us to our world. Anthony was interested neither in my admiration nor in his own pride at his accomplishment. The priest alone could understand and fully resonate with the burdens he bore, the lengths to which he went for his job— and in that Anthony could locate his meaning.

Affective mutuality provides a necessary sense of vitality that mitigates existential aloneness. What we can share is relived (or more fully lived) in the telling. Through our experience, we are "connected" in some way to another person and therefore to the stream of human existence. It is this sense of *us*—a participation in the space between a *you* and a *me*—that affords us a deeper and richer sense of our existence.

Intersubjectivity

Mutuality, existing in the space between self and other, transcends the momentary interaction. The relationship belongs to both the self and the other jointly, not to either solely. Both people carry the relationship with them into all other relationships and activities and are responsible for taking account of the other in whatever might bear on that person's wishes or feelings. Thus I think of my friend if I see something he might like, and maybe I buy it for him. I defend him if someone criticizes him. I take care to guard his secrets. I think of how what I do might affect him. I experience everything through the intersubjectivity of our mutuality.

Surrey (1987) refers to this process as one of "holding a relationship" in a continuous awareness and orientation that "takes the other into account." Mutuality, then, does not exist only in the presence of someone; mutuality changes our way of experiencing.

Children come to their first experiences of mutual empathy and intersubjectivity through building boundaries around their friendships. The rituals that mark this passage center on the telling and guarding of secrets. Adolescents, when asked about their friendships, will tend to stress loyalty and the guarding of secrets. The worst, most unforgivable thing a friend can do is to "tell" what has been privately confessed. I think that the enormity of such a breach has to do with the violation of intersubjectivity. The friend has not considered the other person's feelings, has not carried and taken care of the relationship. When people talk about trust, they are similarly talking about their belief (or lack of belief) that others can carry a relationship intersubjectively, can carry and tend a *we*.

Much of the learning in relational development is learning about intersubjectivity. After we learn that our experience is shareable, that it can be resonated with, we must learn what others will do with the pieces of us that they now carry and what we will do with the pieces of them that are now part of us. We learn about betrayal (a perceived mutuality that was false or that changed) and about the limits to mutuality ("There was only one ticket left for the concert, and I got it," versus "There was only one ticket left for the concert, and I didn't want to go without you.") Mutuality does not involve, after all, a complete union, so misunderstanding and negotiation always take place around issues of how much of the self will be invested in the relationship. What are the rules? Where is the all-important balance?

The vicissitudes of mutuality take place along the boundaries among self, other, and *we*. Resonance resides in the management of the self-other boundary, which we lower (together) so that emotional experience flows unimpeded between self and other into the *we*. But in an ongoing relationship, the gate is always being raised and lowered, as we alternately participate in the *we* and return to the *me* and *you*. Much of the strife between couples is not about the boundary between *you* and *me* but between *we* and *me*. One or the other partner wants more in the *we* than the other. Long-married couples who have gotten this settled seem to outsiders to have *we* and *me* hopelessly confused (indeed, to do separately what one has become accustomed to doing as part of a *we* can be very disturbing).

Mutuality implies trust, confidence that a self entrusted to a *we* will be cherished and respected, not violated or discarded capriciously. Developmental contexts and cultural values set the tone for the emergence and forms of mutuality. Authenticity does not flourish in a climate of manipulation and exploitation; competitive, individualistic societies discourage the cooperation and loyalty inherent in mutuality.

Knowing Each Other

In mutual, resonant relatedness, we know each other partly through what we are told and partly through intuition—that which we just "know." Intuition (Deutsch, 1944) is a result of a permeable, unconscious self-other boundary that allows experience to resonate outside of awareness. As a result, we can intuit another's inner state without verbal exchange. When we are intuitive with another, we do not know how we know. Unconsciously, we have allowed the other to be a part of ourselves momentarily.

Women have traditionally been seen as the more intuitive gender—the ones who are more able to soften boundaries, more able to tolerate frequent but fleeting mergers with others. Bakan's (1966) notion of the female principle is that of communion. Women center themselves in communion—in resonances and mutual exchange with others—not as a substitute for self-definition but as an expression of it. Perhaps that is why women are more apt to live in the space between. Men, while they visit it occasionally, tend not to linger as long.

Most of the time, in order to know and be known, we have to communicate or disclose something about our inner states or experiences. Such disclosure does not guarantee mutuality, but it moves us toward it. Intimacy—the penetration of barriers—implies the capacity to let down defensive walls that keep us from revealing ourselves. Within a relationship of intimate mutuality, we can simply be who we are; we can unselfconsciously relax together. Many important people that research participants included on their charts were described simply as people with whom they felt great openness: "We know everything about each other." Once we know another and that person knows us, we are bonded in an incomparable way.

For some people, having such an open relationship seems to be crucial for survival; for others, it seems not at all necessary. I was astonished (and somewhat distressed) by how frequently my research participants told me things that they had never told anyone else. I asked Nancy, one of these people, if she felt that she had learned anything from the interview. She said, with much anguish, "I wish I had more intimacy in my life." Speaking, I think, for many of the people I interviewed, Nancy wished for more "being with"—not for validation, not for approval, but for the exaltation of what Buber called "meeting."

Friendship

Friend is the name we give to someone with whom we experience ongoing mutuality and resonance. In friendship reside companionship, sharing, self-disclosure, and interpenetration of selves. It may also involve loyalty, affection, competition, envy, and a host of other things. Friendship is *we*—what we have created mutually, the invisible bonds of the space between.

Consider the experience of reunion with a friend we have not seen in many years. There is anxiety as we anticipate her arrival. We remember only a person who used to be. What can she be like now? And yet, within a few minutes, it is as though we had seen each other yesterday. We have not, in that brief time, filled in the details of all the events of each other's lives in the intervening years, but the relationship is nevertheless reestablished. We have "picked up" just where we left off, as though there had been only a momentary lapse. But what exactly is "picked up" here? I think that it is the resonance and rhythm of friendship, the sense that our friend is still quintessentially who she was and we are still quintessentially who we were. So we know what to say to bring a smile; we fall into old idioms. We remember the relationship not cognitively but affectively, and we take it up once more.

My "oldest" friend is now a distinguished physician. I see her only infrequently, because we live on different coasts. Yet when we meet, I still hear in her inflection and her turn of phrase the twelve-year-old, and I remember automatically how to respond. We can still have "fun" together beneath all the layers of adulthood, responsibility, and experience that we have accumulated separately over the years. Like archaeologists, we are joyful to find the old *we* so much present still.

We are not exactly the same person with our various friends. Each friendship has its own language, its own cadence, its own unique *we*. We share ourselves in different ways.[5]

Dissonance and Emotional Isolation

At the opposite pole from mutuality and resonance are dissonance and emotional isolation, experiences that the psychological literature discusses more and understands better. In fact, psychopathology can be seen as the story of failed mutuality. When conflicting needs between people lead not to resonance but to misunderstanding, disappointment, and pain, people become opposed instead of joined; they square off rather than moving side by side. A relationship becomes nonmutual when one of the partners is withdrawn and unable to intermingle the self or if one partner attempts to control (rather than resonate with) the other, to get from rather than be with.

Because of the pleasures of mutuality and the pain of dissonance, most people will usually work to take care of relationships. This taking care includes the effort to balance the experience of the self with the interests of mutual connection. In other words, we put the needs of the relationship on a par with the needs of the self. We may decide not to broach a potentially divisive issue with a friend, for example, or may engage in various compromises in order to preserve harmony.

The management of conflict in the interest of mutuality colors and shades any relationship. In high-spirited, noisy relationships, people manage conflict thunderously but then restore harmony. In quiet relationships, people tiptoe around conflict; they are oversolicitous, stating differences in only the most tactful of terms. Sometimes conflict actually serves mutuality, as when we get to know each other better through disagreement or draw a sharper line between where *we* end and *I* begin. Anger, conflict, and a good fight often bring people closer together.

Mutuality does not imply idyllic experience. It is just that the few words with which we can talk about mutuality, resonance, and communion tend to sound sentimental and idealized. To be sure, the specters of anger, envy, greed, and spite lurk always in the corners. We live with these—we acknowledge or deny them, depending on the mores of our relationship—and try to preserve connection despite our destructiveness.

Mutuality in People's Lives

Culture channels our need for mutuality, giving it form and style. We may find our resonant companions among strangers (making for short but often intense encounters), among family members (joining mutuality to attachment), among lovers (linking mutuality and passion), or, in mutuality's purest form, among friends.

Carol Smith-Rosenberg (1975), in a now-classic paper, describes the intense, intimate friendships between women that characterized female experience in nineteenth-century America. These deep, loving relationships coexisted with relationships with men that had a different emotional texture. The friendships with women were rooted in mutuality, in the exploration of shared female experience in a gender-segregated society.[6] Smith-Rosenberg uses letters to document the intensity and progression of these relationships, many of which lasted a lifetime. In these documents is a record of the women's longing for contact, for knowledge of the other—distilled expressions of their need for mutual exchange. In our own century, people still have such relationships, but what they say about them is both less revealing and less eloquently articulated. When the need for mutuality is expressed in psychobabble catchphrases, for example, it can come to seem trendy or superficial rather than profound.

Whether we talk about it or not, most of us have some mutuality somewhere in our relational lives. People who have no mutuality at all tend not to meet others anywhere in the space between, even within sexual or attached relationships.

If mutuality is a main theme in people's lives, it tends to become interwoven with attachment and/or passion as well. Women, who are particularly likely to have very mutual, resonant friendships, tend to become attached to friends when mutuality exists over time. Increasingly, in today's heterosexually unpredictable world, women turn to mutuality-based friendship relationships for the security of attachment. (In her book *Among Friends* (1986, p. 135) Letty Pogrebin impishly challenges her readers: "I'll bet you have more ex-lovers than ex-friends!")

Mutuality and resonance also adhere to the most successful passionate relationships. In describing their marriages, people are more likely to stress the mutuality, the interdependence, and the companionship of their connection to their spouses than the passionate dimension. For many people, sexuality tends to become background to or expression of the experience of mutuality and resonance. In long-term companionate marriages, there is an ongoing sense of bond even when sexual desire fades or altogether disappears. There is a sense in such couples that the relationship that they have created between them is larger than either individual and is their joint project to nurture and protect. Thus each person acts to take care of the relationship (rather than the other person). Individual needs are subordinated to the good of this entity, which exists between. The French refer to this mutual relational creation as *leur couple*.

Another important repository of adult mutuality lies in one's adult relationships with siblings. I was struck by how many of the research subjects had conflictual, competitive, distant, or antagonistic relationships with siblings as children only to rediscover their siblings as adults and evolve an intimate and resonant friendship. The shared experience of growing up seems to provide a wellspring of commonality from which to build later communion.

Diana

Diana is a vibrant, lively fifty-year-old artist with many interests and projects. Hers was a relational chart filled with friends and connections that she reflected upon thoughtfully.

Diana grew up in a Boston neighborhood of extended family. Her aunts, uncles, and grandparents lived within easy reach, but there were no cousins her own age. Because her parents seemed busy and distant from her, Diana thinks of herself as having a lonely early childhood (despite the number of local relatives). Her happiest times were spent playing "Go Fish" with her grandfather, but she yearned for a playmate who was like her. She developed a longing for a sister and begged and pleaded with her parents until, when Diana was six, her mother produced one.

After her initial euphoria, Diana realized that her baby sister was not going to fix her sense of aloneness. If anything, she exacerbated it, because she took away what little of her mother's time and attention Diana had had. After her sister's birth, Diana's mother had a serious postpartum depression and retreated into her room for a long time. Diana remembers feeling very alone.

At age ten, Diana remembers assorted aunts and uncles in the background, but she did not feel close to any of them. One cousin her own age had moved into the neighborhood, but she soon discovered that he was "a bizarre, freaky genius kid who I have nothing to say to." He could not provide the companionship she craved. Diana had, however, become more venturesome in the neighborhood and had begun to find other children to play with. Angie was her best chum. During summers they went swimming every day. Diana also spent time with her idol, Tammy, a few years older, who was "blond and knew about periods and things like that."

Increasingly, Diana felt her attention focused outside her home. Her father, working hard, was not around much. Her mother, still mildly depressed, was overinvolved with her quiet, docile sister. By her early adolescence, Diana seems to have come to the conclusion that she would have to find gratification of her emotional needs outside the family.

Diana was successful in finding people who meant a lot to her—people who came to be important in different ways. Two people were central at age fifteen: her boyfriend and her best friend. Diana felt a shade closer to her boyfriend, John, than she did to Marcia, her best friend, in part because he was the source of her self-esteem. "He unconditionally loved me. He was supportive. I trusted him not to hurt me. He disagreed with me if I said anything negative about myself. He affirmed me, respected my secrets. I was very dependent on him, wanted daily contact with him." But with Marcia she felt a strong resonance. "We connected more intensely, understood each other, but I worried she might harm me by talking about me behind my back. We were able to talk about our feelings, our inner psyche; we discussed our boyfriends and the nature of our relationships—also a lot of giggling, being silly together."

With John, Diana found constancy, attachment, and validation, but with Marcia she could share and experience deep understanding. With Marcia, she could explore the dynamics of trust, and she could play.

Diana viewed her parents as "a matched pair." At age fifteen, she had an adversarial relationship with them. She viewed them as trying to protect her from John, lest she be sexually active with him. She challenged them at every opportunity, demanding freedom and independence. Her only sense of real connection with her mother was their shared preoccupation with physical appearance. Diana regarded her mother (who was never satisfied with her own appearance) as a makeup artist. Diana was grateful for her mother's understanding of her wish to have plastic surgery on her nose, a venture her father opposed.

At age twenty, now away at college, Diana again experienced two intense connections—one to a woman and the other to a man. She worshiped Ingrid, her Swedish roommate. "I loved her. We were immensely close. I thought she was beautiful, good at making herself beautiful, very feminine, sensual, motherly, sophisticated. She seemed light-years ahead of me. She was also very kind to me, tolerant of my messiness. She shaped me up by making me aware of the impact of my messy behavior on her. She introduced me to things I'd never have known about. She was my soul sister. We connected on many levels." One of the many things that Ingrid offered Diana was permission to consider expressing her sexuality. Raised in a rigid, sexually prohibitive family, Diana felt troubled and frightened about sexuality. Ingrid was able to calm her guilt, which enabled Diana to begin to do some exploring in this area.

Diana had broken off her romantic relationship with John, but he continued to be important to her as a connection to her past. There were people and experiences she could talk about only with him, and they were also able to share their current interests. "If I was feeling unlovable, I could always sidle up to him and feel cared about, but I had a lot of guilt and shame here because of having broken off the boyfriend-girlfriend relationship."

Diana spent much of her time obsessed by George, the love of her life. She felt insanely drawn to him, although there was no mutuality. They had a long, conflicted relationship. "I never had a safe bond with him. He was always ambivalent. He did insanely romantic things, like sending me three dozen roses or serenading me under my window, and then would disappear from my life. I was always trying to be who I should be to appeal to him. I was constantly nervous."

Her lack of mutuality with George stood in contrast to the sense of soul bonding she had with Ingrid and the resonance she experienced with four of her women friends. With Jean, she shared a devotion to music; with Helene, a political consciousness; and with Lynn and Eliza, an interest in nature, talking about human foibles, and discussing their future and their dreams.

Over the next few years, Diana tried to experience the mutuality she had with her women friends with a man. She and Bill began as friends, working and studying together. She could not talk to him as she could to Ingrid or her other female friends, but he was "a pretty good friend." Ready to throw off the burden of her virginity, she chose him as someone she could trust and feel safe with. To her chagrin, she became pregnant, and the couple bowed to her mother's insistence that they marry.

By age twenty-five, then, Diana was married to Bill. Sometimes they really enjoyed being together. They played bridge a lot, for example—usually without arguing. But much of the time, Diana felt that he could not really connect with her. She would tell him something funny that happened during the day, and he would fail to see the humor. She would be burning to talk about some new idea that she had read about in a magazine, and he would fall asleep. He thought that the things she liked to talk to her friends about were silly. He criticized her housekeeping and spent most of his nonwork time watching TV sports. Diana, who hated sports, knew in some deep way that she had made a mistake in marrying him. Because divorce in her family was unthinkable, Diana focused on the positive: she loved being a mother, so she stayed as "pregnant as possible." When the children were small, Bill left their upbringing in her hands. The kids were her real family; she talked to them all the time, even before they could understand. She was determined to seem happy, to *be* happy, and to raise a happy family.

Diana had grown away from Ingrid, who could not bear Bill, and she had become close to Martha, a woman to whom she could confide some of her private thoughts and who responded with her own. Diana's parents and John remained "there" if she needed someone, but they were otherwise not emotionally important (in part because Diana secretly blamed her mother for her marriage).

By age thirty, Diana had four children, whom she experienced as "part of me. They make my life meaningful." She raised them with her belief in mutuality. "As soon as I could, I would do a lot of sharing with them about personal, grown-up stuff as well as childhood stuff so they would know me, and I encouraged them to do the same back so I would know them. I use them as friends, in a way, in addition to being their parent. They feel stable to me. I can't imagine anything happening to these relationships other than death. These are the immutables." She clearly enjoyed her children and loved playing with them, sharing their worlds with them.

Aware of her emotional distance from Bill, Diana tried to reassure herself that all marriages were like this, that *life* was like this. Bill had a successful business and made a good income, and she and Bill were partners in the enterprise of raising the children now that they were a bit older. She increasingly resented what she perceived as his lack of empathy with the children, however. He barked orders at them like an Army sergeant. There was tension at home when he was there (which was not often). Sexually bored with Bill, Diana occupied herself with fantasies of a passionate involvement with a friend of theirs—a passion never consummated in reality.

Diana made friends around this time with an older woman, Evelyn, who took a real interest in her and in her family. Evelyn did not seem to want anything other than to participate with her in her life; they could laugh together and share challenges and tasks. Other women friends were also available for sharing the experiences of child raising and of life. Immersed in these interactions with others, Diana was not at all lonely.

By age thirty-five, Diana was still surrounded by her connections to her children, with whom she felt yet more personally engaged and mutual. Bill had drifted even farther away. She became for the first time close to her sister, who had married and had children; for the first time, they could really share their experiences.

Hesitantly, tentatively, and initially somewhat offhandedly, Diana began to speak to some of her women friends about how empty was her relationship with Bill. He was self-absorbed and uninterested in her, except in terms of her taking care of the house and the children. In these areas, however, he was increasingly critical of her: she never did things exactly as he would have done them. She was more critical of his dealings with the children too. As the kids got older, Bill wanted more of a say about rules for them. He tended to be authoritarian and punitive, while she liked the children to have freedom to explore, so they got into frequent battles. When angry, he could be savage in his words toward all of them. She had sex with him during this time purely out of obligation and fear of his anger. He did not seem to notice that she was completely unresponsive. Meanwhile, she spent more and more of her time in fantasies of a perfect lover who would be interested in her and would share himself and his feelings.

Eventually, Diana entered therapy, but she found her silent, unresponsive therapist unhelpful.[7] She blamed herself for her relationship with Bill, blamed herself for her therapist's silence. Her friend Abigail finally helped her find the courage to consider what had been unthinkable: to leave both her therapist and her husband. (Diana in turn encouraged Abigail to return to college to change careers.)

Nellie, another friend whom Diana enjoyed, had a strong influence on her around this time. "Matronly, plump, arty, and creative," Nellie shared stories of her sex life with Diana. Vicariously living some of Nellie's experiences, Diana renewed her interest in her conflict-ridden sexuality. She felt that Nellie gave her permission to take a lover and "to bring sexuality into my life."

Age forty found Diana divorced from Bill. Two of her children still lived at home with her; the others were off to college and graduate school. By this time, Diana had developed an intense closeness to her sister. They could talk about their childhood, and they also shared deeper experiences than she had ever had with anyone. Diana felt that her sister had stopped judging her and accepted her for who she was. She was likewise able to do the same.

Having renewed her old interest in art, Diana went to work as an art designer for a large magazine. There she met Carl, with whom she was able to experience the resonance she had always longed for. "I wasn't attracted to him right at first. I thought he was funny-looking. But we worked together, and I began to love him. We talked all day and all night; we laughed, had fun, generated ideas, designed beautiful things, dreamed dreams. And we made love too. I was never tired of him."

And still there were friends for sharing, including new friends from among her colleagues; with them, she could share the work part of her life. With each friend, she found a different degree of intimacy, a different kind of sharing. With one, she shared her enthusiasm for art; with another, her interest in working for nuclear disarmament. With another friend came long talks about men and sex. Diana also treasured the chamber music quintet she played in. She spent long hours working on their repertoire and occasionally performing.

When Carl turned forty, he felt an absolute need to create a family, a project that Diana felt was now behind her. They could resonate in so many ways—had been soulmates, lovers, and friends for two years—and yet there was no resolution possible here. With much pain, they parted; and Diana, after a time, resumed her search for a man with whom she could find the resonance and mutuality she had with her women friends and had had with Carl.

By this point in her life, however, at the age of forty-five, there was a real lack of available men. Among those she dated, she found it extremely difficult to find someone with whom she could feel deeply connected. She consoled herself occasionally with affairs with married men. "I enjoy my specialness to them. Usually, we are work colleagues and have a lot in common. Most of these married men have only had affairs with me. There's a halo around me, but I'm distracting, and they are too frightened to have an ongoing relationship."

Now at age fifty, Diana experiences passion with men, but she has not again found mutuality She describes intense romances that paled, passionate one-night stands, and even a few somewhat long-term but empty relationships that she held together just to have the "joy of being close to a man." Still rising in the design world, she has her own projects and skills to exercise. She cannot bear men who try to control her or who interfere with her work; she wants someone who will try to know her, understand her, have some dreams with her to share and to realize—someone who can simply "be with" her in her aspiration and giggle with her in her play.

Diana continues to experience mutuality within her large group of women friends, although these friends change at each period. People serve her intensely as they share her current stage of development; then they fade into the background and eventually disappear. Hers is not a pattern of intense attachment over time. Rather, she connects deeply to whoever can join her—and whoever she can join—where she is.

Late in her forties, Diana rediscovered her father, with whom she had earlier had only the most superficial and distant relationship. Visiting him in the hospital as a dutiful daughter during his illness, she found that he was interested in many of the same aspects of world politics she was. She found that they were "temperamentally attuned"; they even shared a sense of humor. She came to appreciate him and found a way that they could be friends.

Diana's main relationships of attachment are with her children, who have grown into independent, lively, and interesting people. She enjoys their returns home to share their adventures and their hopes. She travels with them, feels fully open with them. They continue to be the "immutables."

In Diana, we see a striving for and prizing of mutuality. Beyond sexuality and attachment, beside her needs for validation and support, Diana needs deep and resonant connections with others. From her earliest memories and wishes for a sister, Diana has longed for a companion—someone "like" her who would make her feel less alone and isolated. She connects with people intensely (although somewhat infrequently and haphazardly) and enriches herself by sharing her interests, needs, and feelings, absorbing in return those of her friends. Hers is a side-by-side pattern; someone is usually "with" her. When she speaks of her friends, she has much to say about them; she wants to tell their stories too. She is very aware of who they are and how she interrelates with them. Hers is a very peopled world, and she lives in the vital spaces that she has created with others. She exemplifies what Surrey (1987) calls participation in mutually empowering relationships; stated simply, she and her friends have an impact on and are responsive to one another. Diana's core world is a relational one. Although she does not have a primary partner and although her children are grown, her core sense of self is defined within the matrix of her resonant interconnections with others.

Mutuality and Psychotherapy

Therapists have long suspected that there is something in the mutuality of therapist and patient that may be the essential healing element (Fairbairn, 1957; Yalom, 1989), but we have been at pains to conceptualize this ineffable (and nonintellectual) aspect of the interaction (see Kaplan, 1988; Jordan, 1986). It is that which Greenson (1967) called the "real relationship": the transaction that takes place between the two people who come together for the work. That felt connection between them, which exists beside empathy and insight and beyond transference, is the essence of the therapeutic encounter.

Here is Diana describing a positive experience in therapy that occurred just last year: "In contrast to that silent lump [her first therapist], we really communicated. We were like collaborators. When we reached a new insight, we had a sense of pleasure together, a sense of figuring something out. As time went on, we understood each other's use of language and imagery better. And we knew better when we really communicated: I could tell when I really communicated with him and when I lost him, and I think he felt the same with me."

Sometimes the most therapeutic moments with patients come when we as therapists are most fully engaged—not losing boundaries, not acting out our own fantasies and needs with our patients, but participating fully in the space between. Significant therapeutic moments might involve the therapist and client sharing a laugh or thinking the same thoughts or the therapist acknowledging a *resonant* feeling. Therapy may be most powerful when it is fully collaborative: when both participants are meaningfully changed by the encounter. But this we are just beginning to learn about.

Chapter 9

Embeddedness

She had only been Frankie. She was an I person who had to walk around and do things by herself. All other people had a we to claim, all others except her. When Berenice said we, she meant Honey and Big Mama, her lodge or her church. The we of her father was the store. All members of clubs have a we to belong to and talk about. The soldiers in the army can say we. And even the criminals on chain-gangs. But the old Frankie had had no we to claim.

—Carson McCullers, *The Member of the Wedding*

Embeddedness, like holding and attachment, is silent rather than active and eventful. It is the framework that gives shape to selfhood, the context in which we define ourselves, the togetherness in which we are alone. The issues of embeddedness are the issues of the individual in group life.

Winnicott (1965b) attempts to put into language the inherent paradox of self with others. We can bear to be alone, says Winnicott, only when we have mastered the capacity to be alone *with* someone. That is, we can be alone only when we are secure enough in relatedness to allow ourselves to forget about the existence of the Other— who is, nevertheless, always there.[1] Our relationships of embeddedness are the relationships of social existence that connect us to all the people whom we may not notice but whose presence makes our existence possible.

The Social Context

In defining the context of all relatedness, our embeddedness in a social context limits and gives meaning to all of our other relationships. Embeddedness is the soil in which other relatedness grows. Our connections to others always exist within a cultural set of meanings that form a web of interdependence as well as a lexicon for interpretation of experience. The tragedy of Romeo and Juliet, for example, is meaningful only to the extent that being a Montague or a Capulet is consequential. Embeddedness involves vital and serious contracts among people; it may (or may not) involve affection or respect.

Buber discusses these phenomena in terms of people being "bound up" with one another.

> To be bound up together means only that each individual existence is enclosed and contained in a group existence. It does not mean that between one member and another of the group there exists any kind of personal relation. They do feel that they belong together in a way that is, so to speak, fundamentally different from every possible belonging together with someone outside the group. And there do arise, especially in the life of smaller groups, contacts which frequently favour this birth of individual relations, but, on the other hand, frequently make it more difficult. In no case, however, does membership in a group necessarily involve an existential relation between one member and another [1965, p. 72].

Instead, it is the collective itself that "lifts them out of loneliness and fear of the world and lostness" (p. 72).

Erikson's (1968) concept of identity similarly grapples with the individual joining society by simultaneously making the self a part of the social world and making the social world a part of the self. We are embedded in our culture, which is embedded in us. This embeddedness creates a sense of identity that, if firm and well integrated, organizes us to such an extent that we become unaware of it. We belong, we are connected, we are "in" the world that is "in" us. We have a socially based perch from which we experience the world (with others).

Being social creatures, we need to find a place within a social context, to join a culture, to entwine our individual experience with an ongoing human narrative. In the learning of language, our first act of embeddedness, we link the expression of our mental states to a preexisting commonality. When we learn to call a horse a *horse* (rather than some noise that suits our own creativity), we join social life (Stern, 1985; Vygotsky, 1986). How we speak, our form of communication, ever after denotes our connection to culture. In a large sense, our language expresses our embeddedness in one nation or another, our accent within that language identifies our social class or place of origin, and our choice of vocabulary links us to certain subgroups. We "speak" from our place within a society. (Embeddedness can also be a link to mutuality, as when we say, "He speaks my language." This expression seems to mean that we share enough similarity in our embeddedness to establish a groundwork for mutuality.)

To be embedded within a social network is to feel included, to share characteristics, to be the same as, to give up some individuality in the service of interconnection. To embed ourselves, we must learn social conventions beyond language: customs, mores, manners. We learn to conform our behavior to our group.

The danger of not being embedded is isolation or ostracism. In social isolation, we have no place; we are without a group. We may have passions or attachments, but without embeddedness we have no place. Camus's "stranger" expresses most clearly the sense of anomie that is the polar opposite of embeddedness.

When one belongs, one merely fits in—undramatically, harmoniously. The moral of Hans Christian Anderson's story about the ugly duckling is that the conspicuous deviant may have a context elsewhere where it is unremarkable. In a group of ducks, the swan is vilified and rejected. With other swans, however, it would be simply taken for granted. Embeddedness, then, is the phenomenological sense of being just another swan among other swans.

The individual who wishes to belong but does not belong has an intense sense of yearning, feels left out of the ongoing process of human life. "I never *belong* anywhere," laments Lena, a bright, funny, insightful member of my therapy group. Only in this group has she ever felt truly a member, and one of the most important aspects of her therapy has been to experience membership somewhere.

Embeddedness

What we feel a part of + what we don't feel a part of re: adoption... people raised w/ those they aren't born to can adopt the embedded value

This yearning to belong is distinct from attachment, holding, validation, and the other dimensions of connection. Its aim is the linkage of the self to a larger social environment. Because of the interdependence of the self and the social world for mutual definition, in embeddedness one is most oneself *with* others.

In group life, there is always a tension between inclusion and individuality. We want to be enough a part of the group to take part but we fear losing our individuality. At the same time, we fear to be so much an individual that we lose our tie to the group. A culture makes demands on an individual and requires repression and suppression of unchecked individuality. In exchange, it holds people together and offers rituals and prescriptions for action; it keeps people from what Buber called "lostness."

Social Constraint

The importance of embeddedness as a dimension of human relatedness varies by society. In very tight, rigidly controlled societies, individuals have relatively little latitude for personal choice and preference. Such societies govern relatedness as well as self-expression, and development becomes a problem of adapting the self to the requirements of social life or risking ostracism. Here group norms of obedience to family mores or religious dictates are held to be far more important for the individual than are interests of the self.

Nineteenth-century novels often center on the effort to carry out relationships in the idioms of "goodness" (as socially defined). Plot tension derives from the collision of individual personality and seemingly immutable social definition. In George Eliot's *Daniel Deronda* ([1876] 1967), for example, the characters struggle continually with how their birth-dictated social position shapes the possibility of relatedness. Gwendolyn, a poor though talented young woman, changes her social standing through marriage, bartering her attractiveness and competence for wealth. She then spends much of the rest of the novel trying to live with a husband who treats her unfeelingly, as an acquisition that he has purchased and controls. Deronda, with whom Gwendolyn feels an empathic bond but has no socially defined connection, is himself struggling with his "fit" in the social world. An orphan raised by a kind English squire, he feels incomplete without knowledge of his origins. Once he discovers that he was born to Jewish parents, he changes his whole orientation to his life, reorganizing himself and his attachments to meet his perceived commitment to this other social milieu. Our social meaning for others, then, can become the central thread of our life story. Beyond attachment and mutuality, belonging can be the primary focus of our lives together.

In the nineteenth century, social place was far more salient as a ground for relatedness in Western societies than individual feeling was. Selfhood was thought to exist in social position, in enduring commitment based on binding obligation (Bellah and others, 1985). In contrast, we in the twentieth century see the experience and expression of feelings as central to the real self. Thus a binding obligation in the service of values, religious duty, or social strictures is passing out of our twentieth-century lexicon of relatedness. While the freedom to connect to others based on emotional experience has been liberating, it has been achieved at the price of social disruption and anomie. Embeddedness, the secure sense of place, results from shared loyalty beyond emotional experience.

In less restrictive societies, we have more and more latitude in the forms of embeddedness open to us. We can be born poor and still aspire to join the exclusive country club or the prestigious professional society, for example. In more fluid societies, embeddedness thus becomes a form of identity formation: we come to be identified by our society as being like those with whom we join. Development in adult life often involves changing contexts of embeddedness. Midlife crises often create disjunction with one's group and an effort to search for another group whose rituals and symbolic life are more compatible with aspects of the self. The successful resolution of such a crisis of embeddedness is a deep sense that "here, with this group of people, I belong."

Within the relational spaces of the research subjects, embeddedness was nearest consciousness at times of identity change or loss of important attachments. Leaving home to pursue a career or an education or changing values or orientation to life makes for wrenching changes in feelings of embeddedness. "My parents were still there in the background," said Mary of her experience at age twenty-five, "but I was living in a whole new world in New York that seemed a million miles from them. I would call them each week and we would talk on the phone and I still knew they were my parents, but when I would go home at Christmas, I felt like I had just landed from another planet." For a long time, Mary felt confused about where she most "belonged"—on the North Dakota farm, with its rhythms of nature and animals, its relaxed Sunday suppers with the family, extended family, and neighborhood (all bringing pots of homemade something), or in the fast-paced New York fashion world, where she was a rising designer, exhilarated by the celebrities, the dinners in high-priced restaurants, and—on off nights—the dinners alone at midnight out of plastic containers.

Embeddedness and Other Forms of Relatedness

Embeddedness makes a lasting and indelible imprint on the context of other forms of relatedness. It is our social conventions that determine whether we will be raised by nannies and governesses or carried on our mother's back all day in the fields. We learn through socialization when, how, and with whom we may express our sexuality, when, if, and with whom we may marry, and when and if we may divorce. We also learn how we ought to view our relationships inside and outside of the family.

It is our broader social world that gives us a vocabulary for our interpersonal experiences. We "feel" toward another to the extent that our socialization has prepared us to express our emotional needs in one form or another. Even experiences as primal as sexual passion have been dictated by culture: passion was directed toward young boys among the Greeks, directed toward married women among the troubadours, and denied altogether among women of the Victorian period. One's mode of expression of passion, then, is both the basic experience of passion itself *and* the intrinsic and silent expression of cultural embeddedness.

ˋMarriage and relationships with children are similarly shaped by cultural embeddedness. Rather than being somehow innate (perhaps driven by human needs for attachment or passion), these are socially defined roles that to some extent express the assumptions of the society and the individual's needs to participate in those social forms. Thus marriage provides a socially defined place that varies by culture. We not only marry a person but also participate in the social institution of marriage. Social expectations about what marriage should provide the individual vary with the time and the place. In the history of human relatedness, marriage has served a variety of human needs, from joining large properties or entwining nations to serving emotional needs for mutuality. Similarly, societies have regarded children variously—sometimes as precious beings deserving of the utmost tenderness, in other times and places as expendable parasites. The human affectional systems, then, are flexible, and they are expressed through the individual's embeddedness in culture.

We may find the social rules either consonant with our predilections or widely discordant. But how we are with others, beyond the relationships themselves, makes a statement about our embeddedness. When we wish to make changes in relationships, we often must find new contexts of embeddedness as well.

Diana, for example (discussed in the last chapter), spoke of her sense that her marriage was as it "should" be. Married at her mother's urging, she stayed married for many years as a way of carrying out the social forms. She felt that she "ought" to be happy in this framework, because—according to the social definitions that surrounded her—she had all that was required. Only later did she allow herself to notice the disparity between her inner expectations—that is, her feelings toward her husband—and the set of feelings she was trying to live out. Her awareness of this disparity, as well as the new friends who took it seriously with her, led Diana to seek an alternate framework of embeddedness—a framework in which leaving Bill would not only make sense but be applauded. This, fortunately for Diana, was readily available in the early 1970s among women who were liberating themselves from stultifying marriages.

Because love and its forms of expression are woven into cultural networks, changes in primary relationships make systemic changes in all other relationships as well. Following divorce, for example, people often lose most of their accustomed social contacts. Newly single people do not "fit" in a coupled world, no matter how intimate and mutual the relationships may have been during their coupled stage. Not only is the newly single an "extra," but the fact of the divorce itself threatens the existence of continuing marriages, taking a chunk out of the context of embeddedness that supports the social institution of marriage. Being surrounded by couples makes a couple feel that—whatever the internal problems and disappointments—this is the way life is supposed to be (Rubin, 1985).

Similarly, social mores affect the possibilities of mutuality by the attention and space society gives to friendship. Holding is also in part determined by the extent to which a society honors nurturance.

Cultural Continuity

Embeddedness not only absorbs culture but gives rise to it. When we are embedded, we share a history with others that makes it possible to elevate our experience of life to a level of symbolic expression. Communal memory is the expression of embeddedness. It is not surprising that Lena, the group-therapy patient for whom embeddedness was such a central therapeutic factor, became the group historian. She remembered for all of us the members who had come and gone, the touchstone incidents and when they happened, when other members might be having anniversary reactions, and so on. Similarly, married couples or old friends often treasure the retelling of past shared experiences. When communal experience is written, we refer to it as literature; the communal memory of a group becomes valued as history. All these forms of memory record the continuity of the *we*.

Our embeddedness within a culture provides us fables and myths by which to evaluate our lives and our relationships and thereby determine if they are "coming out right." Our sharing in this culture becomes another opportunity to create with others something larger than ourselves. Here is a connection with humanity beyond mutuality. We can connect our lives to people in the past as well as to the unborn: we take our place among the generations.

Campbell (1972) points out that in embeddedness, the subordination of the self to the social order becomes a form of self-transcendence. By interpreting our lives in the same terms as those who have come before us and passing on these stories to the next generation, we ensure a continuity of our existence that outlasts ourselves.

And these ideas are borne out in everyday life. Some of the research interviewees reported intense connections, for example, to grandparents whom they barely knew personally; they felt the connection through embeddedness in the same values or group loyalties that the grandparents made paramount in their lives. In the same vein, concentration camp survivors who lost their families in World War II had intense needs for communal involvement. In order to feel connection and continuity across the generations, many of them felt intense ties to parents whom they could only imagine (Moskowitz, 1983).

In a new reading of tragic drama, Simon (1988) locates the essence of tragedy in the threat of discontinuity of generational links. Intrafamilial disputes must be resolved in the interest of continuing the line, preserving the "house." At the center of the *Oresteia*, for example, is the tragic conflict over whether Agamemnon should sacrifice his daughter, Iphigenia, in order to win the Trojan War and thus preserve his "house." Preservation of immortality through children involves coming to terms with "the passions, rivalries, conflicts, and consequent ambivalence of relationships" (p. 3) or risking extinction. Tragic conflict involves the sacrifice of relatedness within the family to protect embeddedness and continuity or, even more tragically, the sacrifice of generations for the sake of the individual. This is the tragic essence of giving our children to fight and die in war.

Individual Identity

When we are embedded, we walk through the world bearing the labels of our connections. I am an American, which becomes a more salient and noticeable aspect of my embeddedness when I am in another country. I am white, which I do not experience nearly as strongly as I would experience my racial identity if I were black. I am distinguishable from others in being a psychologist, which provokes a myriad of reactions from different people: some assume that I must be like Joyce Brothers or Ruth Westheimer (perhaps the only other psychologists they have encountered), and some fear that they will be transparent to me. And I am a woman, the social meaning of which I have seen change (and have struggled to change) profoundly in the past twenty-five years. There are many other contexts in which I feel embedded, where I have joined and belong. But being American in the late twentieth century, I would not put these memberships first in thinking about who I am (as I undoubtedly would have had if I lived a century ago).

Unlike the other dimensions of relatedness, embeddedness is an impersonal experience. It is not eye to eye or side by side; it is abstract. The American predilection for individualism has tended to disown the collective aspects of our identity, valuing personal autonomy and self-realization over notions of place in group. Dion and Dion (1988) discuss the differences in the experience of interpersonal relatedness within the collectivist orientation of Oriental cultures: there the individual self is emotionally real only in terms of role, place, and face within a defined social group.

American anomie, while widespread, is not universal. It is furthered, however, by the tendency of the American idiom (and the idiom of American psychology) to highlight the individual, to treat embeddedness as potential quicksand that threatens to engulf and overwhelm the individual. The social group, in this schema, is viewed as those whose influence is to be resisted, rebelled against, or used as a backdrop for the heightening of the boundaries of the self. Our loyalty to our group or sense of obligation to our role is, at least in certain sectors of American society, experienced as vaguely shameful.

But neither extreme is ideal. An individual not embedded with others is an egoist; too much embeddedness results in blind conformity. A theoretical viewpoint that too rigidly distinguishes between the individual and the group is itself in danger of these pitfalls. The distinction between the individual and the group is, in some ways, merely a cognitive convenience. The group contains the individual, who contains the group (Bion, 1961). And the tensions on the boundary between individual and group provide the fuel that powers human life.

Embeddedness in the Life Cycle

The awareness of embeddedness requires the cognitive capacity to appreciate the ways in which individuals join together and identify themselves and each other. As children, our embeddedness is ascribed—we are born as royalty or paupers—and we are socialized to behave as members of whatever social group we are raised in. Parental control is often explicitly in terms of group identity: "If you eat like that, people will think you were brought up in a slum," "Good Catholics don't do things like that," "Liberals don't say such bigoted things: you may not use that word in this house," and so on. Our embeddedness as children follows our attachments. Those with whom we live, who are our primary caretakers, define what we are in the larger social world. Through childhood, we are "Mr. and Mrs. Smith's child," no matter what we do or think.

It is not until adolescence that we discover that values and attitudes totally unacceptable in the group in which we are embedded are not only tolerated but valued elsewhere. With this discovery, embeddedness often begins to diverge from attachment. The processes of identity formation afford adolescents the opportunity to choose those with whom they wish to associate and be linked.

Although within the larger social world the young person remains identified as an offshoot of the family of origin, the business of finding a place in a group has been taking place since middle childhood. Children even before adolescence (and certainly during) make their own groups of embeddedness, learn to identify each other according to these labels, and rehearse issues of loyalty and exclusion. Clubs and cliques emerge whose sole purpose seems to be that of defining who is in and who is out. Young people begin to define each other in terms of belonging with one or another group, formal or informal. ("She's one of the snobs." "He plays only with the jocks.") Everyone seems to know which are the "in" groups and which the undesirables. Those of us who treat adolescents have to stay current on always-shifting group definitions. Our adolescent patients cannot imagine that a world defined by "heads," "geeks," "preps," "jocks" and so forth is not a universal reality.

Dress, jewelry, and language become symbols of youthful allegiance to one group or another. Although the various adolescent subcultures may look very different from the dominant culture, they are in fact rehearsals for and mirrors of the adult world that the adolescent will soon join. (Adults, after all, have their own codes of dress, jewelry, and language.) In these subcultures, adolescents practice expressing identity with the group, practice joining. Beginning at adolescence and continuing throughout life, it is a grievous experience to belong nowhere at all.

embeddedness

attachment

splits at adolescence

Ideology may also carry the adolescent into new frames of embeddedness. As the adolescent sifts through and integrates emerging identity elements, the frames of embeddedness similarly shift. (This shift is in part what gives adolescents the reputation for being unreliable.) Joining a new way of thinking or valuing often means joining different people as well.

Where the context of embeddedness that adolescents choose is very different from that of their childhood, young people may have to weave a complex relational web to maintain both the new embeddedness and the old attachments. It is often difficult for parents (as well as theorists and therapists) to understand that a major tension of adolescence results from this splitting off of embeddedness from attachment. Adolescents feel (and wish to retain) their attachment to parents, but the needs for special kinds of validation that the parents cannot supply drive them to new arenas of embeddedness. Adolescents may experience a new (and important) sense of belonging, a sense of having a "place" that is uniquely theirs among like-minded others, with friends or groups whose appeal is incomprehensible to parents. Yet these adolescents may be no less "attached" to their family.

For some adolescents and adults, embeddedness and attachment are so overlapping as to be indistinguishable. These people are content to stay close to home, belonging only to the family. In these instances, the family is itself a framework of embeddedness, linked to other such families (or to the institution of the family).

Rita, a thirty-five-year-old research subject, for example, was an "Army brat" whose family moved at least once a year. Her relational diagram was unusual: she included no one to whom she was not related by blood. Her family was central throughout her childhood and until she married and had children. When I asked her why she put only relatives on her chart, Rita added two "bunched" groups that she remembered as having had some importance to her. At age fifteen, there were teammates with whom she played soccer; at age twenty-five, when she returned to school, there was a group of classmates with whom she discussed schoolwork.

But at thirty-five, she could hardly remember individuals in these groups. Her investment in them had faded quickly, and she had moved on again. Rita had learned to "fit in" in many different environments and with many different people, but she felt that she "belonged" only when she was with her family. Familial attachments were the only ones that held vivid emotional reality for her. For Rita, attachment and embeddedness were synonymous.

At the other extreme is Lois. At age forty, unmarried, she lives in Hong Kong and works as a successful accountant for a large international firm. Her world is a glittery one of international high finance, and the people with whom she is most intertwined are friends, colleagues, and associates in the financial world. She left home just after college and has lived abroad most of the time since. She has had many adventures and many complex relationships during those years, but her sense of attachment to her mother, back home in Florida, remains. She continues to call her mother once each week, no matter where she is, and she stops to visit her whenever she is in the neighborhood of North America. When her mother became ill, Lois took a leave of absence from her job and went to Florida to take care of her. Lois felt completely out of place in the North Florida community where she grew up and where her mother was still living, but her sense of attachment and her tenderness were more motivating for her than her embeddedness. Lois felt confident that her place in her other world would remain for her; she carried her sense of embeddedness with her.

Embeddedness is always an internal sense of belonging, although people may choose to make their group attachments more or less visible. Embeddedness is one of the most slippery of the dimensions, because it can masquerade as other dimensions or be so taken for granted that it seems to disappear. It is most apparent in its absence, in the individual without a group, even a fairly abstract group, who experiences anomie and meaninglessness.

Sometimes embeddedness is visible only through the forms of behavior—for example, loyalty and allegiance—to which it gives rise. We may be unaware of the depths of our embeddedness until our group is threatened. Individuals who did not even know that they were patriotic, for example, find themselves willing to die for their country or for a cause. Embeddedness, with its potential for collective action, is a sleeping giant. Roused from its silent slumber, it can become the most powerful of human forces, binding people together in potent unification of will.

Ezra

Ezra was three when his parents immigrated to the United States from Poland, escaping the Nazis. They settled in a small textile-manufacturing town in South Carolina. Thinking back to age five, Ezra said without hesitation that his main awareness was of not feeling part of the group. Even at this age, in his mind were paired the picture of the typical American and his absolute and painful awareness that he was not that. Everything about his family was different—their language, their dress, their ways of treating him and each other. "My parents were close to me, but I wanted them to be like the others. I hated their behavior. They wanted to fit in too, but they couldn't because they were new. I was the only boy in our group not born there. Also, the other kids had self-esteem because they had big brothers and sisters, and I was the oldest and small for my age. There were lots of problems. I was very aggressive and problematic in nursery school and kindergarten and then in school. I was always getting in fights." Ezra remembers his parents as trying to take care of him, but he resisted their help, saw them as the people he wanted to get away from.

By age ten, Ezra had managed to use his skill with a baseball bat and glove to gain some respect in his school group. He still felt like an outsider, however—especially when his parents cheered for his team in Yiddish-accented English. He envied the other boys, who were surrounded by "respectable" people—strong older brothers, distinguished-looking fathers, well-dressed mothers. He felt his parents there as a home base and rested on them, but he resented them as well. "My mother took care of all my physical needs, but I really wanted to be far from the family. She was very intrusive, always wanted to know about everything I did, and I hated it. I wanted to be free, to do what I wanted and not what they wanted."

Around this time a new boy, also an immigrant, joined their class. This boy seemed to take Ezra's place as the class scapegoat, with Ezra often leading the torment against him. "We were really cruel. We would send the dogs to chase him until he cried, and then we would beat him up. I could feel part of the group by being against him. The most important thing was to be part of the group, the leader of the group, to be strong. That's how we felt we had to survive—otherwise, we are nothing. I would do just about anything not to be left out."

Ezra had two brothers by this time: Howard, who was five, and a newborn. Telling about this period of his life with some shame, he recalled hitting Howard often, mercilessly, and uncontrollably. "It would start with play. I was still small and weak, and he was very strong. Then he would cry and everyone in town would hear and know that I was hitting him again. My parents took me to a psychologist, who tried to understand why I hit him so much." I asked Ezra if he had an explanation. "I think it was from love," he said. Hitting Howard was perhaps a desperate effort to make a real emotional connection with him, Ezra surmised. "If anyone else wanted to hit him, I didn't allow it; I defended him."

With the newborn, however, Ezra was exceptionally caring. "I'm sure I took care of him more than any other brother I ever heard of. I would get up at night if he cried and change his diapers. I loved to feed him."

By the time he was fifteen, still not feeling part of the group, Ezra had become almost impossible to contain at school. He did not study, and he fought with all of his teachers. Often he would stay out all night, and he continued to hit and torment Howard. Because his parents could not manage him, it became clear that some change was necessary. An uncle who had immigrated to one of the northern states but had never been close to the family heard about these problems and offered to help by paying Ezra's tuition to boarding school. Ezra relished the idea of getting away.

At his new school, Ezra began a new life and a new self. Telling no one there about his background and previous school experience, he set about establishing himself as an excellent student and a leader of the group. "I liked the school and the people around me. Nobody knew or cared that I had an immigrant background. At boarding school, no one has parents. I was able to use all my potential."

From this age, Lenny appears on Ezra's relational chart. He

and Lenny were roommates for four years. They came to the same room by chance and stayed there. "After three years, we saw that we were friends." They did not talk about anything personal; they just knew that they were friends.

Ezra got into the occasional fight but was mainly able to restrain himself. He was focused on making good, on being able to go back and impress all those people back home with his achievements.

Part of what made him a leader in his group, besides doing well in school and lettering in track, was his success with girls. Ezra had many girlfriends, mainly for sex, but his heart had already been claimed by a girl he had seen at a mixer between boarding schools. He had seen Melissa across the room—blond, blue-eyed, as much an American WASP as one could imagine—and had vowed that he would marry her. "I was very ambitious at that time," Ezra said. He told his friends that he intended to marry Melissa, but he never spoke to her about it. In fact, he never spoke to her at all.

After he graduated, Ezra began to write to Melissa from college, but they did not actually speak to each other for another two years. Then Melissa, who was two years younger than he, ended up at the same university, and they began to date. When she became pregnant a year later (he was twenty-two), they decided to marry. Ezra had always intended to return to the town where he was raised, to "fit in" at last, so they headed south. Returning in triumph with Melissa, some self-confidence, and a business degree, Ezra was invited to join a fledgling carpentry business with the former "leader" of his class. Flattered at having been asked by someone with such a good reputation, Ezra took this on. Now his name was linked with someone who was respected.

By the time Ezra was twenty-five, his business partner had decided to go to California, and Ezra bought out his share of the business. By now another child had been born, but Ezra, working long hours, left the childraising to Melissa.

Ezra's relational chart shows him, at age twenty-five, in a tight circle with Melissa and their children. This circle is inside the circle of the community, which includes his parents and his brothers. Just outside is a circle to represent Lenny, who remained his "best friend" although they saw each other infrequently. This pattern continued without much variation for the next twenty-five years.

Now at age fifty, Ezra is the head of a large, successful construction company and the father of eight children. He has held major community positions in the town, including president of the town council. With his large family increasingly present, he has felt over the years a growing sense of belonging. Now he feels that it is "his" town. (For the most part, he has built it with his construction company and populated it as well!)

He perceives little change or development in his relationship with Melissa over the years, although she herself has changed: she is now active in the town she at first resisted living in. She has headed many organizations and is regarded with respect, as a leader. Clearly, Ezra also admires and values her. He had wanted yet more children, but at age forty-three she said that she was finished with procreation. This is Ezra's only source of disappointment in her.

Ezra continues to go to his parents' for dinner once a week and still struggles against his mother's intrusiveness, but he is on pleasant and warm terms with them. Sometimes his children feel that he is too harsh with his mother; he feels that she has learned over the years to respect his need for distance and is more content to leave him alone. Ezra's brothers have joined him in the business, and they work well together. They trust each other, know that they will always be there for one another.

Every few years he sees Lenny, and they continue to feel like best friends. When they meet, they talk about their lives—not deep feelings, just keeping up with one another—and they know that they can count on each other if need be. When Ezra's son went to college in a city near Lenny's, for example, Lenny checked on him, invited him to his home, introduced him to people—all without Ezra's having to ask. Lenny has a retarded daughter, and Ezra feels that it is important to know about her, to worry, even at a distance, with his friend.

As Ezra reflects on his relationships through his life, he stresses the importance of the faceless community of which he finally became a leader. "I think I finally did all the things I had wanted to do as a child in this town." He sees in one of his daughters, who has had many illnesses and is not very bright, the struggle to be part of the group. He feels that he can understand her more than any of the other children. She, too, is prone to tantrums and angry outbursts. "She reminds me of myself. It's hard to live through as a parent, but I know that sometimes she suffers a lot." Ezra is proud that his is an important family, that they are sought after for social occasions, that they matter in the town.

Ezra is on warm terms with people, and his eyes sparkle as he talks about this. "I see them and I'm happy to see them, and we talk and joke together or go for a beer. But they don't influence me really. Very few people are really, really close to me."

It was hard to end the interview with Ezra. He said that he was surprised at his openness, that he had told me things that he had never told anyone in his life. It was a somewhat wrenching experience for him, because he had never oriented himself to sharing his inner life. Yet despite the absence of an inner life or passionate attachments, Ezra has attained interpersonal contentment.[2] Perhaps he could afford to reveal himself to me simply because I am not a part of his embeddedness: he has no position to place at risk with me. For Ezra, as for many others, embeddedness and intimacy are unrelated. Place and role become a mode of connection with the human community independent of emotional exchange. Fitting in, with its emphasis on sameness and group identity, requires adaptation rather than heightened individuality. The focus is on what is shared rather than what is internal, and life is lived in the comfort of a valued alcove—a place in the world that is one's own. Embeddedness, then, provides identity rather than a means of exploring it.

Ezra's quest for belonging also led him to use his skills and creativity in his work. A "good-enough" culture empowers and energizes the individual through the possibilities of embeddedness that it affords (Kotre, 1984). Motives to join, to belong, and to take and maintain a place with others are all potent forces that impel initiative. Needs to express group ethos and group experience on behalf of all the members give rise to many forms of artistic creativity. A "good-enough" culture offers meaningful ways for the individual to exist through, on behalf of, and within the group.

Chapter 10

Tending (Care)

She openeth her mouth with wisdom,
and in her tongue is the law of kindness.

—Proverbs 311:26

All writing about human relatedness focuses on what we need in order to survive, both physically and psychologically. We need to be held, to be kept from falling; we need the support and encouragement of others; we need others to be reliable attachment figures who will be "there" for us in times of need; we need others to recognize and validate us, to help us structure our own sense of reality; and we need others to embody our ideals, to stimulate us and help us learn how to be. To provide for all these needs, all we have is other people—people no more godlike and no less needy than ourselves. And we do such providing, in return, as best we can, out of our need and capacity to care about and tend to others.

The human need to tend, to offer care, reflects our need to feel needed by others.[1] Rollo May (1969) suggests that care is a combination of love and will. He points out that the word *tend* had the same linguistic root as *intention*. Thus when we tend another, we do so deliberately, intentionally. We *choose* to offer ourselves in the service of another.

Tend is also related linguistically to both *tenderness* and *attentiveness*. Sullivan (1953) uses the word *tenderness* to describe what, besides food and oral gratification, a mother offers her baby. He posits that the "mothering one" has a general need to give tenderness that is complementary to the infant's need to receive tenderness. This "general need" to give tenderness is, in Sullivan's hypothesis, a result of the tension induced in the mother by the tension in the infant.

We also need a word like *tendingness*, which would denote the proclivity to nurture, care, attend, and respond. This orientation to others is a form of connection that is at once a product of ethical decision making and an outgrowth of human emotional organization. An ethical system based on care (Noddings, 1984) places affect at its center. Our need to tend unites emotion and thought. When care comes from the heart, morality arises from the experience of connection (Gilligan, 1982).

The Sources of Tending and Care

Nurturance, like the Nile for so much of its history, is the sustenance of life, yet we have only vague, magical ideas of its source. We know, certainly, that the helplessness of the human infant necessitates a long period of care. And if we have grown and thrived, we have experienced, at least to some extent, the satisfaction of our needs for food, warmth, and comfort—for all that nurturance entails. We know what it is to be cared for.

Psychological theory has, to this point, not proceeded past the fairly straightforward assertion that out of the experience of nurturance grow the wish and capacity to nurture in return (Benedek, 1960).[2] While this undoubtedly is so, it leaves unasked some of the most interesting questions. How does the experience and integration of care change and develop across the life cycle? How is the need to tend expressed under different circumstances? And why has this been so much the relatively unnoticed and undervalued province of women?

What efforts there have been in psychology to investigate the expression of the need to tend have focused on the care of infants. While this may indeed be a prototype situation of tending, care and concern exist in much broader realms of human existence. The equation of care with the tending of children again reflects our propensity to demean and infantilize that which is relational. We *all* need tending—in babyhood and in old age, but in adulthood as well. Beyond that, we all need to tend, to express a side of ourselves, whatever its origin, that bespeaks our human need to care.

Erikson (1964) goes so far as to suggest that our identity is equivalent to what we will tend. Our declaration of what we will stand for in life—our identity, in other words—is a statement about what we will look after. I would add to this that it is not just the *what* but the *who* that is central here.[3] Because we are the object of care and solicitude for so many years, we long to grow into someone who can be the source of caring, of that which is so much valued. Erikson suggests that we create all-caring gods not only out of "persisting infantile need for being taken care of, but also [as] a projection onto a superhuman agency of an ego-ideal" (p. 131). We aspire, in this view, to the godliness of giving.

Like most other theorists, Erikson posits a flow of sustenance from being nurtured to the capacity to care. Melanie Klein ([1946] 1975) similarly suggests that a connection between gratification and gratitude leads to a wish to return pleasure, but she thinks that the capacity to love is innate. In the experience of tenderness, in her view, we offer to others what we experience to be good inside of us: we offer our emotional resources. We may put aside some of our own needs and demands in the interest of others. In return, we experience joy, which is the emotional accompaniment of the fulfillment of caring (Noddings, 1984). When we care, we feel ourselves to be fully in relation to an Other. If we presume that human nature is fundamentally object-seeking rather than pleasure-seeking, tending becomes a link to the Other, another way of making connection (Gilligan, Lyons, and Hammer, 1990; Sharabany, 1984).

A genuinely caring, altruistic connection to another requires devotion, but how much selflessness is necessary? Here we are hovering dangerously on the brink of idealization, and caring is rarely so faultless. Selfless love that demands nothing in return, love focused only on the needs of the other, is an archetypal form of love. In her moving book about the illness and death of her son, Mary Lou Weisman (1982) describes her own struggle with the longing to be able to offer this kind of perfect love. Its wellspring, in her experience, is a "collective nostalgia" for a kind of care that we may never have received but that is rooted in a primordial knowing or yearning. And this form of love, never quite fully experienced, is also never fully achievable. We are able, then, to articulate well either the all-giving ideal (the "perfect mother") or the failure of care (all that we have not done for someone that we ought to have done or that we wish we had done or that they wish we had done, and so on). What we lack is a concept of "good-enough" caring.

Because we tend to equate motherliness and care, our attitudes toward tending are fused with our attitudes toward being mothered. Tenderness is the ideal of motherliness, perhaps, but it is our very conflicts around the experience of being tended and nurtured that make this such a difficult topic to discuss. We are never more vulnerable than when we are in need, and it is our (vaguely remembered) and terrifying experiences of being helplessly *un*tended that lead to our powerful defenses against and denials of our need for care. Speaking from a feminist point of view, Luepnitz (1988) suggests that nurturance is a taboo topic of discussion under a patriarchy that is contemptuous and frightened of mothering. Balint (1959), years earlier, coming from a different continent and tradition, similarly wonders whether the neediness represented by the need for the mother is so primitive or dangerous that no language has words to describe it. Thus, defensively, we disown and depreciate, demean and devalue this dimension of experience. (See also Miller, 1986.) Caretaking jobs are usually the lowest paid and afforded the least respect. Those of us in the "helping sciences" (such as medicine and psychotherapy) publicly emphasize the "science" part of what we do; and we do not acknowledge too openly that we are in the business of taking care.

Tending is rooted in affect rather than action, and this, too, makes it difficult to articulate in language. Tenderness and attentiveness—the experience of tending—is an *attitude,* an offering of ineffable substance of the self. (Mothers can feed grudgingly and resentfully as well as tenderly.) As recipients of care, we *feel* its presence, although it may be invisible to an observer. Similarly, as recipients we may *feel* its absence, although the deeds themselves may appear charitable or generous. Belinda, a patient of mine who longs for understanding from her parents, receives only checks. She sees their gifts as an effort to buy her silence about their neglect of her. Their actions do not feel like care; she feels no tenderness in their financial largesse. (Her parents, however, may well feel that they are being caring, that they are giving what they can.)

Although we idealize motherhood as the fount of tenderness, we nevertheless are most familiar clinically with mothers' failures of nurturance. Nowhere in the psychological literature is an article describing a "good mother." (In fact, if a patient describes his or her mother as good, the therapist writing the case is likely to note that the patient's mother has been "idealized.") Case report after case report in the psychological literature chastises (scientifically) mothers for not giving enough. We end up, then, with a mythology that says that mothers tend and care and a clinical literature that testifies to unmet needs for such care. But, as Sara Ruddick (1989) points out, mothers are usually young women. What should make them automatically or universally or consistently tender? Where, then, does tending originate, and how is it sustained?

People differ dramatically, one from another, in how and how much they can care. But we have no theory with which to understand such variation—especially if we are wedded to the assumption that the need to tend flows from the experience of having been cared for. How do we account for people who were given a great deal of care as children yet grow into relatively insensitive, uncaring adults? Or those who received little yet care much? Here Eleanor Roosevelt, orphaned and relatively untended as a child, is an excellent example. After the early loss of her mother, she was abandoned by her much-adored father, who then died as well. Taken in by a harsh aunt, she knew little warmth or affection as a child. Yet she became in her adulthood a symbol and embodiment of caregiving, able to offer to others not what she had received but what she had lacked (Lash, 1973). Similarly, child survivors of the Holocaust who became good and loving parents give lie to the notion that you cannot give what you did not get (Moskowitz, 1983).

There appears to be nothing automatic about the capacity to love and to care. Like other aspects of personality, it develops through complex sequences and processes that have been largely unexplored. Tending and care develop through struggle and reflection. Care involves the effort to balance the interests of the self and the interests of a (cared-for) other, and it requires thinking and strategy. Ruddick (1989) points out that the scrambling, temperamental toddler in search of poisons under the sink and the school-child left out of a birthday party are more emblematic of the demands on a mother than is the nursing infant, which is what psychological theory is most apt to consider. In overemphasizing the feeding situation, and in equating it with care, we have obscured and overshadowed the intricacies of the interpersonal challenges of tending to another.

Our late-twentieth-century philosophy of the primacy of self-interest simply ignores these dilemmas. At its worst, our popular self-help literature tends to view suspiciously all expressions of care: concern with another's needs may be a symptom of overprotection, codependency, passivity, or self-denial. If we do not know how to create a kinder world, presumably, we might as well just look out for ourselves. We want tenderness and care simply to be there. We do not want to have to look at or for it or watch how it grows.

Tending, the most ubiquitous of human interactions, goes far beyond parenting. We offer our help and sustenance in momentary as well as grand ways many times each day. Tenderness exists in kindness and compassion, in a wink of encouragement, in visiting a sick friend, in a touch of solace to the bereaved, in a special gift that brings pleasure to someone we like. We tend not only by taking care of someone but by taking on their cares (Gilligan, 1990), worrying with them, intervening for them. We tend relationships as well as particular others, by enacting dozens of small, practical rituals that strengthen our bonds: looking after the home, taking charge of the neighborhood get-together, and so on (Bateson, 1989). Tending is everywhere around us, yet few of us will note it in recounting to ourselves the day's happenings. In response to tenderness, we feel gratitude and warmth. In the absence of being tended, we feel cold (and perhaps unloved). In the absence of being able to express care, we feel deadened, unmoved.

In extreme situations of human cruelty, tenderness is most likely to emerge as an affirmation of what is good in human existence. A released prisoner of war, for example, holds on to his belief in human potential, remembering the kindness of one of his jailers. "There was this one nice warden. At night he would sneak into my cell, take off my handcuffs and clean my wounds. For a week they were not bringing me any food, so this warden had pity on me. One night he brought me a cake from the marketplace" (Lieblich, 1990, p. 115). This jailer *cared*, as do people who risk their lives to save a stranger. Our tenderness is what is best in us. It is our capacity to love.

Children seem naturally concerned about the helpless and needy. Anxiously, they ask about the beggar in the street; they feel terror and pity at news photos of starving children. Angrily, they demand to know why we cannot save these people, feed them, house them. We just *can't*, we answer, discouraging further questions. We teach our children to live with others' misery, to screen out others' need. Maturity is hardening ourselves, we imply; growing up is learning to be selective about those we care for. It may be, then, that care is the natural state. Perhaps what we learn with development is how *not* to care.

Rarely a unitary emotional experience, the giving of care involves emotional sequences. In search of the roots of altruism, the Oliners interviewed European Christians who had rescued or protected Jews from the Nazis (Oliner and Oliner, 1988). These rescuers described having felt pity, annoyance, and resentment, as well as responsibility, compassion, and concern, toward those whom they chose to save. In contrast to nonrescuers (people who were in a position to protect Jews but did not), rescuers had a capacity for greater investment in others, which seemed to arise from closer familial relatedness—especially closeness to their mothers. Their families had stressed generosity and the obligation to help others, not only in the immediate family but also within the larger community. The rescuers did not, however, see themselves as having been heroic or having displayed exemplary courage; they were merely more responsive to others' pain.

Even responsiveness to those closest to us involves integration of disparate emotional capacities. Mary Main found that she could predict on the basis of attachment histories who would parent a securely attached child (Main, Kaplan, and Cassidy, 1985). Her studies indicate that adult representations of attachment are more complex than simply good and bad experiences. It is the capacity to integrate positive and negative, general and specific, into some coherent understanding of our early attachment experiences that predicts who will parent a secure child. In other words, parents of insecure children were parents whose need to keep themselves unaware of aspects of their early relationships left them unable to respond sensitively to the attachment needs of their children.

Tending requires first the empathic capacity both to know what another is feeling and to feel moved by it. In other words, in order to be empathic, we must be able to put aside our own experience, at least momentarily, and reverberate to the feelings of another. Having admitted this emotional experience, we then allow our own emotional response—our compassion and care—to come to the fore: in whatever way seems most appropriate, we communicate our understanding and attempt to help or comfort.

In the absence of nurturing connections to others, people sink into self-absorption. Focused solely on themselves, they must hoard all of their resources and orient themselves to what more they might pry from others. But they feel empty. We equate monstrousness with the inability to tend and care. A being without compassion or human feeling, the monster is the most reviled character in our mythology. That is why the worst of human fears is not of being unloved but of being unable to love.

What tenderness we do exhibit is rarely "pure." There is often an intricate relationship between tenderness and hate, for example. A tender response requires an integration of complex affects. Klein and Riviere (1967) view love as an effort to make reparation for the murderous fantasies engendered by infantile envy, while Ruddick (1989) makes the wry but true observation that the first task of maternal care is not to murder one's child, which is a constant adaptive struggle.

The problem, then, is to be able to discuss the need to tend (to attend and to be tender) without sentimentalizing it. Tending is not just a reaction formation against aggression, nor does aggression detract from it. Instead, caring as a form of connection exists in a cauldron of affect that includes rage, boredom, resentment, and other manifestations of our hostility, and these manifestations may be aroused, paradoxically, by the acts of caretaking themselves. This is what is so hard to remember when discussing care: love and hate are parallel, not opposite, streams of experience.

The Connected Self and the Ethic of Care

Carol Gilligan (1982) had an enormous impact on the field of psychology as the first to speak clearly and intelligently about the ethic of care and responsiveness as an organizer of experience. Taking issue with the exclusive focus on fairness and rights as central tenets of moral development, Gilligan showed how a woman's psychological development often resides in the deepening of her understanding of care. Concern for and sensitivity to others, in conjunction with the responsibility for taking care, leads women to attend to voices other than their own in forming judgment. Moral awareness thus becomes an effort to orchestrate and be responsive to people's needs rather than to manifest allegiance to abstract principles. In this view, care evolves out of the experience of living in and maintaining connection to each other.

Moral concerns within the ethic of care thread through issues of selfishness and responsibility as we seek to nurture and to avoid inflicting pain. While a justice orientation invokes homage to abstract principles of fairness, care demands a human face. It requires both an understanding of what is needed by another and an ability to balance one's own capacities and needs with the capacities and needs of another. To tend too much is to risk the martyrdom of excessive self-sacrifice. Because relationship implies preservation of both self and other, selflessness abolishes relatedness and sidesteps, rather than enlarges, the interconnections of care. To tend too little is to incur guilt and the cold mantle of selfishness. (How often my patients inquire of me anxiously whether their actions or thoughts are "selfish." I am aware that within the Weltanschauung of the psychotherapeutic ethical system, a concept of selfishness simply does not exist.) The development of the capacity to care, then, is an ongoing calibration of conflicting needs and interests, a balancing act of never-ending complexity that is the core of relationship. The fundamental question, from this vantage point, is the problem of living in connection with oneself and with others (Gilligan, 1982, 1990).

The ethic of care, the "different voice" that Gilligan (1982) articulated, gives rise to morality based on human connection—a morality that has been frequently denigrated. Freud, for example, was contemptuous of women for showing less sense of justice than men and being easily influenced in their judgments by feelings of affection or hostility ([1925] 1955b). But, as the Oliners concluded in their study of altruism, "the virtue that may arise out of attachments, care and affiliations with other people is no less meritorious or reliable than that which arises out of autonomous abstract thought" (Oliner and Oliner, 1988, p. 258).

Variations in Tending

People tend in different ways. We sometimes misread what is intended as a caring response, or we may feel care but be unsure how to express it. Tending is often a subtle process: a small difference in voice tone or the quality of a smile can create consolation or warmth.

Men and women tend differently. Some of this difference may derive from the fact that the expression of care is not directly translatable into action but resides in an empathic and attentive orientation that allows a person to divine what the other needs or wants.[4] Women, identifying with the mother who was our first nurturer, have little conflict about expressing care. Men, on the other hand, must learn to express care within an idiom that does not threaten their masculine identification (Chodorow, 1978). In our consulting rooms, we often find women trying in vain to elicit a certain kind of responsiveness from their husbands. "She" asks for a token, a gesture, a sign of his affection. "He," trying to comply, brings her flowers. She tells him, in the words of Prufrock, that that was not what she meant at all. The dialogue seems impossible, because the language and symbols are so different.

For men, tending often seems to find expression in both concrete and indirect forms. Men are likely to express care through protectiveness, for example. By shielding those for whom he cares, a man experiences himself as tending. Men tend at a greater physical and affective distance than women, and in different media and different styles. "Didn't you notice that I was sad and needed comforting?" says she. "Well, I washed your car for you, didn't I?" replies he.

Women are more likely to provide supplies and do the validating. They are more apt to promote eye-to-eye closeness (to "listen," to "understand") and to revel in mutuality.

People differ, too, in their perception of care. There are those, for example, who clearly read and experience the caring intent in actions that others ignore. Amy, who described her father as absent, unavailable, alcoholic, and often abusive, nevertheless said, "We knew he loved us." I asked how they knew. "Well, he used to cut flowers from the garden for us and go out to the store for ice cream. Little things. We knew."

Tenderness does not yield its secrets to logical positivism. It has no formula. There are many ways to nurture, because tenderness is orientation and receptivity, not behavior. People are often good at some kinds of caring and poor at others. Some people, for example, are excellent as attachment figures—always dependable, always ready to pick you up at the airport or bring you food if you are sick—but you would never look to them for validation or deep resonance. Other people use apparent kindness in the service of their aggression, hostility, or competitiveness. On the other hand, anger and discipline can be tender: witness, for example, the intense caring behind Mammy's tirades to Scarlett in *Gone with the Wind*.

Efforts to tend can misfire. Because caregivers do not necessarily require a response in order to feel connected, we may give too much or too little. The perception of need may be faulty, for example, or the intention to care may be experienced by the other as suffocating, controlling, or patronizing. ("But I *meant* well.") Tact, timing, warmth, and expressiveness represent major developmental achievements. Successful tending is an exquisitely balanced operation.

Even when our best efforts at tending seem to have no effect on the other, they may remain important to us. Kevin spoke of how he used to put his young daughter on the back of his bike each day and pedal five miles to a playground that she adored. He would stand there for over an hour and push her on the swing; then he would wait another hour while she climbed on the bars and slid down the slide. When his daughter graduated from college, he reminded her of those days, a time when he felt a special connection to her. To his initial chagrin, she did not remember that period at all. But Kevin concluded that her obliviousness to his early devotion did not really matter. It was a special memory to him, and he could treasure it nonetheless.

Fundamentally, caring creates connection between us. Like the Little Prince with his rose, we are anchored by caring. When we tend to others, putting their needs on a par with our own, we have a share of their life, too; thus we enlarge our own selfhood.

Developmental Aspects of Tending

Tending requires the motivation and ability to be aware of and to respond to another's state of need. We know that the capacity to be aware of another's feelings and to respond compassionately exists in very young children (Klein and Riviere, 1967). Studies of infancy have demonstrated that even infants can perceive and attempt to improve their mothers' moods. The capacity to care seems to be present in nascent form from the beginning of life, and it unfolds, gaining in complexity, as development proceeds.

How we are treated as an infant and young child has profound implications for our capacity to respond tenderly to others. Abused toddlers, for example, are unsympathetic to agemates in distress, while toddlers who have affectionate and caring parents make efforts to be comforting (Zahn-Waxler, Radke-Yarrow, and King, 1979). There is at least some research evidence that people treat each other as they have been treated, even from a very early age.

Nurturing and caring children appear to retain those traits. Longitudinal research carried out by developmental psychologists on prosocial behavior demonstrates consistency of altruism through the early years of childhood. The tendency to be responsively concerned about others seems to emerge early in development and to proceed with some predictability across both situations and time (Mussen and Eisenberg-Berg, 1977), but it is always subject to ongoing learning and revision.

Quite early in life, children begin trying to take care. Many of the people I interviewed still recall their first experiences of tending—primarily the tending of younger brothers and sisters. They remember with joyful affection (as well, very often, as jealousy and competitiveness) the arrival of new siblings and the pleasures of caring for them.

In their interactions with other children, children learn about the dynamics of caring and sharing; that is, they learn through *experiencing* what goes on among themselves. From childhood on, but particularly during adolescence, developing young people struggle with the care issues enacted on the playground and in the peer group: inclusion and exclusion, responsiveness, fairness, helpfulness, kindness, and so on (Gilligan, Lyons, and Hammer, 1990).

Sullivan (1953) placed the development of care later than current researchers do. In his view, people first move toward supplying each other with satisfactions just before adolescence. In this "chumship" phase, children between the ages of eight and a half and ten begin to take their first steps toward adjustment of their own behavior to the expressed needs of others. This search for mutual satisfaction involves the practice of attentiveness to another, of sensitivity to what matters to another person. Sullivan saw this occurring at an affective, interpersonal level just for the pure joy of the closeness itself. Robert White (1966) extends this process further along the life course and makes the expansion of caring a central developmental task of young adulthood.

Most efforts to study the development of care locate its origins in the mother-child interaction. Yet the capacity to tend develops continuously. Later sources of love and care may enrich growth and open up new possibilities for caring. Feeling adequately responded to after an emotionally deprived childhood may tap unexpected wellsprings of tenderness. Selma Fraiberg's work with seriously disadvantaged mothers, for example, demonstrates how one can empower even a seriously depressed mother by being emotionally responsive to her (Fraiberg, Adelson, and Shapiro, 1975). Many of the people in the research study similarly reported experiences with people after childhood who "taught me how to love."

Developmental psychology, in contrast to interpersonal psychiatry, most often places tenderness and care within the context of moral development. Tenderness and nurturance are here regarded as values and attitudes that prompt helping behavior. Caring for others, in this approach, derives from needs to avoid guilt and from ego-ideal orientations to express altruistic concern. These forms of caring are cognitively mediated and intellectually determined rather than affective and primary. We help others because we determine that this is the "right" thing to do rather than because it is emotionally and relationally gratifying. Care, in this orientation, becomes an overarching principle that governs behavior. As such, it is generally studied in the laboratory as a form of altruism or prosocial behavior.

These two concepts—care as a form of bonding and care as an ethical system—may have complex interactions and disjunctions. Robert Lifton (1986), for example, describes the psychological mechanism of "doubling," which made it possible for Nazi physicians to torture people in the name of science and still be loving fathers and husbands to their families, regarding themselves, on balance, as ethical and caring human beings. Because we each have the capacity for both love and cruelty, we need to understand more about what calls forth and what suppresses our compassion and care.

How we care, and for whom, is very much determined by social learning and by the transmission of the society's values and ideals. We find enormous variation in caring behaviors across societies (Mussen and Eisenberg-Berg, 1977). In our own country, for example, corporal punishment of children was seen in the nineteenth century as an expression of love and concern ("Spare the rod and spoil the child"); today it is regarded as child abuse. Cultures also vary widely on the value placed on caring behavior—whether tending to others is treated with respect or held in vague contempt.

No society can exist without care, a force that creates the cohesion necessary for society to survive. As people enter adulthood, newer and more differentiated forms of tending are available to them. And tending binds people together; those we care for become part of us. Barbara remembers that she could not really believe that her newborn first child was really *hers*, belonged to her. "Wait until you start getting up with him in the middle of the night," her mother told her. "Then you'll know he's yours." To care is to be owned, in part, by the needs of another. Being needed is one of the most powerful of interpersonal ties.

People I interviewed were most likely to include tending as a central dimension of their interpersonal experience at times in their life when they were just learning about new ways to care.

Teachers valued their students most, for example, when teaching
was new to them. Similarly, patients were most present to therapists
when the therapists were first struggling with what it means to try
to be therapeutically helpful to someone. Friends often took on
additional meaning for someone when they needed extra tending—
in other words, when they went through a crisis that challenged the
person's resources for care.

Riddles of Tending

The great secret is that caring is difficult. It requires empathy of
several kinds. First, we must discover what the person toward whom
we wish to express our care needs and can accept. Then, as Sullivan
understood the roots of tenderness, we must experience an empathy
in which someone else's anxiety becomes our own. When we feel
caring toward others, we sense their state of need and wish to restore
them to equilibrium if they are upset or arouse happiness in them
if their affect is neutral. Because of our emotional attunement,
changes in their affect state bring on corresponding affective
changes in ourselves. But this is not just another form of mutuality,
because it does not involve interchange. Rather, it entails aligning
our own emotional state with that of another. This kind of attunement posits an identity of emotional state such that we rise and fall
together. There is no smile as contagious as one we have produced.

Caring sometimes also demands forms of empathy in which
we contain opposing or unpleasant affects. If we are good tenders,
we may have to hold and contain someone when we would rather
be mutual. We may have to sit by and hear someone struggle with
his or her own discoveries when we long to tell of our own experiences. We may need to recognize that the person with whose care
we are charged needs to experience the boundaries of selfhood while
we remain unobtrusive, even though we would rather join in and
get some warmth for ourselves. This is a painful lesson that every
good teacher or therapist learns. There are times when we long to
assuage our aloneness and say simply, "I'm part of that too." But
at these times we must remember whose needs we are serving. If we
are interested in the growth of the person before us, we might better
simply bound the space (hold) and let the other person grope his

or her way to individual selfhood and experience. One of the great puzzles of caretaking is how to hold without impinging, how to give without smothering. As life progresses, caring poses dilemmas. Would that it were always as easy as feeding a hungry infant!

The cognitive development literature (Piaget, 1965) suggests, correctly, that empathy requires maturation out of egocentrism. Only when we are cognitively able to take the point of view of another are we able to feel from another's perspective. Being able to take another's perspective is necessary for empathy, but it is not sufficient. Our own psychological growth and complexity limit what we are able to "know" of another. In other words, our knowledge of another is filtered through our own conflicts and experience. We can know of another only what we can bear in ourselves. Thus we can know each other only imperfectly; only occasionally can we be fully "with" another.

People are not uniformly empathic. Those of us who supervise beginning psychotherapists can see distinctly the range of empathic responsiveness. One therapist is well able to empathize with grief and helplessness but is deaf to anger; another hears hopefulness and joy but misses guilt. Parents, too, are often specifically rather than universally empathic.

Research evidence clearly shows that empathy underlies the wish to help another. We feel "with" and then try to join or assuage or comfort or protect or cheer. But how to do this? Sometimes the needed action is clear. Sometimes, as in long relationships, comfort is ritualized. But more often we must confront our own clumsiness in tending. This is perhaps why tending is a central aspect of relatedness when it is new and challenging. Learning to care is absorbing because of its challenges.

We must also learn the limits of caring. Those of us in the helping professions learn that there is only a narrow band within which we can help, although we strive (if we are not burned out) to increase the range of our helpfulness. Those of us who become parents discover, however painfully, that we cannot give as much as we wish we could, and we inevitably repeat at least some of the *un*caring of our parents. Still, our effort is to improve our tending; we firm our intention to care and broaden (we hope) our repertoire of caring responses.

The ability to care is sometimes a latent attribute. In extreme circumstances, people can discover an unsuspected capacity for tending. Kathy, American by birth but married to a German man, was working as a freelancer in Austria, writing about high-achieving women. Her husband was a high-ranking bank official, and they had a house overlooking the gardens of Vienna's Schönbrunn Palace. They had two daughters, whom they delighted in, and many friends. Kathy felt that she was living the perfect life. She considered herself to be more intellectual than maternal and was somewhat contemptuous of "traditional" women, whose interests were dominated by "Kinder and Küche." Then her younger daughter—eight-year-old Gail—was diagnosed as having a terminal, incurable cancer. Kathy learned that there was only one place in the world—Baltimore—that treats such children. Within three days, she had moved herself and her daughters to the United States. She and Gail then spent the next three years in the hospital while Gail underwent radical and experimental cancer treatment.

Kathy hesitated to tell me about what this time had been like for her, not only because it was such a painful time but also because she had learned that it embarrassed people to hear about it. This was a time of heroic tenderness as she struggled to care for a dying child, to be strong and supportive for her daughter despite her own exhaustion, terror, needs, and doubts. Kathy had to care for her older daughter as well, who was trying to adjust to a new culture, a new language, and a drastically changed family. Each day Kathy would accompany Gail through painful tests and treatments, would watch and try to comfort as Gail lost her hair, lost her eye, lost her desire to live. Kathy joined with the other parents of terminally ill children in supporting each other and living through their losses with them.

But I was astonished to learn that Kathy does not consider herself a "high-achieving" woman. Gail lived, miraculously; but with many ongoing physical problems, she is unable to be independent. The stress of those years ruptured Kathy's marriage, and she and her daughters have remained in the United States to be near the best medical treatment. Although Kathy's main life focus is care of Gail, she has now returned to some intellectual work. She regrets not finishing the book she began, however, and continues to admire women who are in the political limelight, who write books, who are public figures. A product of our culture, she does not believe that she, too, has "achieved," that her work of caring, of persevering to tend in the face of despair, resentment, and fatigue, has been much harder than writing a book.

To an extent, we always fail at tending; we can rarely give exactly what is needed. If we commit ourselves to caring, we take on the painful necessity of having to come to terms with our own limitations in the face of our most ardent wishes for the good of the other. And our attempts at care may be clumsy. We fear to look foolish. (This is often, I think, what keeps men away from tending. "You write to my sick mother," says he to his wife. "I never know what to say.")

And the results of our tending are often obscured. We seldom know when we have done a good job of care. I say to a friend, "You don't realize it, but something you said to me years ago has stayed with me and strengthened me." She is astonished, does not remember the conversation. For me, it was a watershed moment; for her, it was an unremarked corner of her experience.

In a culture that assumes that people naturally know how to nurture and tend, we cannot openly talk about how to do these things well. Yet we furtively read the how-to books hoping for guidelines, hoping that *someone* knows. I had a patient who told me that she and her husband had waited exactly four years between children, because that is what one of the childrearing advice books recommended. Generations of mothers have bowed to expert advice on timing feedings, holding babies, swaddling, not swaddling, breastfeeding, not breastfeeding—anything to do it *right*. We cannot really talk in this way about care, however, because no one really "knows" how to do it. It is unrelated to intelligence or socioeconomic status. It is not automatic, but it is not "learned" either.

Unlike the other dimensions of relatedness, tending is active (although it may not involve action). We offer ourselves to fulfill a need. In order to tend, we must *attend* to need and *intend* to find something within ourselves to *extend*.

Our debates about caring center around one or the other of these facets. Couples, for example, argue about what was intended and what was extended: "Maybe you wanted [intended] to help me, but you didn't say [extend] anything." ("I didn't know *what* to say.") Or "I really wish you'd take an interest in my work [attend] and ask me about it once in a while [extend]." ("Work is all you seem to think about; you never seem to care about me [intend].") Thus we miss each other.

Caring can also wear many masks, making us unsure of the intention behind what was offered. The behaviors of tending and caring can differ widely from the underlying intention. We may extend care in action while our motivation is uncaring. Linda spoke of her different experiences mothering her three children. Laurie was born when Linda was twenty-one and not yet ready to have a child. "I rocked Laurie because she cried and I had to, I rocked Lloyd because he liked it, and I rocked Kim because I was tired and wanted to sit down."

When tending goes along harmoniously, "automatically," this aspect of relating fades into the background. Only when others' needs are urgent, unfamiliar, or extreme or when we are forced to recognize the limits and difficulties of tending does this theme claim our attention.

Wendy

Wendy remembers at age five feeling happily "together" with her mother, whom she regarded as sweet, kind, gentle, and easy to get along with. The younger of two children, Wendy was viewed in the family as easy to love, in contrast to her sister, who was jealous, had tantrums, and misbehaved. Wendy thinks of her father as having been "out in the world. He had no thought of being involved with the kids. He was never a large figure for us, kind of mercurial, just kind of there. Later I learned that he was alcoholic, but I didn't know that until recently."

Wendy's mother's family was a traditional Italian family— very loving, very family-oriented. Her maternal grandfather, however, was a free spirit, kind of wild. "He would grab us and dance with us. No one could keep up with him."

Her Uncle Mario, kind, calm, and peaceful, was an important model for Wendy. "I gravitated toward his kindness. He was the basis of my ideal husband. He was kind and stable and never changed. He was like my mom. I wanted the peacefulness that I sensed that some people had."

Other relatives were also important in shaping bits of Wendy's character. Her father's sister, Aunt Julia, who was conservative and opinionated, taught her "that a woman can speak out, doesn't have to go about pleasing people." Aunt Mary, the black sheep, had many lovers, including her own daughter's boyfriends. "I got a kick out of her. She was fun, glamorous. She was everything that women in the family secretly wanted to be."

When Wendy dreamed of a self in the future, she wanted to have the joy of life of Aunt Mary and her grandfather, the earthiness and creativity of her mother, and the peacefulness and stability of Uncle Mario and Aunt Julia.

When Wendy was ten, her mother remained most important as someone who was "always there, nurturing, accepting, affectionate, encouraging." It was clear at this point that her parents were not getting along, and Wendy tried to mediate between them. She felt especially chagrined by the unhappiness she sensed in her mother, which she knew was due to her father's erratic behavior. She wished that she could offer something to her mother, make up for her pain. She turned to Uncle Mario for help, and he tried to act as a peacemaker. He also encouraged Wendy's intellectual pursuits and tried to rechannel her energies away from her parents' problems.

Meanwhile, Wendy was noticing the families of her schoolmates. She saw that some people were different and lived differently; she saw that some mothers and fathers were happy with each other and could give to one another.

By age fifteen, school friends had become extremely important to Wendy. She spent most of her time with four other girls.

> I spent most of my time with them. They were my life. We were a support group. We had fun, shared everything. We put our heads together and figured out what our childhoods were like. We were very different but got along so well. We'd spend the night at each other's houses. We were like sisters. We stayed close all

> four years of high school. Their parents let me come
> and fit right in. I disliked being home. Home was not
> happy. My sister was having problems, abortions,
> running away. My mom was stressed. She and my dad
> were fighting all the time. I didn't like my dad any
> more. He was always making everyone unhappy,
> making them cry. He threw all my mother's makeup
> in the garbage, cut up her credit cards, hit me in the
> face occasionally. My mother and I became each oth-
> er's lifeline.

Looking back, Wendy realizes how confusing it was for her to come to terms with her father and with her parents' marriage. On the one hand, her father was brilliant, analytical, and witty. On the other hand, alcohol made him nasty and unpredictable. She got the message from her mother that this kind of suffering was the way life is.

Wendy was slow to date. Her first boyfriend came from the "wrong side of the tracks," but he was "sweet. He accepted and supported me. He was always there for me. One of my friends dated his brother. We were a foursome. If I hadn't been forced to go to college, I might have married him."

Wendy's mother remained her lifeline and role model through age twenty.

> I came to her when things got rough in the outside
> world. She'd accept me and say how rotten everyone
> was. I thought I was supposed to be acquiescent and
> mild-mannered and deferential to men. I had dated
> but was terrified of men, a virgin, afraid to cross the
> line to a real commitment.
>
> Cliff and I were students together and friends at
> school for two years. I was attracted to him, but very
> concerned with being how I was supposed to be. I
> made him into my father figure, behaved toward him
> the way my mother related to my father. He had a
> good sense of humor, came from a troubled family,
> full of alcoholics, which I didn't know at the time. He

was stable and serious, seemed like a good anchor, attractive, well liked. It seemed like I was just following along and everything was going fine, so I married him.

At this age, Wendy enjoyed her schoolmates and friends more than anyone else. She was always drawn to women who were free spirits and independent, unlike her mother. But something in her told her that she had to follow the road her mother had taken—to do it better, perhaps. She chose the same kind of man that her father was: "glib, good-looking, nice on the outside." Wendy had been identified as a talented writer, but "I had accepted that my lot in life was to be like my mother."

When Wendy married Cliff, they moved to Virginia and bought an old mansion that they ran as a small hotel. By age twenty-five, she had three children, eighteen months apart. Cliff soon lost interest in the hotel and got a traveling sales job, leaving Wendy with the children and the hotel. Declining in quality, the hotel became a kind of boarding house for people down on their luck, and Wendy found herself taking care of many people with problems. She took care of alcoholics and teenage runaways; she talked people out of killing themselves and delivered others to therapists. Each person who came, it seemed, was in need of care. Wendy did all the caring, but she felt burdened by the demands made on her.

Joy in life came from her children, whom she enjoyed taking care of. She relished the family fun. Her children were happy, spontaneous, and healthy, and with them she felt an effervescence that she had not had enough of as a child. When they were doing things as a family, she and Cliff could feel close; otherwise, their relationship was deteriorating. Regardless of the growing problems with Cliff—his overburdening her, his refusal to coordinate his activities with hers and to share in the workload—the success of her children made it all worthwhile. With the sense that she was building a healthy family, Wendy felt fulfilled.

But then Cliff, whose alcoholism was now apparent, started to become violent. Of him, she said, "I didn't know he was an alcoholic. I just thought he was a bastard." After he beat her for the second time, Wendy realized that she had to leave him—yet she stayed on. She was increasingly aware that it was she who had the competence in the family. She was the one who was keeping the family together.

Only with the help of Al-Anon was Wendy able to understand the way in which she had fallen victim to the isolation that alcoholism imposes. Taking care of everyone else, she had neglected to take care of her own emotional needs. Now, at age thirty, however, she was faced with a terrible choice: to divorce Cliff or to stay with him and try to help him. Either way, she could not have the picture-perfect family that she had longed for, and it was inevitable that her children would suffer.

Choosing to hold her family together, Wendy addressed issues of care for the next five years. She could not find a way to take care of Cliff, however. He resented and feared her independence, yet she was too frightened of his instability to allow herself to rely on him. Despite her efforts and urging, he refused to acknowledge his alcoholism or to seek help. Foremost to Wendy was her wish to care well for her children. She tried to protect them from his outbursts and to interpret for them his distance. When family concerns overwhelmed her, she could distract herself by trying to help the people in the boarding house with their problems.

At age thirty-three, Wendy made the decision to leave Cliff. She turned then to women friends she had met in Al-Anon and to her old high school friends, who were themselves going through conflicts and changes. With these friends, she found support and solace as she faced the issues of care necessitated by her divorce. How best to raise these children? How to help them cope with the family division without tearing them apart? And what about the economic problems: how would there be enough money to go around?

Although her children were still her first priority, Wendy found herself too exhausted by age thirty-five to be the mother she wanted to be. "I didn't have the energy to make everybody happy. I started to have problems with the kids. I couldn't make it right for anyone."

To try to solve the financial problems, Wendy shut down the boarding house and trained as a real estate agent. She found in her boss, Lucy, a mentor who was "brilliant, successful, and outspoken." Wendy began to conceive of her life differently—in terms of achievement, which seemed more attainable than her fantasies of care.

When Wendy's father died and her mother moved in with her to help with the children, Wendy realized that her mother had always looked on her as the stronger person. While she welcomed her mother's help, she often felt that she had gained a fourth child—one she had perhaps had all along.

Wendy did the best she could to raise her children, but she is clearly disappointed now, at age forty-two, in the direction of their growth. Her older daughter ran off and married a man who got her pregnant and then left her. Her second child, a son, is alcoholic at age nineteen. Her younger daughter has lived with her father for the past year and has had little contact with Wendy. Still, Wendy tries to care for them where she can. She has taken in her older daughter and her baby. Wendy's mother cares for the baby while her daughter tries to finish her studies. Wendy, having discovered the necessity of marketable skills, wants her daughter to be able to make something of herself. Wendy has been able to draw her son into Alcoholics Anonymous and hopes that he is on the road to recovery. She retains her faith that her youngest child will return to her in time. It has all been more difficult than she had imagined.

Two years ago, Wendy had another disappointing romance. She met a very nice farmer at an Al-Anon meeting. "He had downhome values and a wonderful, accepting, loving family. I was drawn by the sense of a huge family full of love and acceptance. They were intrigued by me and proud of me. I was a city girl, doing well in real estate. He was very affectionate and warm. He was a big, broad shoulder to cry on, but intellectually it was empty. And after a while I began to realize that he had some serious mental problems. Now I realize he was schizophrenic. Once again I had attached to someone who seemed powerful and expected him to carry me along."

Her real support had come from her circle of very close women friends, with whom she shares everything. "We hold nothing back. We are like soulmates. We share a sense of humor, a sense of being part of a larger world, a sense of goodness, and a sense of being a loving, caring, generous person."

She is trying to have a similar relationship with Robbie, a man she met several months ago. She feels more cautious with him; they seem to be growing and learning together. Because she can talk about how she feels with him, she does not see the relationship as one person taking care of the other. "We can identify how we are oversensitive and have low self-esteem. At the same time, we are very affectionate. With him I have a very strong sexual relationship for the first time."

At age forty-two, Wendy is still very much struggling with finding a way to care. From early childhood, she has sensed the need in others around her—others on whom she has depended. Always she has wanted to heal the pain around her, hoping that something in her could bring out the lovingness in others. Her unconscious attraction to troubled men has led her to have to learn the limits of what her care could accomplish. Even her wish to tend her children has left her, in middle age, with a more mature sense of the complexities of care. Her tending has not created either a perfect family or perfect children. Still, Wendy has come to accept herself as the "loving, caring, generous" person she set out to be. The omnipotence of her tending ideals has been tempered. But instead of reciting a litany of despair, bitterness, or withdrawn egoism, Wendy takes pleasure in offering what she can.

In Wendy, the dilemmas of care are etched clearly. They exist, however, in one way or another, in us all.

Pathologies of Care

We can care too much or too little. If we care too much, we are seen (by psychology, at least) as overprotective, compulsively caregiving, codependent, or intrusive. We can kill with kindness, to be sure, and care can be used in the service of a wide range of neurotic and defensive operations. Many people care for others in order to deny or overcome their own neediness, for example. We assume, but do not know, that this is always a pathological situation.

In the consulting room, psychotherapy with families often involves strategies for persuading parents (usually mothers) to care a little less or for inducing parents (usually fathers) to tend a little more. The challenge in care is to recognize and be responsive to the needs of another without losing one's self-boundaries in the process—a sequence that can misfire at many points and in many ways.

In the procession of life, people negotiate a great deal about care—who will do what for whom and how. Being a loving person is never a completed task. Mary, a patient of mine, complains bitterly about how much Peter has to travel in his job. She is constantly tired from having to get up with him at 4 A.M. to make his breakfast before he gets on the road. Why, I ask naively, doesn't Peter make his own breakfast? (After all, they have a microwave.) Mary is dumbfounded; this is unthinkable. Being in charge of Peter's food is an unquestioned part of her caring for him. In her view, not making his breakfast would be an act of insurrection and great hostility.

Warren, a research interviewee, spoke of how his effort to care for his widowed, frightened, and isolated mother began to interfere with his relationship with his own family. Each day after work he would stop by his mother's apartment, get her what she needed from the store, and then sit with her to keep her from being alone. By the time he returned to his own home, he often found a cold dinner, as well as anger and resentment from his children and his wife. For many years, Warren has struggled to get his caring in balance, but he often feels overwhelmed with guilt; he worries that he is always letting someone down.

Roy grew up trying to get away from what he experienced as the incessant bear hug of his large, smothering Jewish mother. Even today, at the age of fifty, if he leaves her alone in his house, she will rearrange his closet and clean up his desk. Throughout his life, he has had to push her away and try to define boundaries. Never has he confided in her or approached her with a problem, although he continues to visit his parents out of his sense of attachment and loyalty. Roy expressed no positive feelings at all toward his mother throughout his interview, but his warmth and love for his children—his devotion to them and joy in them—were intense. Where, I asked, did he think all this lovingness came from? "I think from my parents," he answered immediately, and then laughed with some embarrassment. "The overdoing of my mother and my father—I think it's influenced me. I don't like it, but . . . I feel I

deliver this to my children—the love. I really appreciated the love,
I guess, but . . ."

In Roy's confusion is the confusion of all of us who would
try to understand care. Sometimes it is too much, but. . . . The
enigmas remain: How do we hold without suffocating? How do we
teach without imposing? How do we bring our passion to others
without overwhelming them? How do we touch, how do we participate fully with another tenderly, without doing harm?

Chapter 11

Sex Differences in Relatedness

The word love has by no means the same sense for both sexes, and this is one cause of the serious misunderstandings that divide them.

—Simone de Beauvoir, *The Second Sex*

If it were possible to obliterate all overt clues to the gender of subjects in my relational interviews, there would still be no doubt as to whether the speaker was male or female. There is great variability among both men and women in how they organize their relational lives, of course, and it is important not to either overstate or understate the differences between them. When we talk about sex differences, however, we usually do a little of both, and I do not pretend that I can avoid these pitfalls here.

Relatedness and connection, centrally important to both men and women, are experienced by all along the same relational dimensions, but they seem to be qualitatively different nonetheless. Some of this, of course, may be a function of verbal orientation. Even highly articulate men would become tongue-tied when trying to describe the importance of their wives, for example. "She's just wonderful—important in every way," was sometimes the most they could say. Women are more accustomed to talking about relationships—this is what they often do with each other—so the interview was a more familiar enterprise.

Beyond familiarity and fluency, however, lay more profound differences of approach. Women tend to shade and nuance their experience of relatedness, to feel and describe their connection to others as multifaceted, complex, and often contradictory and par-

223

adoxical. By contrast, men view their connections in simpler terms, with fewer shadings and layerings. Women are more likely to describe relationships in terms of their evolution, as though they were living entities that unfold over time. Men, on the other hand, are more likely to see relationships as fixed structures—products or givens that, once formed, stay pretty much the same.

Beyond how men and women talk about relatedness, male and female relational spaces have different configurations, highlighting and focusing on different dimensions. Before looking at how these differences manifest themselves within each dimension, we must consider the dichotomies in male and female psychology that underlie the variance in the two approaches to relatedness.

Gender Differences That Affect Relatedness

In general, there seem to be four interrelated central factors. First, men tend to internalize and experience relatedness in more abstract and conceptual terms, whereas women exist in the more affective, ineffable realms of connection. I have anguished over whether this, too, is a matter of articulation and verbalization. I am left with the ancient dilemma that, being a woman, I can never know the experience of a man. But I have heard enough of male confusion over the affectivity of women in relationships and of female mystification over male obtuseness to conclude that this is a difference that reflects some real disparity in experience.

As an example, only men put authors, poets, and philosophers on their relational maps. These were people by whom they felt profoundly moved and with whom they were often in intense internal conversation. For men, intellectual intercourse "feels" relational; women, on the other hand, seem to require at least a dollop of affective coloring (real or imagined) to feel themselves in relationship to another.

This greater abstractness in men is a result of a second important aspect of gender difference: individuation and separateness. Men define themselves as more separate from others and at a greater emotional distance from them than do women. Ever since Chodorow (1978) pointed this out, gender differences in relatedness have made a great deal more sense. Because boys and girls are parented primarily by mothers, who are women, girls have continuity between affection and identification while boys must define themselves as distinct from the person they first and most love. This has the utmost impact on the way in which the two sexes come to experience themselves vis-à-vis others. The boy has the painful task of detaching himself from the warm fluidity of his connection to his mother in order to claim his masculinity. The fear of being once again engulfed by her maternal embrace and returned to an unsexed state haunts his psychic development ever after (Dinnerstein, 1977). Then, having laid stake to his masculinity through his renunciation of maternal closeness, he returns again to his mother with his newly won sexuality, only to find a larger, more powerful father-rival already there, threatening his masculinity in a new way. Thus the problem for the little boy is to resist both the mother-engulfer and the mother-seductress and to identify with his rival and potential castrater (Chodorow, 1978). He must therefore draw tight and defined boundaries around himself and learn to relate to others across a gulf that both separates him and guards his masculinity.

The little girl, by contrast, has a very different developmental task. Mother is her first love object *and* her object of identification. The little girl learns to become and be herself within the matrix of connection. She develops within the paradox that she is both merged and distinct, connected and separate. She never has to renounce the smooth flow of emotional dialogue with her mother, never has to step outside, forcefully and determinedly, and declare herself different. The Oedipus complex is not a universal issue for women, as I noted earlier; in fact, it may be an important developmental sequence for only a very few.[1] Women do not, as Freud thought, renounce their mothers (Apter, 1990; Josselson, 1987), although their continuing connection to them may involve elements of renunciation and differentiation. To this continuing intense relationship is added a (sometimes passionate) connection to a man, which makes the female inner world at least tripartite (and large enough to encompass multiple connections). And in all these connections, female relating means interweaving selves, blending and blurring boundaries, being self and Other simultaneously—and finding this experience not threatening but exalting.

The exigencies of defining oneself as masculine require not

only separateness from mother but also action. One has to *do* to be masculine, while femininity is given as a whole. Joseph Campbell (1972) points out that in mythic and early artistic representations, the female is shown as naked and unadorned. She is a given, mythic in herself. The male, by contrast, is costumed. He has to gain his powers and represent some specific social role or function through action. In sexual/reproductive functioning, the male is the active partner who has to perform, to *do* something. Femininity, by contrast, is a given: a woman does not have to do anything at all to become pregnant except be penetrated by a male. The third important factor of difference, then, is that the masculine self is so much defined by doing; the feminine, by being. Men (even as boys) know themselves through their actions, while women (even as girls) know themselves through others. When the boy turns away from his enmeshment with his mother, he moves to exploration of what his own initiative can produce in effects on the world. What happens when he hits, when he builds, when he throws a ball this way instead of that? It may be nice when others notice his accomplishments, but that is not the thing itself. (Thus a grown man turns to his bank balance to know how well he is doing in life.)

The girl, by contrast (who does not catapult herself out of the matrix with her mother), knows herself through her effects on her mother and, later, on others. She "feels" who she is through the responsiveness of others to her. And their responsiveness is rarely directly related to her actions. The girl is more likely to feel most herself when she experiences a warm emotional exchange with mother rather than when she performs a concrete action in the world. Thus the being-with-others self is the fundamental one; the action-doing self exists in a different layer of self-experience.

As the girl grows, she learns to locate herself in a shifting, inexpressible world of affective linkages. The young girl of seven or eight begins to notice that some girls are "liked" more than others, but the antecedents of their being liked remain unclear. Girls are not liked for being smart or good at soccer, as boys are, but for ill-defined qualities, such as responsiveness to others, self-confidence, playfulness, and charm. And the girl understands, quickly and deeply, that she, too, will be labeled and located in this slippery interpersonal universe. She will be responded to for how she is deemed to *be*, not for what she wills or for her skills.

This contrast between *doing* selves and *being* selves has been a major obstacle in our ability to study the differences between male and female. Because our science is empirical, we can better think about doing than we can about being. When we think about such things as identification, therefore, we think about identification with what people *do*. We think, for example, about girls identifying with their mothers as baby-tenders or as cooks.

But what women tell me that they admire in their mothers is not their *doing* but their interpersonal attitudes, their way of being with others. "My mother was always so even-tempered. Just by looking at you in a certain way she could make you laugh, could make you forget what hurt. You just couldn't ruffle her. No matter what the emergency, she stayed calm, and you just felt that everything would be all right. She was the pillar of strength." Now this kind of description has nothing to do with watching one's mother change diapers and wanting to *do* like her, which is what so much of our social and developmental psychology tends to suggest when it considers a concept such as identification with the mother. Instead, the description covers ways of being, expressed in action but not definable as sums of behavior.

Similarly, when girls talk of other girls whom they admire, they speak of how the girls are with others rather than what they can do. "Dora was someone whom everyone liked. She was kind of weird, always laughing. She just drew people to her. I wished I could be like her." If we were to dissect a statement such as this in "doing" terms, we would surmise that the girl who wished to be liked as much as Dora was ought to commence laughing frequently (which, indeed, many girls have tried). But it is not the laughing behavior that makes Dora likable; rather, it is some essence in her that is likable, which is also expressed in her laughter. What the speaker is aware of is that it is desirable to be liked and that being liked is a subjective response from others, but the causal determinants of being liked are unclear. Not only that, but who is liked changes frequently and changes over time, as any adolescent girl will tell you. This is the world in which the growing girl must find her place.

For boys, by contrast, valuation is based on skill. Boys admire the one who is strong or smart or who directs a ball of whatever shape where he wants it to go. Masculinity exists in action. It is earned through clear rules for success and failure.

The fourth major area of relational differences between males and females lies in their widely divergent developmental histories of sexuality. As I discussed before, sexuality for men is more tangible, visible, urgent, and guiding, while for women it is more internal, private, malleable (women can be either unresponsive or multiply orgasmic, as the culture wishes), and above all diffusible. Male sexuality is more vulnerable to perversion and disorder; female sexuality is more mysterious. Males tend to have to deal with sexuality first in a relationship, whether by extending it, denying it, disowning it, or sublimating it. Women only later become aware that their strong feelings toward someone might include sexual ones. Women put relatedness and attachment before sexuality; men do the reverse.[2] For men, sexuality is clearly located in the genitals. For women, it is more likely located in the heart.

These multiple differences between men and women are apparent in the conflicting male and female perspectives on the following story—a relational "Rashomon":

One of Connie's most treasured memories is of an evening she spent (at age twenty-three) with Vince, her mentor. A man twenty-five years older than Connie, Vince had been a substitute father to her. Having recognized her talent as a musician, he then taught her, encouraged her, and dried her tears through years of training and struggling up the ladders of competition. They performed in public together and shared their innermost selves in private. They sometimes flirted with each other, but playfully and unseriously. Both were married, and neither wanted to disrupt either their marriages or their own friendship and colleagueship. The year before the evening in question, Connie had moved away because of her husband's career. Depressed about having left Cambridge, she kept in constant touch with Vince for support. The move had highlighted the underlying emptiness in Connie's marriage, and after half a year away she decided to leave her husband. She was uncertain where she would go or what she would do next, however.

In the midst of this turmoil, she had to return to Cambridge to perform a final recital for her doctoral degree. Vince, of course, offered her a place to stay with his family. Connie arrived anxious about the recital and somewhat panicky about decisions she was making. She was emotionally exhausted, frightened of the future, and less confident and more alone than she had ever been. What she remembered later as the brightest moment from this whole troubled period of her life was the night before her recital. She sat in Vince's living room in her bathrobe, watching Monday Night Football with Vince, his wife, and his two sons. She felt such warmth and comfort that she wished that she could stay there forever, being Vince's talented daughter, held in the circle of family, routine, and profound acceptance. Remembering Vince and what he had meant to her as she recounted this story, Connie became tearful.

My reading of this episode is that it is a moving story of idealization (of Vince), of validation (Vince recognized her as a talented violinist), of holding (note the family circle, Cambridge, and the professional world represented by Vince), of mutuality (she and Vince played together and shared themselves), and of deep attachment (Vince offered her an emotional "home" and a secure base). Connie felt overwhelming affection and gratitude toward him.

"But wait," says a male colleague and friend of mine, a much-respected psychologist and expert in the analysis of human relatedness. "None of that is what is going on in that scene—at least not for Vince." For Vince, my friend asserts, this is a poignant and painful scene of inhibited lust. Connie is not his daughter after all, but a very attractive twenty-three-year-old sitting in his living room in her bathrobe, seemingly oblivious to his sexual fantasies about her. She may think that she is in touch with him, my colleague argues, but she could not be further from the mark.

I present this because the debate between my colleague and me recapitulates the story of Connie and Vince and may indeed epitomize the enigmatic gulf between men and women. This is a friend and colleague with whom I usually see eye to eye, but our years of training and experience with the human psyche cannot override our genders. No doubt Freud, if he were here, would have agreed with my friend.

If Freud could say that he could never understand what women want, I must similarly acknowledge that my gender prohibits me from fully understanding male sexuality. And the fact that neither gender will ever be able to completely empathize with the other's experience of sexuality is a two-edged sword. On the one hand, it means that we will eternally be driven toward each other and never come to the end of Otherness. But is also means that our answers to questions about how the genders differ in relatedness will always be distorted, filtered through the gender-lens of the speaker.

Gender and the Eight Dimensions

Gender differences exist in all of the dimensions of relatedness, and these differences grow out of the factors mentioned above. Most profound are the differences in the passions, in eye-to-eye experience, and in mutuality. Identification, tending, and embeddedness come next, with scant differences in attachment and holding.

Passionate experience, intensely sexual in its origin, is more a primary motivating force for men than for women. When women are aroused to passionate expression, it is usually passion connected to other dimensions as well. That we as a profession could have lived so long with a theory that saw others as objects of drive gratification attests to the dominating power that metaphors of male sexuality can exert.

Passionate experience for women tends to be romantic—a merger in which one is penetrated not only physically but emotionally, known and possessed spiritually, and then kept and cherished eternally. Thus elements of holding, validation, and mutuality are intricately woven with arousal and the longing for enduring union.

Women are more at home than men in the world of mutuality and eye-to-eye experience. In fact, it is perhaps in the realm of mutuality where the greatest tensions between the sexes exist today. Survey reports document that everyone seems to be unhappy with what is acknowledged as male inhibition in mutuality. Men (as a group) are seen, by both men and women, as unresponsive, unable to disclose their feelings, unwilling to reveal personal experience, and uncomfortable with the sharing of inner states that is intimacy

(Hite, 1987; McGill, 1985; Farrell, 1986). In place of emotional interchange, men substitute instrumental activity, such as sex or the
giving of presents (McGill, 1985). By contrast, women are seen to
speak naturally to each other in a "female patois"—a language that
takes account of the emotional climate of the topic and is punctu-
ated by personal sharing (Eichenbaum and Orbach, 1987; see also
Jourard, 1964). For men, sharing and confiding is a struggle—the
result of deliberation, risk, and decision making. For women, it is
unremarkable—the essence of interaction.

Men avoid the emotional and personal when these produce
feelings of vulnerability, because they fear being known in their
weaknesses (or what they fear are weaknesses). Men also retain profound fears of the nonsexual merging that accompanied their pre-
oedipal closeness with their mothers. In resonance, two notes make
a chord; they merge their sounds. The chord *is* the two notes, and
if we ask about the separate contribution of each, we lose the concept of *chord*. For men, this is the essential problem. The temporary
relaxation of separateness necessary to an emotional coming together invokes deep anxieties and often rigid defenses (Dinnerstein,
1977).

For the men who allowed me to study them, mutuality existed in relationships only in carefully bounded circumstances.
Friendships existed around a shared sports activity or around an
intellectual sharing of ideas. Ruefully, my male subjects admitted
that they had never tried to "really talk" to their "best friends"
about their feelings and experiences. Recall, for example, Tom,
who maintained loyal and loving attachments to male friends
throughout his life. But he shared with his lifelong friends his
conflicts and anguish about getting a divorce only *after* he had
implemented a decision. Theorists advance the hypothesis that men
cannot be emotionally close to other men for fear of the stigma
attached to homosexuality. There are powerful cultural taboos reg-
ulating men's closeness with each other.

Once I had the opportunity to observe a group of experienced
male psychotherapists participating in a men's group convened to
explore male intimacy. By the end of the two-hour group meeting,
most of the women observers were in tears, torn by the pain of
watching psychologically sophisticated, emotionally available men

so sincerely reaching for each other and so poignantly unable to make contact. What these men were saying about their lives and in their behavior was that they had never experienced a truly emotional mutual connection with another man. Pogrebin (1986), after a study of friendship, concluded that "the average man's idea of an intimate exchange is the average woman's idea of casual conversation" (p. 260).

Men bond in the mutuality of "the hunt." They are together by cooperating and doing together actively. War, with its intense arousal, danger, affirmation of masculinity, and need for cooperation, offers the supreme opportunity for male bondedness. Similarly, men can touch, caress, kiss, and hug each other when their sports team has been victorious.

Men can be close and mutual, then, when their attention is jointly focused on something external. Women, on the other hand, are most bonded when the focus is on the relationship. Men invite each other to play tennis, to "do" together. Women get together to talk, to "be" together.[3]

For women, the interpenetration of selves, the regulation of closeness and distance, and the shared experience of emotion is the essence of relating. What do I talk about when I'm "with" my friend? Whatever has moved me strongly since the last time we spoke. My friend responds by sharing in the affect, enlarging it with her own associations and responses, and we somehow experience it all together. Louise Bernikow (1980) points out movingly that this nonlinear, intimate language that women speak to each other has been absent from representation in literature. This mode of expression has been so relegated to the private realm over the centuries that women's voices have been silenced in the larger culture. If women speak this language only to other women, no wonder "what women talk about" has remained so mysterious to men.

But when women, with their predilection for resonant experience, come together with male instrumentality, the interpersonal war is kindled. "He won't listen to my feelings," says the misunderstood wife. "I don't know what she wants me to *do*," replies the perplexed husband. She brings up an experience for savoring and chewing. He takes it as a problem to be solved or advised about.

Because the man fears becoming too involved in what he

perceives to be feminine chaos and boundarylessness, he either attempts to control and dominate or he withdraws to silence or alternate activity. Over and over again, for those who see couples clinically, the wife drags in her unresponsive husband and asks that we therapists teach him mutuality.

Those men who do express themselves intimately in mutual relationships tend to do so with a woman friend—that is, a woman with whom they are not romantically involved.[4] Clear boundaries for men protect against too much vulnerability.

Alongside their pleasure in mutuality, women need each other and need men for eye-to-eye validation. Because women get to know themselves as they are for others, the responses of others are the nourishment for the female sense of self. This is a very marked sex difference.[5] Men rarely speak of valuing others for valuing them—for "making me feel good about myself," "giving me confidence," "knowing me as I really am," "really understanding how I feel," or other phrases that indicate the need for mirroring or personal validation. Men attempt to know who they are through what they do. The male self is realized in activity—in pursuit of accomplishment or adventure. Glory comes ultimately from recognition, of course, and not from directly regarding the self in the looking glass of the other.

But because their sense of self is more rooted in doing, men are much more attuned to issues of idealization and identification. Goals and ambitions are more abstract, and they grow out of identification with idealized heroes. Ideology, for men, is often interchangeable with relatedness. People are apt to be loved because they embody perfection. From the earliest period of recorded history, male writing about love has confounded the person and the ideal. Philosophers could not tell whether the beloved was the actual person or an incarnation of an abstract possibility (Singer, 1987).

Idealization of the beloved is part of what energizes male heroism. And the need to be a worthy hero invokes a deliberate quest for the shape of the self that drives men to consider a wide array of others as potential models. Women are less likely to look beyond those people at hand for models, and their identification with these models is more likely to be with essence and orientation than with specific behavior or activity. Thus we witnessed Allison experiencing her role as a college president as within the metaphor of being a mother to everybody, as her own mother had been a mother to her extended family. In contrast, we recall Sam spending years in intense conversation with D. H. Lawrence as he tried to decide how much he owed to others, how much he could allow himself to pursue his own pleasures.

Throughout these interviews, I found men much more likely than women to highlight people as important because of the ideas they carried and discussed. Women tended to mention the importance of others' ideas only when they were ideas about how to relate to others. (Diana, for example, mentioned that the ideas of others had helped to free up her inhibited sexuality and allow her to have an affair.) Even the most successful, highly achieving women did not tell a story of identifying with someone, trying to become like him or her, and then succeeding. Rather, they told of being encouraged, validated, perhaps pushed in a certain direction, invited to action or performance—all within a web of connection. Allison's story was the closest to having a central theme of identification and idealization among those told by women, and she interlaced her identifications with both mutuality and care. Where women emphasized the importance of their work, it tended to be because they felt appreciated rather than because they were satisfying an internalized aspiration.

Women, then, tend to grow and stretch themselves by seeking closeness and connection with those they admire, while men tend to identify at a greater emotional distance with those they idealize. In so forcefully separating from the mother of infancy, men (and boys) must grow in a space apart from others. Mechanisms of idealization and identification allow this closeness and interaction at a distance and so play a similar role to the one that more direct forms of validation play for women. Women must thus remain closer to others and grow in relation, as they did in their first connection with their mother.

As a result of these different strategies for defining the self, the experience of embeddedness differs for men and for women. For men, the achievement of an impersonal role is a high form of participation in a society or group. Men aspire to roles in which people take their place not as private individuals but as agents of collective principles or laws (Campbell, 1972, p. 57). Rituals of investiture of various kinds ensure that people are installed in such socially defined and essentially impersonal roles to act "in the name of" something other than themselves. Such rituals in behavior lift people out of themselves so that their conduct is not personal but *of* the society or profession or group; that is, it is fully expressive of embeddedness. In "taking part," men take "*a* part" and thereby merge themselves with what is abstract.

Women, however, are embedded *personally* and tend to resist the experience of themselves in roles. They take their place in the family group or a larger group in which they can take part and still maintain personal relationships. Even in childhood, girls are more likely to view "the group" as a network of dyadic friendships, while boys experience "the group" in terms of loyalty and solidarity (Rubin, 1973). This parallels Gilligan's (1982) contrast between the male focus on rights and responsibilities as a form of moral orientation as distinct from the female focus on concern and care. Morality and ethics are the threads of embeddedness—that which we join to become part of a society or group. The male strives to find his place by giving over his selfhood and personal nature to impersonal concern with rules, rights, and justice; the female takes her place personally, through care.

Gilligan makes a profoundly important point about our gender mythology regarding the personal in the face of impersonal Truth. She points out that the central biblical myth for males is that of Abraham and Isaac, in which the father is prepared to sacrifice his much-loved son as a testament to his commitment to faith, to higher principles, to an abstract Good. For females, by contrast, a nameless woman stands before Solomon the judge, prepared to sacrifice Truth for the sake of her baby.

Again and again through the years, as researchers have looked for the interpersonal in the masculine half of our species, we find instead ideology. And when we track ideology in women, we find the interpersonal. For men, the personal is background to the drama of the impersonal: Penelope waits at home while Odysseus voyages and adventures. For women, the personal, in the shape of relatedness, *is* the drama: Medea can take revenge on the man she loves only by killing the children she loves.

There is no evidence that either men or women are any more or less attached, although women tend to have more attachment figures than men do. The man who has only one attachment figure (usually his wife) is more dependent on her and will tend to replace her quickly if there is a loss. Men are also more likely than women to want to base relationships in attachment alone; that is, they may want to have their wife "there," to have her available, but may not wish to initiate more interaction with her. Both clinically and in this nonclinical sample of interviewees, we find husbands who ask for little sex or conversation from their wives. They are quite content with the sense of stability, security, and basic affection that comes with feeling "married."

Both sexes also need to be held, and in adult life, this is experienced as support. In times of crisis, women will tend to turn to the important people in their life for support. Men, on the other hand, will just as likely find support in their important holding environment, in their work, in keeping in physical shape, or in substances. Following a divorce, women turn to their friends. Men turn to organizational service or other activity (Weiss, 1968). For many men, being held by others comes perilously close to loss of autonomy and separateness.

In issues of tenderness are the most perplexing sex differences. Everyone turns to women to be nurtured and comforted. Both men and women—in this study and in all others that I know about, and at all ages, from adolescence to very old age—look to women for soothing, consolation, and help for pain. Having a close woman friend or even having interaction with women is an antidote for loneliness, for both men and women (Wheeler, Reis, and Nezlek, 1983). Girls are most often "best friends" for both adolescent boys and girls.[6] Mothers are confidantes for both their sons and their daughters. Women clearly have the emotional supplies that all people, both men and other women, need.

This would all be rather straightforward were it not for the fact that men experience themselves as tending and nurturing. There is not a man in the study who did not mention someone who was important to him because he took care of him or her. Most of the men talked of how important their children were to them, of the special bonds they felt with them. Yet most also spoke of their own experience of absent fathers, unavailable fathers, fathers who they knew "loved" them but whom they rarely saw.

So men think of themselves as caring for others, but others do not experience men as nurturing. Are we overlooking male nurturance, or do men have an illusory idea of what they are offering to others? Do fathers think of themselves as involved while they are viewed as peripheral by their families, or do men underestimate how much of their emotional input is required before they are felt as a reliable presence by their families? Do we as a culture undermine male nurturance?

Men are more apt than women to view tending to others as activity, as something they do. Women, although they are more likely to idealize caretaking, are less likely to notice their own activity in this sphere. It is as though taking care of others were a form of respiration, automatic and invisible. If we ask a woman what she did during the day, she is unlikely to report that she reassured, comforted, disciplined, heard, empathized, worried about, and cherished others. Men, being more action-focused, are likely to report that they spent some time playing with their children or talking to a friend.

Women and Men in Relationships

What of the traditional notion that men define themselves in work and women in love? I think that this is a defensible assertion, if we understand broadly both what *love* means and who it is who is loved. Person (1988) asserts that, for many women, life's central quest is the search for an ideal love relationship—an assertion that matches our popular conceptions of women. I agree that women do demand more of relationships than men do, but I think that women quest for ideal love relationships in the same ways that grown men long to be baseball heroes. Ideal romance exists at some level of excitement and fantasy, but it does not form the basis for the organization of most women's lives. Women read romances to escape from their quotidian lives and to reassure themselves that the humdrum nature of daily life is indeed the expected outcome of the most passionate romance: the heroine gets married and lives happily ever after, with the usual ups, downs, satisfactions, and disappointments (Radway, 1984).

But the love through which women define themselves goes far beyond romantic love. Much confusion about the psychology of women has resulted from too narrowly construing what is meant by a woman's "inner space" and her "self-in-relation." When we concentrate exclusively on the centrality of husband and children, we miss the true complexity of women's relational life. Women exist within a network of relatedness of which her spouse (if she has one) and her children (if she has them) form only a part. That women define themselves "in relation" does not mean that women should stay home and out of the public sphere. Rather, such a concept allows us to understand, for example, why women medical students do better in person-oriented situations, where their skills are used in personal contact with someone, while equally able male medical students, by contrast, thrive in more abstract mastery and competition-driven situations (Inglehart and Brown, 1987). We are just beginning to learn about the ways that harnessing women's relational capacities in the publicly noticeable work world rather than denigrating and isolating them can change our accustomed ways of doing and thinking.[7]

Women center themselves in connection to others but require complex contexts for the realization of themselves in relation (Bakan, 1966). Part of what provoked the backlash among women in the modern age was the cult of domesticity that isolated them in suburbs, confining them to a sphere that excluded all but the nuclear family. In a previous generation, there were lots of people available for relating. Women were not just "home with the children." They were also home with their mothers, sisters, aunts, neighbors, friends, cousins, nieces, and nephews, and together they shared the tasks of childraising and homemaking and tending one another. Families extended into communities and created intricate social networks within which people could form life-enhancing relationships. In our current age, work involvements take the place of this community, providing tasks and interactions that enlarge the sphere of women's relatedness and open the way for validating aspects of herself, for mutuality, and for new identifications.

Women are empowered in and by relatedness, and they use

relatedness to empower others (Surrey, 1987). Whereas male notions of power are rooted in competitiveness and domination ("power over") or in personal authority to define the self in action, women feel empowered *with* others. The feminine model of power requires "power with"—a way of being in which each person in the relationship feels enhanced, has greater understanding and knowledge, and is more able to act. Women often find it difficult to act within traditional power structures, in which having "power over" diminishes the other and interferes with action to increase the other's sense of powerfulness.

The female predilection for mutuality as a central dimension of relatedness makes a shambles of male hierarchies based on power and competition. Highly talented women function best in an environment that allows them to realize their own abilities and to preserve and empower others (Inglehart, Nyquist, Brown, and Moore, 1987). Women tend to act and work in *connection* with others, viewing relationship and activity as enriching rather than mutually exclusive. The common finding that successful women tend to attribute their successes to factors other than their own efforts may also reflect this awareness that their actions derive from and are nourished by a relational context.

Psychoanalytic theory has traditionally understood psychopathology to derive from one of two developmental lines: conflicts relating to guilt and disappointment in one's own capacities or achievements, or distress resulting from disappointments and losses in relationships (Blatt, 1990). The first has typically been manifested by men; the latter, by women. Women have difficulties when they do not get enough of what they need from others. Men worry more about keeping their boundaries clear, controlling others, and clarifying issues of self-expression and self-definition. We are beginning, however, to understand more clearly that a woman's disappointment in getting what she needs is not a simple result of oral dependency or hysterical neurosis. It is due, in part, to the fact that women are forced to express themselves in a society that works against feminine modes of self-expression. Similarly, we are beginning to understand better the ways in which a man's preoccupation with separateness, control, and boundaries helps him defend himself against intense relational involvement and cover over conflicts about mutuality and tenderness.

As to research into these gender differences, we need to look more at what takes place in peer interactions. We understand that boys have less opportunity to practice relational interaction, having separated themselves so definitively from their mothers and having only distant and identificatory interchanges with their fathers. But there are also strong messages from other boys that vulnerability is dangerous, that boys who feel or who care about others are "sissies." Males are very vulnerable to shame; indeed, shame is often the source of male violence. Is our culture subtly shaming men for their tenderness?

And what of the peer experience of girls? We are just beginning to learn about the ways that girls can become enslaved by their dependence on being liked by others, on seeking a liking that is not in any way contingent on their actions or skills. We have been trying to encourage girls to discover themselves in activity and ability as well as in the responsiveness of others, but we must also learn to respect more in our social institutions the needs of females for mutuality and interaction. Girls achieve when their teachers and mentors take a personal interest in them; girls learn when they are permitted to cooperate rather than forced to compete.

The male model of selfhood views connection as the antithesis of power, self-assertion, and control. The feminine mode of selfhood views relationships and activity as components of a whole. Action takes place within a web of interpersonal interconnections, which, if properly tended, give rise to further (and more meaningful) action. But this "moving *with*" (as opposed to "getting ahead of" or "gaining control of") others has not been encouraged in academic (Belenky, Clinchy, Goldberger, and Tarule, 1986) or social (Bellah and others, 1985) institutions. As we as a society become able to take this feminine orientation more seriously and to treat it with more respect, the implications for changes in our ways of living together are far-reaching. From this "female" vantage point, it is clear that we have come to the edge of our capacity as a species to wield power over one another or to solve problems with force and domination. Either we live interdependently or we all vanish. Our survival necessitates seeing what connects us, looking at what occupies that space between.

Chapter 12

Notes on Love

My love to my husband was not only a matrimonial love, as betwixt man and wife, but a natural love, as the love of brethren, parents and children, also a sympathetical love, as the love of friends, likewise a customary love, as the love of acquaintances, a loyal love, as the love of a subject, an obedient love, as the love to virtue, an uniting love, as the love of soul and body, a pious love, as the love to heaven, all which several loves did meet and intermix, making one mass of love.

—seventeenth-century Englishwoman, quoted in
Marriage and Love in England by Alan Macfarlane

Love glitters because of its many facets; it captivates us because it is always unique, always singular in its expression. The question is not, What is love? but, What are loves? So much of human misunderstanding, however, derives from the mistaken assumption that *love* has a universally shared definition, as do words like *run* and *dog,* or even affect words such as *angry* and *happy.* But my experiences with love and needs for love are *not* the same as yours. Indeed, each person has a highly individual love "recipe" that idiosyncratically intermingles the eight dimensions of connection to others. The quality of love changes when it is composed of different dimensions.[1]

Although the cult of individualism often stresses that we should find the all-encompassing love in one individual, few individuals can satisfy all the love needs of another.[2] Yet people often feel like failures if their primary relationship does not satisfy all their relational needs. We need different dimensions of connection (in various combinations) from different people, and in turn we offer highly individual forms of responsiveness to others.

Many people have pointed out the irony in the fact that our language is so limited that we say both "I love you" and "I love ice cream," as though the two sentiments were identical. Worse, perhaps, are the many languages that do not even distinguish linguistically between *love* and *like*: "I love my husband" and "I like to dance" are then verbal equivalents.

What people seem to mean when they say that they "love" is that they are feeling intensely, in either a yearning or joyful way. "I love" means that someone (or something) matters a great deal to me or provokes a strong positive response in me. Indeed, in languages that do not discriminate between *like* and *love*—where one cannot ask the question, "Is this love or just strong liking?"—the verb *like/love* is modulated expressively. In other words, affective intonation indicates the degree of emotional intensity that one feels; in the sound rather than the semantics lie the quality and strength of feeling. (The line that often appears to exist between "liking" and "loving" seems to be a function of the presence or absence of passion in the relationship.)

Our common understanding of love implies either that the loved one is held in high esteem and intensely valued by the one who loves *or* that the love is a bond of attachment that can be taken for granted (along with the loved one)—a relationship neither esteemed nor necessarily intense. In addition, the common view of love presupposes a measure of exclusivity of the loved one, a sense of being special and different from those who are not loved.

When people talk about loving, however, they seem to experience little contradiction in the fact that they love their mother, their father, their grandmother, their aunt, their friend, their husband, their children, their mentor, and so on. All of these, however, are qualitatively different relationships that serve vastly different needs and exist on different dimensions of relational connection.

Students of love (as far back as Plato) find that they must, at the outset, define the kind of love that they wish to discuss, extracting that particular form of love from all the other types that exist. But the question of what is *really* love remains unresolvable.

There is no other word that is used for such a variety of

emotional experiences. Love is the passion of one lover for another, the tenderness of parent for child, the attachment of old friends, the mutuality of shared experience, the gratitude for understanding and validation, the security of being adequately held, the admiration for someone who seems wonderful, and the joy of feeling at home. Perhaps what we mean when we say that we love is that we feel that the person we love is in some way essential for our existence.

In this fundamental existential sense, we can love and can be loved on any of the dimensions, exclusively or in combination. We love the one who holds us, because without that person we could not exist; and we love those we hold, because we mean so much to them. We love those to whom we are attached, because they are our emotional "home," where we will be taken in no matter what, and they are the people with whom our lives are intertwined. And we love those who mirror and recognize us, because without them we could not be. All these people we love with gratitude, for they give us ourselves. We also love those who are the objects of our passions, because they arouse and excite us and seem to embody all that would complete us. This person we wish to possess, exclusively and eternally. And we love those who embody our ideals, who stimulate us to reach beyond ourselves, who represent our becoming. We love those with whom we share ourselves, in play and in knowledge of one another. These are the people who walk with us through life, and they are irreplaceable. And we love those whom we tend and nurture, because they contain a part of us and testify to our value as human beings. We love, too, those with whom we are embedded; these people we love less personally but, especially in times of group distress, no less profoundly.

It may be that there are higher and lower forms of love, each building on the other. People who grew up deprived of adequate attachment experiences, for example, seek, above all, enduring attachment in later life. Such people—for example, child survivors of the Holocaust whose parents were taken from them and murdered—speak little as adults about a quest for passion or mutuality. For them, feeling bonded to special others in new attachments overshadows all other forms of relatedness (Moskowitz, 1983).

Maslow (1962) was working with the idea of higher and lower forms of love in his notions of deficiency and being needs.

While healthy development requires some relational connection on all of the dimensions, the higher orders of mutuality, passion, and tenderness, for example, are probably available only to those who have had adequate experiences of attachment, holding, and (later) embeddedness. (Perhaps there are also forms of self-actualization that we have not yet conceptualized in loyal bonding or in serving group goals.)

The labyrinths of our relationships with each other are created by our unique recipes for love. The arguments between spouses, between brothers and sisters, and between friends all begin with built-in—perhaps even unconscious—expectations of how one would treat and be treated if love bound the relationship. Thus "If you loved me, you would . . ." is a fundamental phrase of human misunderstanding.

Love and Culture

We have to be wary of love ideology that is based on cultural assumptions. Only recently, with the triumph of "therapeutic" ideals (Rieff, 1966), has "authentic feeling" become the ideological basis of love relationships. In contrast to previous eras, in which kinship or class or duty served to lead people to each other, our age anchors relationship in feeling.[3] The ideal is the heterosexual pair who are "in love," experiencing passion, tenderness, and attachment. Real relatedness among people—relatedness that sustains life, powers development, and shapes identity—is, however, far more complex.

Expectations about love are, to a large extent, dictated by culture.[4] That is dangerous only when people are confused as to what is a cultural ideal and what they can expect in reality. People are alarmed when they find themselves loving differently from others, for example. They are also confused by the idealization of love in a materialistic environment. When love is promoted as a commodity, it is hard to know when we have gotten our share. How much exactly are we entitled to? How do we know whether to stay with a relationship and try to improve it or simply move on? Beneath the symptoms of psychopathology is always relational pain— wounds inflicted through commission or omission by another. But our actions with others exist in a context of interpretation. Between our experience with another and our integration of that experience are multiple steps of meaning-making. Consider the following stories of Sandra and Janet:

Sandra is married to Jack, a businessman who is preoccupied with his work and spends most of his time at his office. He makes a large income and gives Sandra complete freedom in spending it. He has been generous about financial assistance to Sandra's brother, who is always on the brink of bankruptcy, and he is forbearing about taking in other members of Sandra's family in their recurring crises and disasters. He is devoted to Sandra and tries to comply with anything she asks of him. But what Sandra wants most from Jack is emotional investment in her. She wants him to talk to her about his feelings, to initiate sex, to try to get to know her more deeply, to plan activities for them. Sandra works part-time as a nurse, takes college courses, and has many friends. But she feels depressed and unfulfilled, in conflict over whether she should leave Jack and find a partner with whom she can have a more emotionally intense and mutual relationship.

Janet was thrilled when Marty, the high school football hero, finally asked her to marry him. Their friends viewed them as the ideal couple, and Janet thought she had everything she would ever want. Two years after their marriage, they had a much-wanted son, but Marty began spending more and more time at work and playing golf. Now Janet is feeling increasingly isolated. With great simplicity and great pain, she speaks of the collapse of her dream: "I thought we would be together and build a family together. Now I hardly ever see him."

If they were members of another society or subculture, Sandra and Janet would not expect anything else from their husbands. (Men are similarly culture-bound in their expectations of women and in their interpretation of opposite-sex behavior. We might remember that Freud could not figure out what women want.) If they were Victorian women, for example, they would expect to be living their emotional lives apart from their husbands in distinct, sex-segregated worlds (Slater, 1970). They would expect to satisfy their interpersonal needs through kinship, friendship, and community. The relational networks of our highly mobile, loosely organized society force people into increasingly smaller units of relational connection and at the same time idealize these units beyond their capacity to deliver. The current emphasis on marital "togetherness" often burdens the relationship beyond its endurance and so gives rise to an industry of self-help books and marriage counselors to try to keep it intact.

Similarly, the nuclear family is now asked to perform functions formerly carried out by a whole community, and when it fails in its task, it is usually the mother who is "blamed" (Luepnitz, 1988). As the extended family was fading out of existence in urban America in the 1950s, in response to rapidly increasing geographical mobility and the turn to the suburbs, the extremely popular television program "Father Knows Best" was romanticizing the nuclear family. No other television program has appeared so frequently in my patients' associations—associations related to their intense disappointment in their own families for not being like the TV family. They yearned for the calm understanding and compassion of that all-wise, ideal father, whom they were afraid all others had and they alone lacked.

We all secretly suspect that the reason that we do not get more from others is that we are undeserving, unacceptable. ("If only I could lose ten pounds, I would be loved as much as I want.") We compare our own experience of what others offer us with media images and come up short. We are ashamed to compare our experiences with others, because we may be exposed in our inadequacy. Thus many people live with the painful sense of having less loyal and interested friends than others do, less passionate spouses, less reliable attachment figures. To comfort and distract themselves, they seize on the current cultural and therapeutic message that what we really ought to do in life is learn to do it all ourselves. Love ourselves, take care of ourselves, draw wider boundaries. Be our own best friend! (I wonder how anything so absurd could have captured so many people.) Let's just not need each other, our culture urges.

Conflict and the Irrationalities of Love

The dimensional model of relatedness emphasizes the yearning for connection, but power, competition, and conflict are also present throughout. Within each of the dimensions of connection lurks the threat (and experience) of the opposite. We are most aware of being held when we begin to fall or feel smothered, for example. Nothing sharpens our sense of ourselves and our meaning for others as much as a heated argument or contest. Sometimes we most heighten our experience of a dimension of love when we veer into its absence or excess. (For those who like to think in diagrammatic form, Resource B lists all of the dimensions along with their "absent" and "excess" pathological poles.)

Conflict is itself a form of connection, existing on each of the dimensions. Anger, envy, and contempt color all relationships. To speak of relational connection is not to imply seamless harmony or warm fuzziness or anything static and unchanging. Above all, relationships *move*. We discover the self through our connections with others, and our heightening of self-knowledge makes possible more complex and deeper ways of reaching others. As we grow, we refine and modify our connections. We never fully bridge the space between us, but we experience within our lives many ways of reaching across. I agree with Bowlby (1988) that we are not inherently aggressive. Rather, our fears of aloneness and loss make us rageful, and we learn to use our anger to try to compel others to meet our needs.

To be unloved is unbearable because it means that we have no real meaning or importance to anyone. As humans, we are stuck with our inescapable need for the emotional responsiveness of another—a need kindled by the sparkle in our mother's eye, a need that serves no biological purpose and often causes us tremendous pain. But unless we know that we are somewhere part of the affective life of another, we cannot feel our own existence. This is why people who fear that they are unloved often work to be hated (hate being just another face of love in its intensity and its selectivity).

Conflict between us and those whom we take into our relational networks, conflict among the dimensions of our relational needs—these conflicts generally must be lived with rather than "resolved." We can try to achieve a higher order of understanding and integration, or we can tear ourselves apart trying to insist on relational illusions or relational consistency.

People live with both their fantasies of love and their experiences of love. Inner representations of loving relationships may have little to do with how they appear to observers (or even to the other person in the relationship).[5] What we learn about love, then, depends a great deal on what we ask people. Studies of the mythology of love tell us little about people's actual experience. We sigh cathartically over *Antigone* or *Casablanca* but carry on with the less romantic folks at home.[6]

Marge, a thirty-five-year-old research subject, told of her own dreams of love. For years, while she was in her twenties, she was involved with a married man whom she idealized. He was in her profession, and she was always very stimulated talking to him about ideas. There was much mutuality between them, and wonderful sex. Yet she knew that his attachment to his wife was so strong that he would never leave her. What Marge was focused on was wanting just once to hear him tell her that he loved her. She felt that these would be the magic words that would let her know that she was a person of value. (He often told her that he loved being with her or loved making love to her, but he never said that he loved *her*.) Finally, after a five-year relationship, he said the magic words. And Marge said that she felt nothing. The declaration meant nothing. As in the wonderful "Do You Love Me?" song from *Fiddler on the Roof*, it did not change a thing. And she left him.

Consider also the insightful scene in the movie *Tootsie* where the Jessica Lange character confides to the female Dustin Hoffman character that her deepest fantasy is that someday a man will come up to her and say, with no ritual or small talk, "The simple truth is—I find you really interesting—and I'd really like to make love to you." Some days later, the Dustin Hoffman character, back as a man, obligingly does just that. And she throws her drink in his face.

Relatedness and love may be to psychology what chaos is to physics—a new but necessary frontier where the phenomena will not hold still for analysis. (In physics, if they do hold still, they change.) To understand relatedness, we must be able to encompass paradox and contradiction. Inner and outer, self and other, love and hate, fantasy and reality, rational and irrational, conscious and unconscious—all coexist within the relational frame.

Always there is the fear that love, in its many manifestations and dimensions, is not very scientific. And so we try to make love problems appear to be something else. People go to psychiatrists because they are lonely and feel unloved, and they are given medication: the "scientific" response.

A patient consults me for intractable stomach pain that physicians have been unable to treat medically. I am her fifth therapist. Others have told her that her problem is her oral dependency, her inhibited sexuality, possible sexual abuse (which she does not remember), repressed rage. She is talented, attractive, and sensitive but has no friends. What does she feel she needs? I ask her. "I need to have someone in my corner," she says. And that, I think, is the essence of it. So do we all.

O Love is the crooked thing
There is nobody wise enough
To find out all that is in it
For he would be thinking of love
Till the stars had run away
And the shadows eaten the moon

—W. B. Yeats, "Brown Penny"

About Relational Space Maps and Interviews

Instructions to Interviewees
on Drawing Relational Space Maps

You might remember that when you were in school, you used to see diagrams of the planets that looked like this. [The interviewer should draw a fresh picture while the subject looks on.]

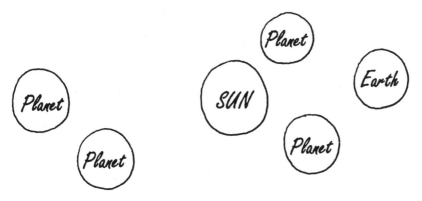

I'm going to ask you to make similar diagrams, only instead of putting the sun in the middle, I want you to put yourself there. Around yourself, I want you to arrange the people who were important to you at that time of your life. By *important*, I mean people who were in your mind, whom you would have been thinking about. So the distance from you on the page that you put the im-

251

portant people in your life should reflect their inner presence for you rather than who was physically there, how far away they lived, or similar factors.

What you will end up with is a diagram that looks like the planet scheme, all with circles. Please label each circle with the name of the person who belongs there.

There are two additional kinds of circles that you might find yourself wanting to draw. One is a "dotted circle" to indicate someone who mattered a lot to you at that time of your life but who was not there at all as a physical presence. This might be someone whom you talked to in your head or thought about a lot even though you had no real interaction with him or her at that time.

Another kind of circle you might like to draw is the group circle. This you might draw to indicate people who were important as a group but didn't really matter as individuals. This might be needed if, for example, you want to indicate the importance of the swim team or a youth group or something like that.

I would like you to do these drawings in five-year intervals beginning at age five. They will go better if you think of yourself at those particular ages rather than trying to do the years in between. So imagine yourself at age five, try to fix yourself in time, and then pretend to interview yourself, asking yourself about who is in your mind at that time. Then imagine yourself at age ten, fifteen, twenty, and so on up to your present age.

Instructions to Interviewers

The interview following the drawing of the circles focuses on *how* each person drawn on the relational map was important. Keep questioning until the "how" becomes clear. If necessary, ask for specific instances or illustrations of the nature of the relationship. As you go through the drawings with the subject, be sure to inquire about how people came to appear on or disappear from the map. Notice and record affective responses that may occur.

Sample Relational Maps: Paul

Paul Age 5

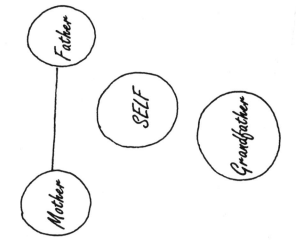

Paul Age 20

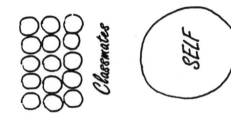

SELF

Classmates

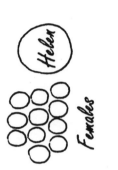

Females

Helen

Paul Age 30

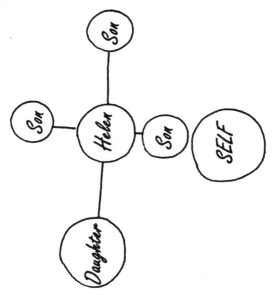

Patients

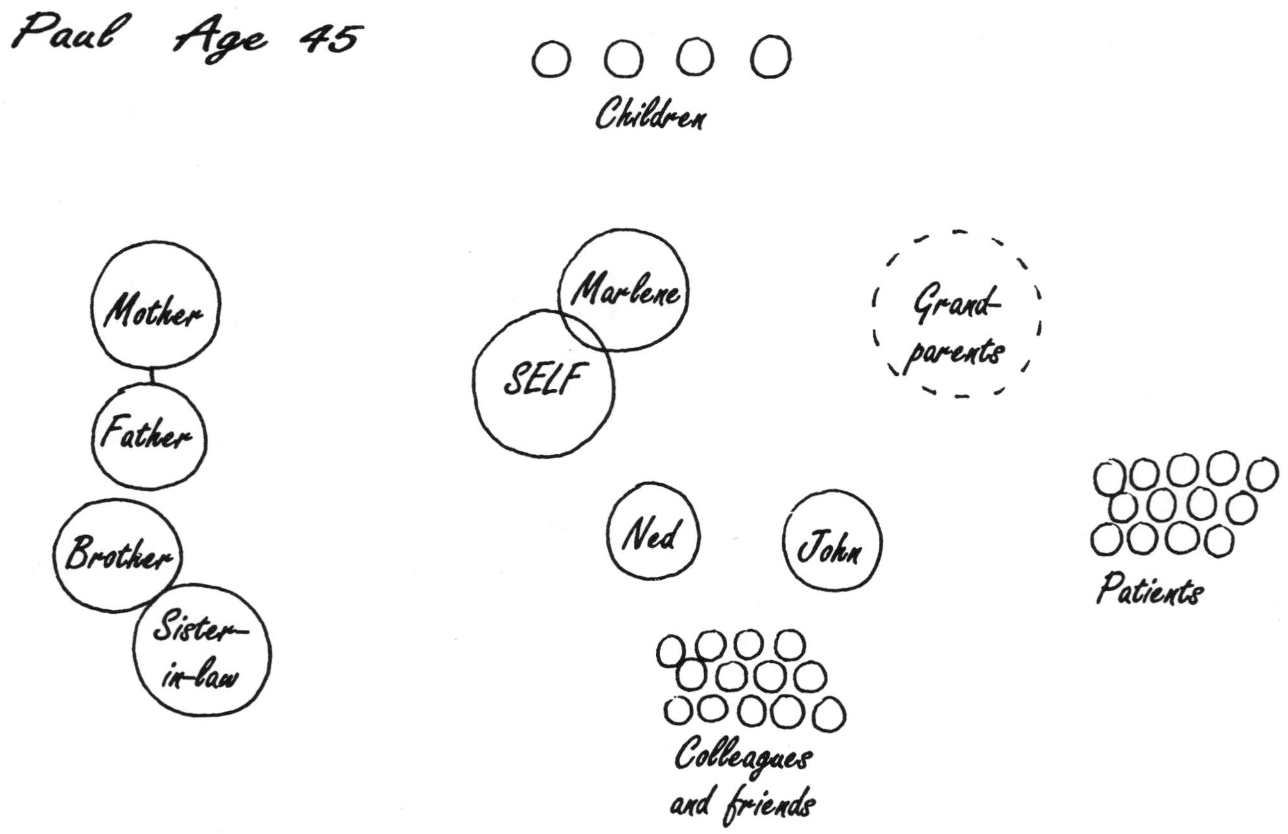

Paul Age 45

Children

Grand-parents

Patients

Marlene

SELF

John

Ned

Colleagues and friends

Mother

Father

Brother

Sister-in-law

Tom Age 5

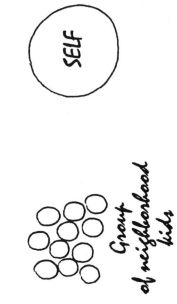

Vera

Mother

Aunt Gloria

SELF

Father

Group of neighborhood kids

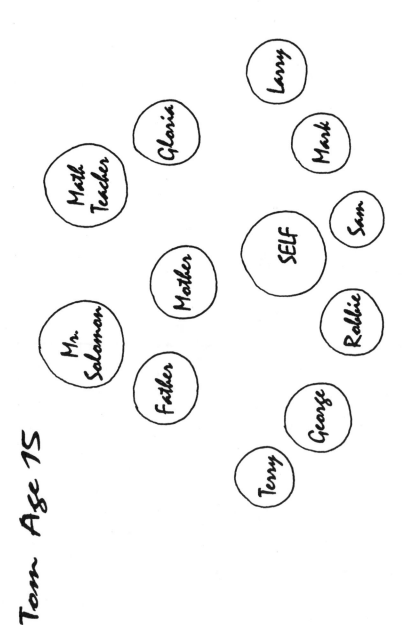

Tom Age 15

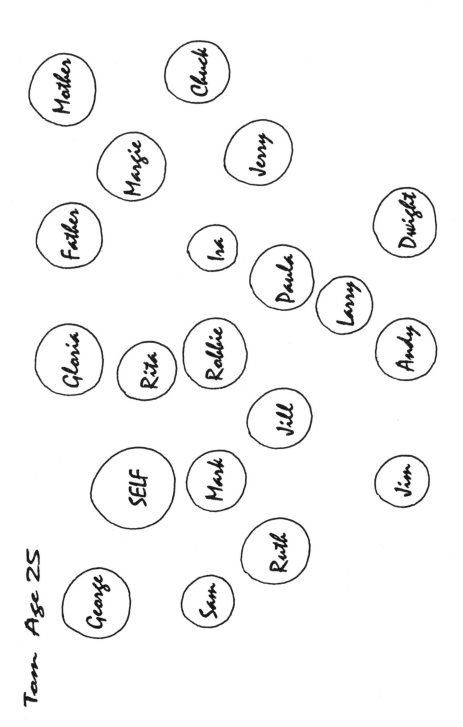

Tom Age 25

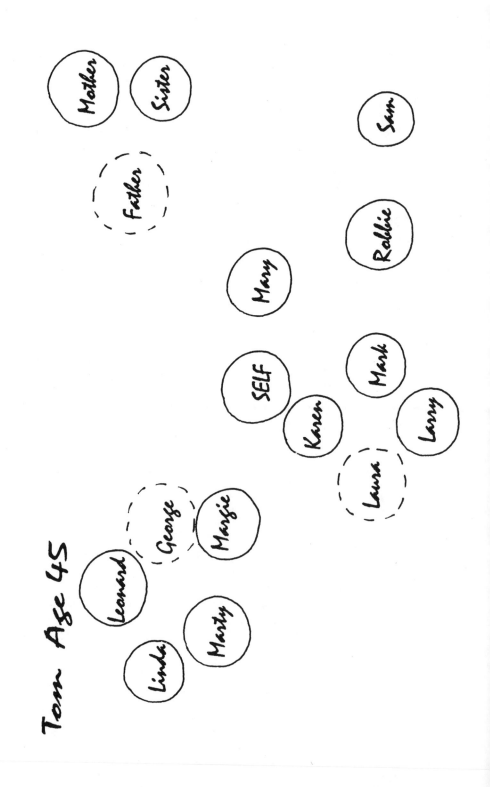

The Dimensions and Their Pathological Poles

absence	*DIMENSION*	*excess*
falling	HOLDING	suffocation
aloneness, loss	ATTACHMENT	fearful clinging
inhibition, emotional deadening	PASSIONS	obsessive love
annihilation, rejection	EYE-TO-EYE VALIDATION	transparency
disillusionment, purposelessness	IDEALIZATION and IDENTIFICATION	slavish devotion
loneliness, dissonance	MUTUALITY and RESONANCE	merging
alienation	EMBEDDEDNESS	overconformity
indifference to others' needs	TENDING (CARE)	compulsive caregiving

Notes

Chapter One

1. With regard to physical health, mounting evidence demonstrates the role of relatedness in physical well-being. A proliferation of studies in psychosomatic medicine suggests that disruption of emotional bonds to others could be causative of or exacerbate a great many medical disorders, from heart disease to cancer (Hojat and Vogel, 1987). One of the most dramatic studies along these lines is Lynch's (1977) demonstration that men who are lonely are more likely to die young, even when all other risk factors are taken into account. In a study even more far-reaching in its implications, Graves, Thomas, and Mead (1990) show that inner representations of others can predict who will get cancer more than fifteen years later. They suggest that one's inner sense of relationship alone, separate from the real attributes and experience of relatedness, can act as a biological regulator of physical health or illness.

2. This is entirely consistent with the theoretical predictions of Bowlby and Kohut, both of whom view aggression as reactive to the pain of unfulfilled relational needs.

3. Erikson, Erikson, and Kivnick (1986) studied a group of old people who had been interviewed decades earlier. They found that their subjects tended to remember their marriages as intimate and affectionate despite earlier documented reports of dif-

ficulties and dissatisfaction. They conclude that the need to integrate a sense of love across the whole life cycle may involve the recasting of earlier experiences "to such an extent that these experiences become unrecognizable to the outsider" (p. 111). Thus the current representation of a relationship in the life cycle serves the psychological needs of that period, stabilizing and balancing the self.

Chapter Two

1. Often this manifests itself most plainly in decisions about individual versus group therapy or individual versus family or couple therapy as the treatment of choice for a particular person. As the culture has become more individualistic, it has often become harder to persuade patients to enter group therapy. They want their "own" therapist. They find it hard to see how "other people with problems" could be part of their own growth.
2. Kegan (1982) has made the most heroic efforts to keep both of these narratives alive and interacting in one theory of development. Blatt (Behrends and Blatt, 1985; Blatt and Behrends, 1987; Blatt and Blass, 1990) has recently been writing from a model that depicts separate lines of development for relatedness and for self-esteem based in action. He makes a strong case for the importance of relational development, highlighting the ways in which the development of the self and the development of relational capacity are recursive and interdependent.
3. I am indebted to Guntrip (1971) for this term.

Chapter Three

1. The phenomena described here also showed themselves in a previous study of identity formation in women (Josselson, 1987).
2. This is an example of the holding function of a transitional object, to use Winnicott's terms.

Chapter Four

1. In general, attachment theorists simply include holding as an aspect of attachment. As long as we are considering infant development, that distinction probably does not make too much difference, because the primary holder is generally also the primary attachment figure. In adult development, however, these threads often diverge quite widely, and it is important, therefore, to conceptualize them separately.

2. Attachment theorists discriminate between attachment *relationships* and attachment *behavior*. Attachment behavior can be activated in the absence of an attachment relationship, as when a person (of whatever age) seeks proximity to a familiar other in order to feel safe or secure. Thus a child might cling to a known adult in the absence of his or her mother; adults alone at a conference might be delighted to see someone they hardly know. Similarly, attachment relationships can exist in the absence of attachment behavior. People with a pattern of avoidant attachment pointedly ignore the people they feel attached to. At some level they may feel attached, but they express this by staying away (Ofra Mayseless, personal communication, June 1990).

3. Ainsworth's "strange situation," and research derived from it, remains controversial. For a complete review and discussion, see Lamb and others, 1984.

Chapter Five

1. There has always been debate about exactly what Freud meant by *libido*. Did he mean only sexual, pleasure-seeking striving, or did he include all of Eros and the life forces? In Bakan's (1966) view, Freud meant libido to be agentic, associated with mastery, reduction of tension, and the urgency of sexual desire. In his later work, specifically in *Group Psychology and the Analysis of the Ego* ([1921] 1955a), Freud seems to subtly shift his meaning to include love in the concept of libido.

2. See M. Balint, 1953.

3. Thus we have a long literature discussing the importance of

"mature" (that is, vaginal) as opposed to "immature" (clitoral) orgasm in the female—a literature that later work on the identity of clitoral and vaginal orgasms has discredited. See Fisher (1973) for a complete discussion.

4. Kernberg (1980) has made the most serious attempt at this, but his conceptualization has been criticized as idealized (Arlow, 1980). Bergmann (1987) explores psychoanalytic ideas about passionate love in the context of myth and culture.

5. Kernberg (1980) discusses this in detail.

6. Kernberg (1980) makes an important distinction between crossing the boundaries between discrete selves in passionate encounter and the dissolution of self-object boundaries in psychosis. He cautions that madness is not in continuity with passion. This line of thinking might help us understand why some grand passions are vitalizing and enriching, as Person suggests, while others are obsessive and destructive. What we still lack is a clear way of describing and representing degrees and qualities of merging across boundaries.

7. See Bergmann (1987) for a thoughtful and complete discussion of the relationship between transference love and love in real life.

Chapter Six

1. The term "gleam in the eye" is borrowed from Kohut (1966).

2. I am indebted to Josephine Klein (1987) for the m(Other) form of notation.

3. Winnicott (1965c) was the first to discuss this phenomenon as the relational context within which the baby grows. Primary maternal preoccupation, however, requires a holding context for the mother that allows her to become absorbed in a unit with her baby.

4. Blatt and Blass (1990) give a fuller discussion of the dialectic between processes of separation and processes of relatedness, making the point that others can be utilized not for relational satisfaction per se but in the service of firming the self.

5. Margaret Atwood, in *Cat's Eye* (1989), is one of the few authors

to have realistically captured the tyranny of preadolescent interpersonal control.

Chapter Seven

1. Melanie Klein ([1946] 1975) thought that idealization was one of the earliest features of object relations, but she viewed it as a defensive flight from frustration or anxiety.

2. Freud initially understood identification as a defensive response to loss of an object. To become like the lost object was a way of preserving it. In this usage, identification becomes a form of incorporation and serves a holding function. This is different from the forms of identification and idealization under discussion here.

   Later, Freud emphasized the oedipal basis of identification and idealization, but more recent writers have stressed these dilemmas more in terms of power and capacity than in terms of drive and defense (see Simon, 1991). The essence of the oedipal problem may be that the adult is bigger and more powerful and thus entitled to satisfaction.

Chapter Eight

1. Daniel Stern (1985), the most prominent and integrative of the infancy researchers, does not take a position on whether the "being-with" that is mutuality has a psychobiological root or whether its origins can be understood theoretically.

2. Whether mutuality exists among other species is impossible to know, because we cannot know what other species might *feel*. And mutuality exists only in subjectivity. Because ethologists are very cautious about this, they try to understand play behavior as preparing the individual for behaviors that will later on be important for survival and reproduction (Michael Figler, personal communication, June 1991).

3. Piaget has discussed the "decentering" that takes place as the baby becomes cognitively able to use a system of coding the world with something other than the self at the center.

4. Lowenthal and Haven (1986) found that simply having a confidant is predictive of better mental health.

5. This is what has made the scientific study of friendship so difficult. Because friendship exists along a continuum of mutuality, it is never clear what people mean when they call someone a friend. See Rubin (1985) for an excellent review and discussion of this dilemma.

6. The psychoanalytic premise that intense same-sex friendship represents latent homosexuality has not only eclipsed our ability to think about friendship, it has also been destructive of friendship itself. All humans begin with the capacity to love persons of both sexes. If we start with Fairbairn's (1954) premise that libido is object-seeking rather than pleasure-seeking, we have no problem conceptualizing relationships that are pleasurable without their being sexual in origin.

7. I am indebted to Hadas Wiseman for pointing out that therapy, in the psychoanalytic framework at least, does not involve mutuality. It may be that people with high needs for mutuality find it most difficult to work with psychoanalytically oriented therapists (personal communication, Mar. 1990).

Chapter Nine

1. This would apply to the dynamics of holding as well, which was probably more what Winnicott was thinking about. But the formulation, I think, applies to all of the relational contexts of selfhood.

2. Storr (1988) comments that a great many people who have a place in the work world that affords them superficial relationships live satisfying lives without intimate attachments. This pattern often fits highly creative people.

Chapter Ten

1. This need links tending to the eye-to-eye validation dimension: when we tend well, we are mirrored in our experience of ourselves as caring people. The link between these dimensions has led some to the conclusion that the fact of receiving validation

as a caring person must therefore imply that this is the motivation for taking care. While this may sometimes be so, it is not always. People often continue to give to thankless others. The human propensity to care cannot be reduced to other dimensions, although it may contain elements of them. The "selfish" aspect of tending is the connection itself.

2. Evidence from experimental social psychology tends to confirm that prosocial behavior in children is related to being raised by nurturant parents who are good models of prosocial behavior, use reasoning in discipline, maintain high standards, and encourage their children to accept responsibilities for others early (Mussen and Eisenberg-Berg, 1977). See also Sharabany (1984) for a thorough review of the altruism literature from an object-relations point of view.

3. Erikson, Erikson, and Kivnick (1986) find this in their study of old age. In their search for the meaning of generativity, they find that procreativity eclipses all other activities as a source of life satisfaction. Older people, regardless of their professional contributions, saw their major domain as "taking care of the world" in their children and grandchildren.

4. Surrey (1987) calls this response/ability.

Chapter Eleven

1. See Simon (1991) for a fuller discussion of current psychoanalytic views of the female Oedipus complex.

2. See Schofield (1965), Hass (1979), and Coles and Stokes (1985) for data that support these conclusions.

3. Lillian Rubin (1985) reports the same findings based on her data. See also McGill (1985), Hite (1987), Bell (1981), and Pogrebin (1986).

4. My being a woman undoubtedly had much to do with the fact that so many men were so revealing in their interviews with me. In a sense, I provided the ideal conditions for self-revelation: I am a woman, responsive, nonjudgmental, not romantically available, and they will never see me again. These factors all maximize the boundaries necessary to male openness.

5. Blatt (1990) defines the anaclitic path of development as one in

which feelings about the self are defined in terms of the quality of interpersonal experience, and he views this path as more typical of women. Kohut (1977), however, regards the need for mirroring responses from others as universal. It is possible that men couch their need for mirroring and validation in other terms, deriving it indirectly.

6. This is true even in a sample of Turkish adolescents (Hortacsu, 1989).

7. See, for example, Sara Ruddick's (1989) ideas about how maternal thinking can be applied to politics in a nuclear age.

Chapter Twelve

1. Sternberg (1986) develops a theory that similarly schematizes love as multidimensional, resulting from different mixtures of ingredients. He describes eight forms of love by combining the following three components: intimacy (closeness, the emotional component), passion (arousal, the motivational component), and commitment (deciding to stay together, the cognitive component). His three factors seem best to correspond to what I call mutuality, passion, and attachment, respectively.

2. See Marris (1982) for further discussion of the ideological contexts of love relationships.

3. This idea is explored carefully and thoughtfully by Bellah and others (1985).

4. One central way in which a culture regulates how love is expressed is through its attitude toward homosexuality.

5. Lillian Rubin found, for example, that people who were named by someone as a close friend often did not include that person in *their* list of close friends. Similarly, others have pointed out that there are always two versions of a marriage: his and hers.

6. See also Radway's (1984) thoughtful analysis of how romance fiction serves to maintain quite unromantic domestic arrangements.

References

Ainsworth, M.D.S. "Attachment: Retrospect and Prospect." In C. M. Parkes and J. Stevenson-Hinde (eds.), *The Place of Attachment in Human Behavior*. New York: Basic Books, 1982.

Ainsworth, M.D.S. "Attachments Beyond Infancy." *American Psychologist*, 1989, *44*, 709–716.

Ainsworth, M.D.S., Blehar, M. C., Walters, E., and Wall, S. *Patterns of Attachment: A Psychological Study of the Strange Situation*. Hillsdale, N.J.: Erlbaum, 1978.

Apter, T. *Altered Loves*. New York: St. Martin's Press, 1990.

Arlow, J. "Object and Object Choice." *Psychoanalytic Quarterly*, 1980, *49*, 109–133.

Atwood, M. *Cat's Eye*. New York: Bantam Books, 1989.

Bakan, D. *The Duality of Human Existence*. Boston: Beacon Press, 1966.

Balint, A. "Love for the Mother and Mother Love." In M. Balint, *Primary Love and Psychoanalytic Technique*. New York: Liveright, 1953.

Balint, M. *Problems of Human Pleasure and Adaptation*. New York: Liveright, 1952a.

Balint, M. "Sex and Society." In M. Balint, *Problems of Human Pleasure and Adaptation*. New York: Liveright, 1952b.

Balint, M. "On Genital Love." In M. Balint, *Primary Love and Psychoanalytic Technique*. New York: Liveright, 1953.

Balint, M. *Thrills and Regressions*. London: Hogarth Press, 1959.

Bateson, M. C. *Composing a Life*. New York: Atlantic Monthly Press, 1989.

Behrends, R. S., and Blatt, S. J. "Separation-Individuation and Internalization," *Psychoanalytic Study of the Child*, 1985, *40*, 11–39.

Belenky, M. F., Clinchy, B. M., Goldberger, N. R., and Tarule, J. M. *Women's Ways of Knowing*. New York: Basic Books, 1986.

Bell, R. *Worlds of Friendship*. Newbury Park, Calif.: Sage, 1981.

Bellah, R. N., and others. *Habits of the Heart*. New York: Harper-Collins, 1985.

Benedek, T. "The Organization of the Reproductive Drive." *International Journal of Psychoanalysis*, 1960, *41*, 1–15.

Benne, K. D. "The Uses of Fraternity." *Daedalus*, 1961, *90*, 233–246.

Bergmann, M. S. *The Anatomy of Loving*. New York: Columbia University Press, 1987.

Bernikow, L. *Among Women*. New York: HarperCollins, 1980.

Bion, W. *Second Thoughts: Selected Papers on Psychoanalysis*. New York: Aronson, 1957.

Bion, W. *Experiences in Groups*. New York: Basic Books, 1961.

Blatt, S. "Interpersonal Relatedness and Self-Definition." In J. L. Singer (ed.), *Repression and Dissociation*. Chicago: University of Chicago Press, 1990.

Blatt, S. J., and Behrends, R. S. "Internalization, Separation-Individuation, and the Nature of Therapeutic Action." *International Journal of Psychoanalysis*, 1987, *68*, 279–297.

Blatt, S. J., and Blass, R. B. "Attachment and Separateness: A Dialectic Model of the Products and Processes of Development Throughout the Life Cycle." *Psychoanalytic Study of the Child*, 1990, *45*, 107–128.

Blos, P. *On Adolescence*. New York: Free Press, 1962.

Bowlby, J. *Attachment and Loss*. Vol. 1: *Attachment*. New York: Basic Books, 1969.

Bowlby, J. *Attachment and Loss*. Vol. 2: *Separation*. New York: Basic Books, 1973.

Bowlby, J. *Attachment and Loss*. Vol. 3: *Loss*. New York: Basic Books, 1980.

Bowlby, J. *A Secure Base*. New York: Basic Books, 1988.

Buber, M. *I and Thou*. New York: Charles Scribner's Sons, 1958.

Buber, M. *The Knowledge of Man*. New York: HarperCollins, 1965.

Campbell, J. *Myths to Live By*. New York: Bantam Books, 1972.

Chodorow, N. *The Reproduction of Mothering: Psychoanalysis and the Sociology of Gender.* Berkeley: University of California Press, 1978.

Coles, R., and Stokes, G. *Sex and the American Teenager.* New York: HarperCollins, 1985.

Csikszentmihalyi, M. "Love and the Dynamics of Personal Growth." In K. S. Pope and Associates (eds.), *On Love and Loving: Psychological Perspectives on the Nature and Experience of Romantic Love.* San Francisco: Jossey-Bass, 1980.

Deutsch, H. *The Psychology of Women.* Vol. 1. Philadelphia: Grune & Stratton, 1944.

Dickens, C. *Great Expectations.* San Francisco: Chandler, 1861.

Dinnerstein, D. *The Mermaid and the Minotaur.* New York: HarperCollins, 1977.

Diogenes, L. *Lives of Eminent Philosophers.* Vol. 5. New York: Putnam, 1925.

Dion, K. L., and Dion, K. K. "Romantic Love: Individual and Cultural Perspectives." In R. J. Sternberg and M. L. Barnes (eds.), *The Psychology of Love.* New Haven, Conn.: Yale University Press, 1988.

Eichenbaum, L., and Orbach, S. *Between Women.* New York: Penguin, 1987.

Eliot, G. *Daniel Deronda.* Harmondsworth, England: Penguin, 1967. (Originally published 1876.)

Erikson, E. *Insight and Responsibility.* New York: W.W.Norton, 1964.

Erikson, E. *Identity, Youth, and Crisis.* New York: W.W.Norton, 1968.

Erikson, E. H., Erikson, J. M., and Kivnick, H. Q. *Vital Involvement in Old Age.* New York: W.W.Norton, 1986.

Erlich, H. S. "Boundaries, Limitations, and the Wish for Fusion in the Treatment of Adolescents." *Psychoanalytic Study of the Child,* 1990, *45,* 195–213.

Erlich, H. S., and Blatt, S. J. "Narcissism and Object Love." *Psychoanalytic Study of the Child,* 1985, *40.*

Fairbairn, W.R.D. *An Object Relations Theory of the Personality.* New York: Basic Books, 1954.

Fairbairn, W.R.D. "Freud, the Psychoanalytic Method, and Mental Health." *British Journal of Medical Psychology*, 1957, *30*, 53–62.

Farrell, W. *Why Men Are the Way They Are*. New York: McGraw-Hill, 1986.

Fisher, S. *The Female Orgasm*. New York: Basic Books, 1973.

Fraiberg, S., Adelson, E., and Shapiro, V. "Ghosts in the Nursery: A Psychoanalytic Approach to the Problems of Impaired Infant-Mother Relationships." *Journal of the American Academy of Child Psychiatry*, 1975, *14*, 387–421.

Frank, A. *Anne Frank: The Diary of a Young Girl*. New York: Pocket Books, 1952.

Frank, J. *Persuasion and Healing*. New York: Schocken, 1963.

Frank, S., Avery, C. B., and Laman, M. S. "Young Adults' Perceptions of Their Relationships with Their Parents: Individual Differences in Connectedness, Competence, and Emotional Autonomy." *Developmental Psychology*, 1988, *24*, 729–737.

Freud, S. "Group Psychology and the Analysis of the Ego." In James Strachey (trans. and ed.), *The Standard Edition of the Complete Psychological Works of Sigmund Freud*. Vol. 18. London: Hogarth Press, 1955a. (Originally published 1921.)

Freud, S. "Some Psychical Consequences of the Anatomical Distinction Between the Sexes." In James Strachey (trans. and ed.), *The Standard Edition of the Complete Psychological Works of Sigmund Freud*. Vol. 19. London: Hogarth Press, 1955b. (Originally published 1925.)

Fromm, E. *Escape from Freedom*. Troy, Mo.: Holt, Rinehart, & Winston, 1941.

Fromm-Reichmann, F. "Loneliness." In W. G. Bennis, E. H. Schein, F. I. Steele, and D. E. Berlew (eds.), *Interpersonal Dynamics*. Belmont, Calif.: Dorsey Press, 1968.

Gaylin, W., and Person, E. *Passionate Attachments*. New York: Free Press, 1988.

Gilligan, C. "In a Different Voice—Women's Conceptions of Self and of Morality." *Harvard Educational Review*, 1977, *47*, 481–517.

Gilligan, C. *In a Different Voice*. Cambridge, Mass.: Harvard University Press, 1982.

Gilligan, C. "Teaching Shakespeare's Sister: Notes from the Underground of Female Adolescence." In C. Gilligan, N. P. Lyons, and T. J. Hammer (eds.), *Making Connections.* Cambridge, Mass.: Harvard University Press, 1990.

Gilligan, C., Lyons, N. P., and Hammer, T. J. (eds.). *Making Connections.* Cambridge, Mass.: Harvard University Press, 1990.

Gilligan, C., and Stern, E. "The Riddle of Femininity and the Psychology of Love." In W. Gaylin and E. Person (eds.), *Passionate Attachments.* New York: Free Press, 1988.

Goldstein, R. *The Mind-Body Problem.* New York: Dell, 1983.

Graves, P. L., Thomas, C. B., and Mead, L. A. "Familial and Psychological Predictors of Cancer." *Cancer Detection and Prevention*, 1990, *15*, 59-64.

Greenson, R. *The Technique and Practice of Psychoanalysis.* Vol. 1. Madison, Conn.: International Universities Press, 1967.

Grinberg, L., Sor, D., and de Bianchedi, E. T. *Introduction to the Work of Bion.* New York: Aronson, 1977.

Grotevant, H. D., and Cooper, C. R. "Patterns of Interaction in Family Relationships and the Development of Identity Exploration in Adolescence." *Child Development*, 1985, *56*, 415-428.

Guntrip, H. *Psychoanalytic Theory, Therapy, and the Self.* New York: Basic Books, 1971.

Harlow, H. "Syndromes Resulting from Maternal Deprivation: Maternal and Peer Affectional Deprivation in Primates." In J. H. Cullen (ed.), *Experimental Behavior: A Basis for the Study of Mental Disorders.* New York: Wiley, 1974.

Hass, A. *Teenage Sexuality: A Survey of Teenage Sexual Behavior.* New York: Macmillan, 1979.

Heilbrun, C. G. *Writing a Woman's Life.* New York: W.W.Norton, 1988.

Hite, S. *Women and Love: A Cultural Revolution in Progress.* New York: Knopf, 1987.

Hojat, M., and Vogel, W. H. "Socioemotional Bonding and Neurobiochemistry." In M. Hojat and R. Crandall (eds.), "Loneliness: Theory, Research, and Applications." A special issue of the *Journal of Social Behavior and Personality*, 1987, *2*, 135-145.

Hortacsu, N. "Targets of Communication During Adolescence." *Journal of Adolescence*, 1989, *12*, 253-263.

Inglehart, M. R., and Brown, D. R. "Gender Differences on Values and Their Impact on Academic Achievement." Paper presented at the 10th annual meeting of the International Society of Political Psychology, San Francisco, July 1987.

Inglehart, M. R., Nyquist, L., Brown, D. R., and Moore, W. "Gender Differences in Academic Achievement—The Result of Cognitive or Affective Factors?" Paper presented at the meeting of the Midwestern Psychological Association, May 1987.

Jones, G. P., and Denbo, M. H. "Age and Sex Role Differences in Intimate Friendships During Childhood and Adolescence." *Merrill-Palmer Quarterly*, 1989, *35*, 445–462.

Jordan, J. "The Meaning of Mutuality." *Work in Progress*, Stone Center Working Paper Series, no. 23. Wellesley, Mass.: Stone Center, 1986.

Josselson, R. "Tolstoy, Narcissism, and the Psychology of the Self: A Self Psychology Approach to Prince Andrei in *War and Peace*." *Psychoanalytic Review*, 1986, *73*, 77–95.

Josselson, R. *Finding Herself: Pathways to Identity Development in Women*. San Francisco: Jossey-Bass, 1987.

Jourard, S. M. *The Transparent Self: Self-Disclosure and Well-Being*. New York: Van Nostrand Reinhold, 1964.

Kaplan, A. G. "Dichotomous Thought and Relational Processes in Therapy." *Work in Progress*. Stone Center Working Paper Series, no. 35. Wellesley, Mass.: Stone Center, 1988.

Kegan, R. *The Evolving Self*. Cambridge: Harvard University Press, 1982.

Kernberg, O. "Boundaries and Structures in Love Relations." In O. Kernberg, *Internal World and External Reality*. New York: Aronson, 1980.

Klein, J. *Our Need for Others and Its Roots in Infancy*. London and New York: Tavistock Publications, 1987.

Klein, M. "Notes on Some Schizoid Mechanisms." In M. Klein, *Envy and Gratitude and Other Works*. London: Hogarth Press, 1975. (Originally published 1946.)

Klein, M., and Riviere, J. *Love, Hate and Reparation*. London: Hogarth Press, 1967.

Kobak, R. R., and Sceery, A. "Attachment in Late Adolescence: Working Models, Affect Regulation, and Representations of Self and Others." *Child Development*, 1988, *59*, 135–146.

Kohut, H. "Forms and Transformations of Narcissism." *Journal of the American Psychoanalytic Association*, 1966, *14*, 243-272.

Kohut, H. *The Restoration of the Self.* Madison, Conn.: International Universities Press, 1977.

Kohut, H. *How Does Analysis Cure?* Edited by A. Goldberg and P. Stepansky. Chicago: University of Chicago Press, 1984.

Kotre, J. *Outliving the Self.* Baltimore, Md.: Johns Hopkins University Press, 1984.

Laing, R. D. *The Divided Self.* Harmondsworth, England: Penguin Books, 1965.

Lamb, M. E., and others. "Security of Infantile Attachment as Assessed in the 'Strange Situation.'" *The Behavioral and Brain Sciences*, 1984, *7*, 127-171.

Lasch, C. *The Culture of Narcissism.* New York: W.W.Norton, 1978.

Lash, J. P. *Eleanor and Franklin.* New York: New American Library, 1973.

Lee, G. R. "Marital Intimacy Among Older Persons: The Spouse as Confidant." *Journal of Family Issues*, 1988, *9*, 273-284.

Lieblich, A. *Only the Birds.* Tel Aviv, Israel: Schocken House, 1990.

Lifton, R. J. *The Nazi Doctors: Medical Killing and the Psychology of Genocide.* New York: Basic Books, 1986.

Lindon, J. A. "Does Technique Require Theory?" *Bulletin of the Menninger Clinic*, 1991, *55*, 1-21.

Lowenthal, M. F., and Haven, C. "Interaction and Adaptation: Intimacy as a Critical Variable." *American Sociological Review*, 1986, *33*, 20-30.

Luepnitz, D. A. *The Family Interpreted: Feminist Theory in Clinical Practice.* New York: Basic Books, 1988.

Lynch, J. J. *The Broken Heart: The Medical Consequences of Loneliness.* New York: Basic Books, 1977.

Lyons, N. P. "Listening to Voices We Have Not Heard." In C. Gilligan, N. P. Lyons, and T. J. Hammer (eds.), *Making Connections.* Cambridge, Mass.: Harvard University Press, 1990.

McGill, M. *The McGill Report on Male Intimacy.* New York: Holt, Rinehart & Winston, 1985.

Mahler, M., Pine, F., and Bergman, A. *The Psychological Birth of the Human Infant.* New York: Basic Books, 1975.

Main, M., and Cassidy, J. "Categories of Response with the Parent at Age Six: Predicted from Infant Attachment Classifications and Stable over a One-Month Period." *Developmental Psychology*, 1988, *24*, 415–426.

Main, M., Kaplan, N., and Cassidy, J. "Security in Infancy, Childhood, and Adulthood: A Move to the Level of Representation." In I. Bretherton and E. Waters (eds.), *Growing Points in Attachment: Theory and Research*. Monographs of the Society for Research in Child Development, serial 209, 66–104. Chicago: University of Chicago Press, 1985.

Marris, P. "Attachment and Society." In C. M. Parkes and J. Stevenson-Hinde (eds.), *The Place of Attachment in Human Behavior*. New York: Basic Books, 1982.

Maslow, A. *Toward a Psychology of Being*. New York: Van Nostrand Reinhold, 1962.

May, R. *Love and Will*. New York: W.W.Norton, 1969.

Miller, J. B. *Toward a New Psychology of Women*. Boston: Beacon Press, 1976.

Miller, J. B. "The Development of Women's Sense of Self." *Work in Progress*, Stone Center Working Paper Series, no. 12. Wellesley, Mass.: Stone Center, 1984.

Miller, J. B. "What Do We Mean by Relationships?" *Work in Progress*, Stone Center Working Paper Series, no. 22. Wellesley, Mass.: Stone Center, 1986.

Miller, J. B. "Connections, Disconnections, and Violations." *Work in Progress*, Stone Center Working Paper Series, no. 33. Wellesley, Mass.: Stone Center, 1988.

Mitchell, S. A. *Relational Concepts in Psychoanalysis*. Cambridge, Mass.: Harvard University Press, 1988.

Moskowitz, S. *Love Despite Hate*. New York: Schocken, 1983.

Mussen, P., and Eisenberg-Berg, N. *Roots of Caring, Sharing, and Helping*. New York: W. H. Freeman, 1977.

Noddings, N. *Caring*. Berkeley: University of California Press, 1984.

Nussbaum, M. *The Fragility of Goodness: Luck and Ethics in Greek Tragedy and Philosophy*. Cambridge: Cambridge University Press, 1986.

Oliner, S., and Oliner, P. *The Altruistic Personality*. New York: Free Press, 1988.

Palmer, R. E. *Hermeneutics: Interpretation Theory in Schleiermacher, Dilthey, Heidegger, and Gadamer.* Evanston, Ill.: Northwestern University Press, 1969.

Parsons, T. *Social Structure and Personality.* New York: Free Press, 1964.

Person, E. S. *Dreams of Love and Fateful Encounters.* New York: W.W.Norton, 1988.

Piaget, J. *The Moral Judgment of the Child.* New York: Free Press, 1965.

Plato. *The Symposium.* (W. Hamilton, trans.) Harmondsworth, England: Penguin Books, 1951.

Pogrebin, L. *Among Friends: Who We Like, Why We Like Them, and What We Can Do About Them.* New York: McGraw-Hill, 1986.

Radway, J. *Reading the Romance: Women, Patriarchy, and Popular Culture.* Chapel Hill: University of North Carolina Press, 1984.

Rich, S. "Daughters' Views of Their Relationships with Their Mothers." In C. Gilligan, N. P. Lyons, and T. J. Hammer (eds.), *Making Connections.* Cambridge, Mass.: Harvard University Press, 1990.

Ricks, M. H. "The Social Transmission of Parental Behavior: Attachment Across Generations." *Monographs of the Society for Research in Child Development,* 1985, *50,* 211–227.

Rieff, P. *The Triumph of the Therapeutic.* New York: HarperCollins, 1966.

Rogers, C. *Client-Centered Therapy.* Boston: Houghton Mifflin, 1951.

Rubin, L. B. *Just Friends.* New York: HarperCollins, 1985.

Rubin, Z. *Liking and Loving.* New York: Holt, Rinehart & Winston, 1973.

Ruddick, S. *Maternal Thinking: Towards A Politics of Peace.* Boston: Beacon Press, 1989.

Salzman, J. P. "Save the World Save Myself: Responses to Problematic Attachment." In C. Gilligan, N. P. Lyons, and T. J. Hammer (eds.), *Making Connections.* Cambridge, Mass.: Harvard University Press, 1990.

Schofield, M. *The Sexual Behavior of Young People.* Boston: Little, Brown, 1965.

Schultz, N. R., and Moore, D. "Loneliness—Differences Across Three Age Levels." *Journal of Social and Personal Relationships,* 1988, *5,* 275-284.

Schwaber, E. "Self Psychology and the Concept of Psychopathology: A Case Presentation." In A. Goldberg (ed.), *Advances in Self Psychology.* Madison, Conn.: International Universities Press, 1980.

Sered, S. S. "Ritual, Morality, and Gender: The Religious Lives of Oriental Jewish Women in Jerusalem." *Israel Social Science Research,* 1987, *5,* 87-97.

"Sex vs. Hugs: Landers Survey Raises Questions." *Baltimore Sun,* June 16, 1985, p. 1B.

Sharabany, R. "The Development of Capacity for Altruism as a Function of Object Relations Development." In E. Staub, D. Bar-Tal, J. Karilowski, and J. Reukowski (eds.), *Development and Maintenance of Prosocial Behavior.* New York: Plenum, 1984.

Sharabany, R., Gershoni, R., and Hoffman, J. E. "Girlfriend, Boyfriend: Age and Sex Differences in Intimate Friendship." *Developmental Psychology,* 1981, *17,* 800-808.

Simon, B. *Tragic Drama and the Family: Psychoanalytic Studies from Aeschylus to Beckett.* New Haven, Conn.: Yale University Press, 1988.

Simon, B. "Is the Oedipus Complex Still the Cornerstone of Psychoanalysis? Three Obstacles to Answering the Question." *Journal of the American Psychoanalytic Association,* 1991, *39,* 641-669.

Simpson, E. *Orphans.* New York: New American Library, 1988.

Singer, I. *The Nature of Love.* Vol. 3. Chicago: University of Chicago Press, 1987.

Slater, P. E. "Some Social Consequences of Temporary Systems." In W. G. Bennis, E. H. Schein, F. I. Steele, and D. E. Berlew (eds.), *Interpersonal Dynamics.* Belmont, Calif.: Dorsey Press, 1968.

Slater, P. E. *The Pursuit of Loneliness.* Boston: Beacon Press, 1970.

Smith-Rosenberg, C. "The Female World of Love and Ritual: Re-

lations Between Women in Nineteenth Century America." *Signs,*
1975, *1,* 1-30.

Spitzberg, B. H., and Hurt, H. T. "The Relationship of Interpersonal Competence and Skills to Reported Loneliness Across Time." In M. Hojat and R. Crandall (eds.), "Loneliness: Theory, Research, and Applications." A special issue of the *Journal of Social Behavior and Personality,* 1987, *2,* 157-173.

Stern, D. *The Interpersonal World of the Infant.* New York: Basic Books, 1985.

Stern, L. "Conceptions of Separation and Connection in Female Adolescents." In C. Gilligan, N. P. Lyons, and T. J. Hammer (eds.), *Making Connections.* Cambridge, Mass.: Harvard University Press, 1990.

Sternberg, R. J. "A Triangular Theory of Love." *Psychological Review,* 1986, *93,* 119-135.

Storr, A. *Solitude.* New York: Ballantine, 1988.

Sullivan, H. S. *The Interpersonal Theory of Psychiatry.* New York: W.W.Norton, 1953.

Surrey, J. "Relationship and Empowerment." *Work in Progress,* Stone Center Working Paper Series, no. 13. Wellesley, Mass.: Stone Center, 1987.

Tolpin, M. "Discussion of 'Psychoanalytic Developmental Theories of the Self: An Integration' by Morton Shane and Estelle Shane." In A. Goldberg (ed.), *Advances in Self Psychology.* Madison, Conn.: International Universities Press, 1980.

Tolstoy, L. *What Is Art? and Essays on Art.* (A. Maude, trans.) London: Oxford University Press, 1930.

Uchalik, D. C., and Livingston, D. D. "Adulthood: Women." In K. S. Pope and Associates (eds.), *On Love and Loving: Psychological Perspectives on the Nature and Experience of Romantic Love.* San Francisco: Jossey-Bass, 1980.

Viederman, M. "The Nature of Passionate Love." In W. Gaylin and E. Person (eds.), *Passionate Attachments.* New York: Free Press, 1988.

Vygotsky, L. *Thought and Language.* Cambridge, Mass.: MIT Press, 1986.

Weisman, M. *Intensive Care: A Family Love Story.* New York: Random House, 1982.

Weiss, R. S. "Materials for a Theory of Social Relationships." In
W. G. Bennis, E. H. Schein, F. I. Steele, and D. E. Berlew (eds.),
Interpersonal Dynamics. Belmont, Calif.: Dorsey Press, 1968.

Weiss, R. S. "Attachment in Adult Life." In C. M. Parkes and J.
Stevenson-Hinde (eds.), *The Place of Attachment in Human Behavior*. New York: Basic Books, 1982.

Weiss, R. S. "Reflections on the Present State of Loneliness Research." In M. Hojat and R. Crandall (eds.), "Loneliness: Theory, Research, and Applications." A special issue of the *Journal
of Social Behavior and Personality*, 1987, *2*, 1-16.

Wheeler, L., Reis, H., and Nezlek, J. "Loneliness, Social Interaction, and Sex Roles." *Journal of Personality and Social Psychology*, 1983, *45*, 943-953.

White, R. W. *Lives in Progress*. Troy, Mo.: Holt, Rinehart & Winston, 1966.

Winnicott, D. W. "The Capacity to Be Alone." In D. W. Winnicott,
*Maturational Processes and the Facilitating Environment: Stud-
ies in the Theory of Emotional Development*. Madison, Conn.:
International Universities Press, 1965a.

Winnicott, D. W. *The Family and Individual Development*. New
York: Basic Books, 1965b.

Winnicott, D. W. *The Maturational Process and the Facilitating
Environment*. Madison, Conn.: International Universities Press,
1965c.

Winnicott, D. W. "The Theory of the Parent-Infant Relationship."
In D. W. Winnicott, *Maturational Processes and the Facilitating
Environment: Studies in the Theory of Emotional Development*.
Madison, Conn.: International Universities Press, 1965d.

Winnicott, D. W. *Playing and Reality*. New York: Tavistock Publications, 1971.

Winnicott, D. W. "Birth Memories, Birth Trauma, and Anxiety."
In D. W. Winnicott, *Through Paediatrics to Psychoanalysis*.
London: Hogarth Press, 1975a.

Winnicott, D. W. "The Observation of Infants in a Set Situation."
In D. W. Winnicott, *Through Paediatrics to Psychoanalysis*.
London: Hogarth Press, 1975b.

Winnicott, D. W. "Primary Maternal Preoccupation." In D. W.

Winnicott, *Through Paediatrics to Psychoanalysis.* London: Hogarth Press, 1975c.

Wolf, E. "Developmental Line of Selfobject Relations." In A. Goldberg (ed.), *Advances in Self Psychology.* Madison, Conn.: International Universities Press, 1980.

Yalom, I. D. *Existential Psychotherapy.* New York: Basic Books, 1980.

Yalom, I. D. *Love's Executioner.* New York: Basic Books, 1989.

Youniss, J. *Parents and Peers in Social Development.* Chicago: University of Chicago Press, 1980.

Zahn-Waxler, C., Radke-Yarrow, M., and King, R. A. "Childrearing and Children's Prosocial Initiations Toward Victims of Distress." *Child Development,* 1979, *50,* 319–330.

Index